THE EXCEPTIONAL APPLICANT

Recommended Reading for High School Students and Parents Seeking an Edge in the College Admission Process

THE EXCEPTIONAL APPLICANT

FOR COLLEGE ADMISSION,
YOU DON'T HAVE TO BE **PERFECT**,
YOU JUST HAVE TO BE **ORIGINAL**

DR. DEBORAH BEDOR

Bestselling author of *Getting IN by Standing OUT*

Published by Advantage, Charleston, South Carolina.
Member of Advantage Media Group.

Printed in the United States of America.

10 9 8 7 6 5 4 3 2 1

ISBN: 978-1-64225-407-5
LCCN: 2022912368

Cover design by Megan Elger.
Layout design by Wesley Strickland.

To my students, past, present, and future: You are meteors!
Your dreams, dynamism, and openness to possibilities make
my work a joyous adventure.

CONTENTS

PREFACE

If all you read about the experience of preparing yourself for college comes from salesy clickbait ads by college application essay mills or news reports on the increasing worthlessness of a top-tier degree, you might miss the bigger picture. It's about who you become while you're preparing.

How to Read This Book

- Ten pages at a time
- Five chapters at a time (with a latte)
- With your friends
- With your parents
- With a highlighter
- Aggressively dog-earing
- In one sitting (maybe you should switch to decaf?)

I know that all the wonder, curiosity, and creativity you *could* possess cannot be ideated and contained in two hundred, three hundred, or even three hundred and fifty nine pages of a book—but you have to start somewhere. 😊 And because your interests span several fields of study, I have made sure my advice does too!

If you need unique résumé-building suggestions; essay inspiration and strategy; innovative ideas for intellectual projects; and guidance in the fields of technology, mathematics, environmental studies, science research, law and debate, the arts, or business, you will find it here.

I have provided volumes of personal statement and supplementary essay examples; action steps to social good; and the latest available credentials, awards, and competitive programs, plus additional wisdom from subject experts in the very fields you will be pursuing for a remarkable high school career and an exceptional college application.

Is it a thick book? Oh yes! Will it empower you on the journey toward your dream colleges? Absolutely!

INTRODUCTION

My college roommate knew to keep the door ajar when it was a late night at the library for me; otherwise, I'd have to kick it open. I'd enter with armfuls of precariously balanced assigned tomes, "knocked about" notebooks, and titles by scholars I had not yet read—neither mumbles nor masterpieces but magical to me. Those old, hauntingly beautiful editions from a different time and stunningly different cultures that I studied in college prepared me to look at life and the human condition in all their evolving complexity. Yellowed palimpsests awaiting new interpreters, carefully preserved texts from 3000 BCE asking the same questions we ask today, a panoply of dictionaries, and scholarly Festschriften borrowed from the shelves of Van Pelt Library all kept me happily awake and writing into the wee hours. The next morning in class brought the rewards—the great excitement that came with asking the right questions. Nothing made my professors and mentors happier than hearing a question or point they had never thought of ("That's it!" my professor would exclaim, climbing up onto the seminar table with yellow pad and pen aloft.

"That's the question of the hour, Miss Bedor. Let's write a book!"). Such elicited excitement always came when students started creating value that moved beyond the documents they studied.

The most important voices behind my career in academia have been my University of Pennsylvania professors, many of whom I am lucky enough to call my mentors. We bonded by "nerding out" over the great curiosities of ancient texts, their social and literary messaging, and translations of the linguistic nuances that made such analysis possible. I learned to love the way human beings communicate across time; for me, there are no dead languages, only people with messages to impart. These subject experts taught me how to ask meaningful questions, get lost in books, and become an explorer of literature. They also inspired me to advise and mentor future bright young lights on their way to our nation's great universities and in need of equal care and dedication.

My mentors pushed me with such confidence that by the beginning of sophomore year, I was not only helping them do the research for their new works but was offered the chance to submatriculate and go directly into the master's degree program, graduating from college in four years with both a bachelor's and master's before moving on to doctoral work.

The rigor of my undergraduate years instilled in me a respect for the wisdom of experts and mentors. No students will reach their goals alone, yet many of you reading this book may not know where to find the experts in your areas of interest. Not all mentorships grow organically from a faculty member you've impressed or a nonprofit director who sees leadership potential or a local politician who observes a spark of greatness in you. In high school, more frequently than not, you will need to seek out subject experts, college advisors, science research professionals, physicians, technologists, or eminent music teachers and preconservatory programs. You might need specialists and advisors who guide you to build authentic passion projects and differentiated college essays, advance your coding skills, lead you through the rules and methodologies of engaging in research, coach you on debate and persuasive communication, prep you for mathematics competitions, connect you with business internships, or work with you to awaken hidden social, creative, or intellectual interests.

It is difficult to find the right mentors. I know that. But the pursuit and development of your interests at the highest possible level are what ultimately make you THE EXCEPTIONAL APPLICANT. Today, as you read, you will be receiving important kernels of mentorship not only from me but also from a few of the finest subject experts I know. Use the following pages like a textbook—highlight passages, assimilate information, and even feel free to contact these nationally recognized professionals if you would like to find your strengths. They are here to take you one step up.

This is an "anthology of activation" that takes the pieces of high school life and shows you how to thread them together into a remarkable whole to which Admissions will not be able to say *no*. There are big, bold, creative ideas for intelligent students stuck in a standardized educational world and a little philosophy that I hope will lead you toward a growth mindset. You'll find college application timelines, competitions to enter, inspiring passion projects that will help you launch your own, and tons of sample Common Application essays and excerpts to guide you toward more thoughtful, quirky, and creative drafts. I've also included interviews with some of my top-tier and Ivy League college students who share high school dos, don'ts, and "should haves" through their rearview mirror, and wisdom from subject experts who teach students just like you—those who want to differentiate themselves in the admissions process through projects in computer science / machine learning / artificial intelligence, research sciences, mathematics for national competitions, debate, athletic leadership, business, and music. There's a potpourri of possibilities before you. Use them well, and you'll never be viewed as a cookie-cutter applicant!

My deepest thanks to the dedicated and talented mentor-contributors in this book: Wes Carroll (MIT, mathematics competition specialist), Brian Skinner (Stanford University, founder of Breakout Mentors for computer science, machine learning, and artificial intelligence), Bo Eason (former safety for the Houston Oilers, bestselling author and speaker), Pamela Stein Lynde (Peabody Conservatory/Johns Hopkins University, classical voice coach and composer), Jessica Meyer (the Juilliard School, GRAMMY-nominated violist and composer), Alec Urbach (Princeton University, young entrepreneur, author, and speaker), and Julian Dotson (Tuskegee University, president, District of Columbia Urban Debate League). You are all gems! The time you gave to craft your chapters and the wisdom you offer will inspire some of the greatest young minds of this generation.

Segments of this book's advice will come at you in flashes of action steps and insights; other advice will be more cerebral and require some time to think about and assimilate. Stick with it! I always "teach up" to my students because young people embrace the climb. It's my hope that this book will meet you where you are and take you where you want to be. Please don't think this advice is geared toward one type of student. We all need to explore when we are curious, push boundaries when we believe we're capable of more, and learn how to compete while still engaging our humanity.

Now, let's pull back the curtain on how top Admissions committees think and what you can do to capture their attention.

Ready to make the magic happen? Buckle up!

PART ONE:

DEVELOPING YOUR EXCEPTIONAL APPLICANT MINDSET

You Do You

It was a chilly December evening, and I was finishing up my student meetings at the Penn Club in NYC. A couple of my students who lived nearby decided to surprise me and came to hang out in the library and chat. We talked TV series and must-read books, restaurants in the Village with the best ramen, and ideas for new STEM adventures. Then, I told them I was headed off to Bryant Park to meet my husband and have hot chocolate from one of our favorite food trucks. "You're going to sit outside in twenty-five degrees and drink hot chocolate?" my student Kara asked incredulously. But before I could answer, she smiled and added, "Okay, Dr. B. You do you!"

That made me laugh because it is the very thing that I encourage in my students.

This time is all about you doing you. The ambition to follow your own quirky path and intellectual passions will take you to a new place with new adventures that bring new successes—successes that will differentiate you from every other student in your class. College success will happen too, but it should be a by-product of finding out just how much you've got to give during your young, supercurious, idealistic, and scrappy years.

So how do you make high school all about you? You brainstorm ideas that stir your curiosity. Don't take the road you've traveled more; take the road you've never traveled. Write a thesis on that offbeat topic you study after school that beckons you down rabbit holes and makes you a fascinating person to talk to; train for mathematics competitions; start a speaker series, a high school mobile art exhibit, a podcast with interesting scientist-communicators, a fashion show for a cure, an international news discussion forum with those friends of yours from four different countries, or a vegan ice cream pop-up business. What does it matter? Admissions will love it all because you loved doing it. There is no right combination of things that gets a student accepted to a top college. There is only the right student for that college, and Admissions finds you by reading about your unique journey.

LESSON: You do you!

The Superhero Student Syndrome

I know you feel as though you need to leap tall buildings in a single bound **just to reach final committee** at your dream schools. Those sentiments are creating the most stressed-out generation we have had in many decades. You need to learn how to adapt to the latest college admissions process. You need a new toolbox.

I promise that there are ways for you to chart an intentionally creative and impactful path to college acceptance. Be ready to have new academic and entrepreneurial adventures, engage in research, attend Zoom lectures, watch TEDx Talks and then create your own, and learn about new ideas and fields. Improvise on demand. We've dwelt underground and in trees, created fire and the wheel, and built computers that bring populations and information together around the globe and physically farther than the moon. We are creatures capable of extraordinary change, and Admissions knows it and expects it.

I promise that there are ways for you to chart an intentionally creative and impactful path to college acceptance.

If you stay in your comfortable little universe, taking your honors and AP classes, joining the volleyball team and yearbook without ever reaching beyond, you will be living your high school life according to the movie playing in everyone else's mind, and your application will read like everyone else's too. Is that what you really want? Is that the way to spend four of the most epistemically curious, creatively vibrant, and socially passionate years of your life?

Secretly, admissions officers are asking the same questions when they read your applications. They expect to see you evolve in intellectually and socially fascinating ways during high school. Their supposition is that you live with your life for a long time, so you might as well make it as interesting as possible.

So how do you do that? You see, there's much about college admissions you don't know, or you don't know you don't know, or you think you know, or you used to know. **But what *should* you know?**

How do you design the right paths in high school to open the right doors for college?

Stoic philosopher Epictetus said, "Now is the time to get serious about living your ideals. How long can you afford to put off who you really want to be? Your nobler self cannot wait any longer." Students, Epictetus had it right: you're young with nothing but possibilities ahead. What are you waiting for?

Who knows? Maybe you will evolve into a force for good in your community, a young healer to someone in need, or an innovator and builder in STEM. Without leaping tall buildings in a single bound, you might just become someone's hero.

Your Dream Board!

Have you ever heard of a dream board? A dream board is where you pin all the important, life-changing goals you want to accomplish during high school: your scientific research, travel adventures, talent development, building of apps or businesses, founding of organizations, or succeeding on your standardized tests.

Next to each entry, you place a timeline for when you expect to reach your goals, and then check them off once you've succeeded! And at the bottom of your dream board will be a list of your dream colleges, and you'll keep your eye on that prize until April 1 of senior year.

The wonderful thing about all your dreams is that, if you act on them, they will not only show you how vibrant, fascinating, and powerful you are, but they will give you a major bump on your college applications.

The single most important mantra for college admissions is "The things that make me different are the things that make me."

The experiences and accomplishments you have in your first three years of high school are the things you will be writing about on your college application. So, it's up to *you* to try to make your high school experience as meaningful, impactful, and authentic to you as possible. Just **talking about** cool leadership, science research, app building, or entrepreneurial ideas won't move the dial on your life or on your college acceptances. Do it! **You don't need to be perfect. You just need to be original!**

To be original, you need to have experiences. And that doesn't just mean the very necessary experience of studying hard for your rigorous AP or International Baccalaureate (IB) courses. It means experiences outside the walls of your high school that will shape you, change your perspective, and peel away the layers of who you are as an intellectual, leader, and empathic human being. Your essays and your ResuMotiv[1] will introduce your original experiences to Admissions and serve as your voice in an impersonal and overwhelming application process. If you know how to make your high school career speak, you will get the attention of Admissions and of your best-loved and best-fit schools!

When you see acceptance rates of 3.9 percent or 5 percent at schools like Harvard, Yale, Princeton, Stanford, MIT, or at any of our world-class universities, that is often for the students who never built or created anything unique in the intellectual, entrepreneurial, social good, or artistic arenas. Those are not necessarily the percentages for

---

1 The ResuMotiv is the elegant multimedia résumé many top-tier students use to display their high school successes and achievements: www.resumotiv.com.

you. Try to remember that all students are judged by the value they offer a university. Now, let's dig in!

Here are two mountains.

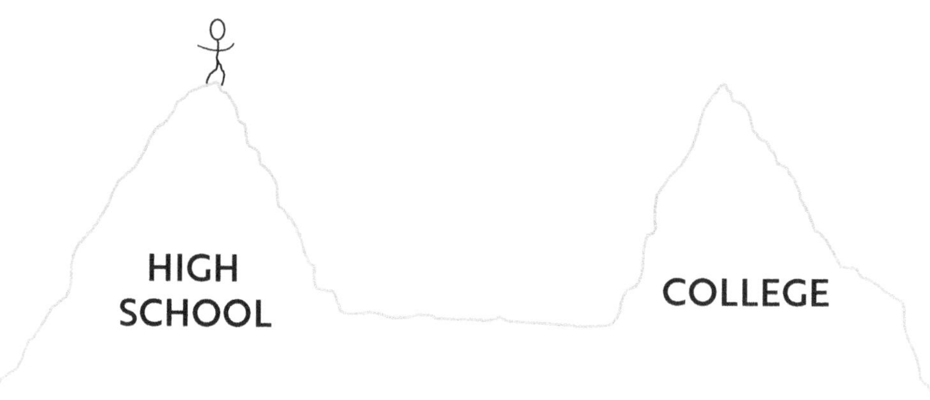

I know they're not works of art, but I drew them just for you. You're welcome!

This is a typical high school achiever's mindset:

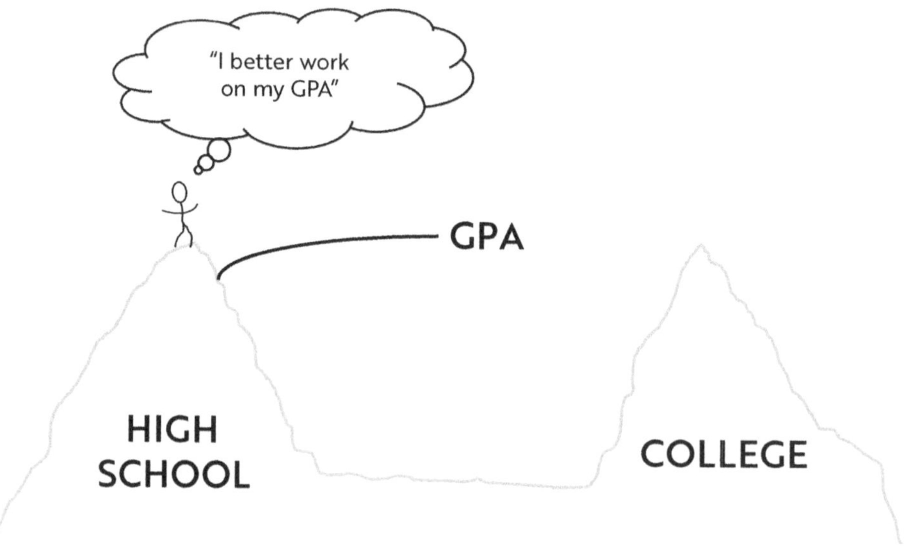

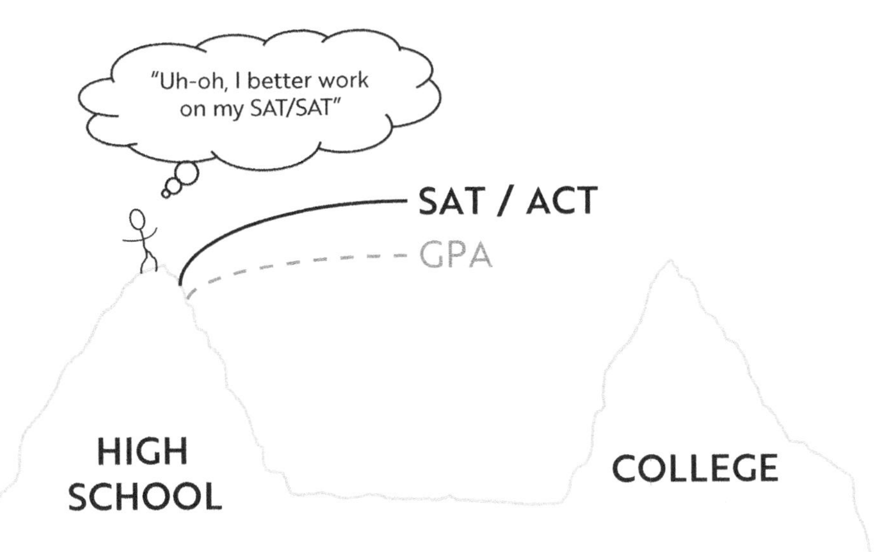
"Uh-oh, I better work on my SAT/SAT"
SAT / ACT
GPA
HIGH SCHOOL
COLLEGE

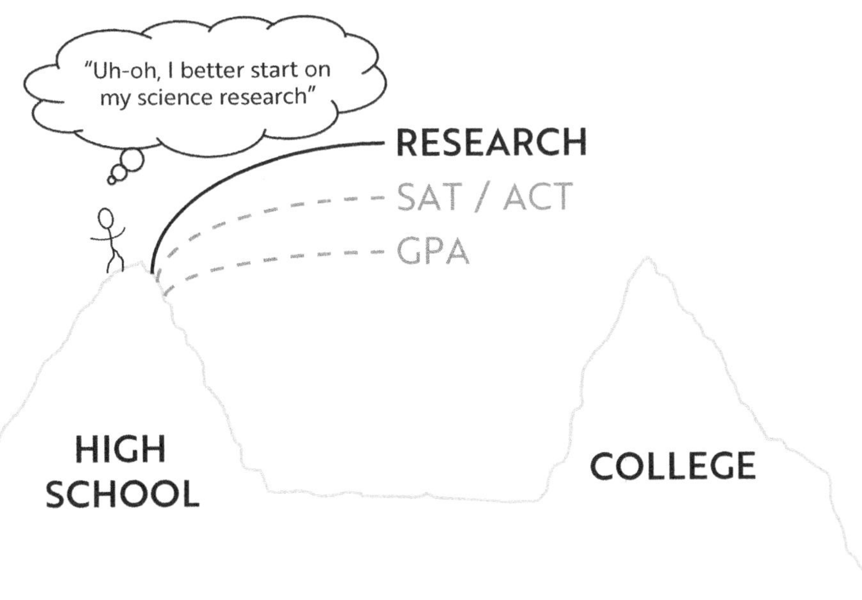
"Uh-oh, I better start on my science research"
RESEARCH
SAT / ACT
GPA
HIGH SCHOOL
COLLEGE

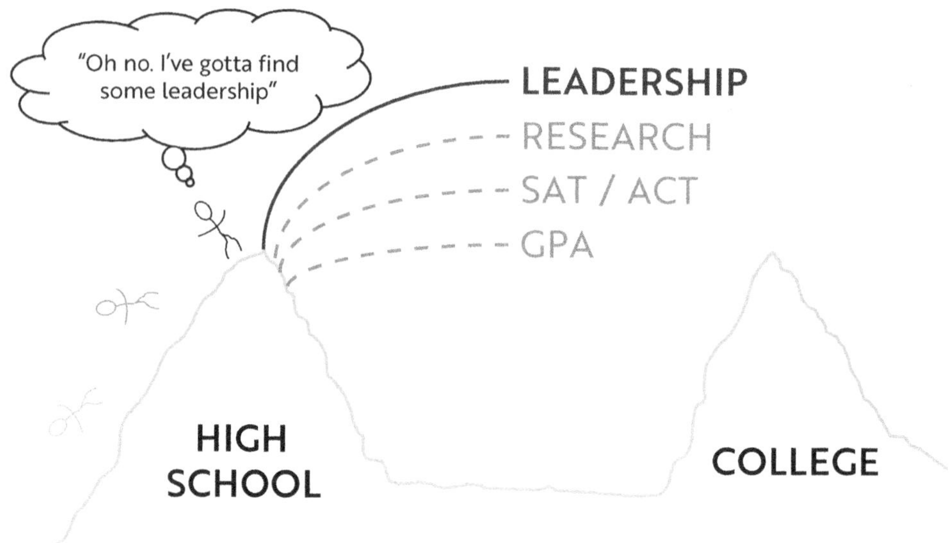

What's wrong with this picture? That's right! None of the bridges makes it over to the other side! You start building one bridge but then shift to building the second bridge before the first is completed.

Stop creating half-built bridges! Pick one bridge, and take it from beginning to most successful conclusion. Let's explore the summer bridge, for example:

- Maybe you're going on a mission trip to a developing-nation clinic—well, don't just go; keep a detailed personal journal of the trip and the people you meet so that you can use that material on a college essay. Write about how you were impacted and how you made an impact!

- Maybe you're conducting science research in a lab—don't just be part of a research team; ask for a small piece of the project that is original research and write a research paper according to Regeneron International Science and Engineering Fair (ISEF) regulations so that you can compete with your research the following year!

- Maybe you're taking a college course—firstly, make sure it sounds fascinating to you, and secondly, make sure it's at a top school and that you receive a transcript with a grade (hopefully, an A) so it can become a meaningful part of your academic résumé.
- Maybe you're traveling to learn about the origins of a particular type of music or healing—well, don't just go and have the experience; create a documentary or audio-interview library with the performers or medical practitioners that you can then share with classmates upon your return. What an imaginative way to spread the state of healthcare, art, and social perspectives with students back home!

You see, you've got to plan your dreams from this moment: build a base camp, strategize, *climb*, build your next step, strategize, *climb*. If you don't carefully and thoughtfully plan your journey through high school to your dream colleges, it'll be like trying to reach Mount Everest without strategy and supplies. You won't make it, and you'll get frostbite.

In this way, you will not just become one of the thousands of college applicants whose résumés and applications look like every other top student's. You will become aggregators of attention in the Admissions office! Everyone on the committee will want to hear about your high school adventures.

Some of you might be succumbing to an inner voice that suggests, "These factors for success are just tools to get into college. I don't want to have more stress during high school trying to outdo the best students in the country just to get into a name-brand university. I'm perfectly happy being who I am now, and then finding myself in college." Okay, as an educator and longtime advisor, I respect that (as my students know), but I also respect the concept of not selling yourself short. You do not **have to** study with field experts in computer science, data science, robotics, music, art, or your preferred areas of interest. You do not **have to** apply for college summer programs (many of which provide needed financial aid) or procure science research advisors, debate coaches, or drama classes. If you have a computer in front of you and assemble a home library full of gently used paperbacks on the fields that fascinate you (and then read them all), or you have the determination to teach yourself several programming languages, or write an anthology of short stories, or research and craft a minithesis on a niche topic of interest, or build small community projects that address gaps in education or social services, you can put into practice many of the creative suggestions that are in this book. There are few boundaries for you these days if you are intellectually curious or advocacy driven and ready to make mistakes while working to make impact. Just remember not to expect your success to always come in the form of immediate gratification—deep learning of a new field of study or building an original project requires patience, a thoughtful approach, and small steps that will include successes and failures.

Listen to the advice of thought leader and entrepreneur James Clear: "If you [break] down everything you could think of that goes into riding a bike, and then improve it by 1 percent, you will get a significant increase when you put them all together."[2] Riding a bike … learning ML (machine learning) … okay, they are different, but having the patience to improve your skills incrementally will bring success in both pursuits. What are your options for learning faster,

---

2 James Clear, *Atomic Habits* (New York: Penguin Random House, 2018).

better, more creatively? What new communication skills, mathematics, or coding languages do you need to learn first? What gaps in knowledge are you dealing with? Identify and fill them; they can be the keys that unlock your successes.

Whether you hope to conduct bench, behavioral science, or environmental research or write an algorithm that will help physicians understand skewed data, you can reach out by email to professors and lab directors at universities within driving distance of your home and ask for an opportunity to intern (but only after you have conducted a science literature review on their work). You can peruse HarvardX and find numerous free courses at an introductory (but sophisticated) college level in diverse fields of interest. If you want to pay for a certificate in the course, you can do that as well. If politics and world affairs are more your thing, you can join debate and Model UN in school and receive coaching while you spend time on your own researching your subject matter to become articulate in your presentations. These are all meaningful narratives that you can discuss on your college supplements as well.

Your Six Make-or-Break College Application Factors

- **Grades in the most rigorous courses (AP/IB/college courses) are most important to colleges.** Past success in rigorous courses is the best predictor of future success in college courses. As a point of interest, if you read the *Harvard Crimson* about admissions procedures, you will notice that to score an academic 1, an applicant must be a "potential major academic contributor" with "summa potential and near-perfect scores and grades." It also helps if the high schooler has "national or international level recognition in academic competitions." So, if you have your eye on the Ivy League, please keep these words in mind.

- **Rigor of curriculum.** Colleges want students who have challenged themselves with the most rigorous courses available at their high school. If your high school offers fifteen APs and you've availed yourself of only three or four, that's an issue. However, if your high school offers few or no APs and you have pushed intellectual boundaries by taking college courses at a nearby college or online in a certified program like Stanford University Online High School and receive a grade for each, then Admissions will take note of that in a big way too.

Colleges want students who have challenged themselves with the most rigorous courses available at their high school.

- Now, a word about the AP madness. If you are taking five APs in a year and you *know* that taking one additional AP class will overwhelm you, don't take it! I don't care how many kids in your school are taking AP Psych as a sixth AP. They are likely not creating the kinds of leadership opportunities that we are talking about in this book—the ones that swing admissions decisions in your favor! That's because they don't know about them. Well, that's your ace in the hole—not another AP course in an AP-laden year.
    - How much time does an extra AP class cost you? Let's say beyond the normal class, there's an extra six to eight

hours per week of homework and studying for tests, and thirty-six weeks in a school year. Let's say in preparation for the AP test, you also study for an additional ninety hours. In total, this means an extra 378 hours.

- How much could you accomplish with your leadership project/organization/business/research with an extra 378 hours of time? The possibilities are mind boggling.

- **Standardized test scores.** Your SAT/ACT scores are still considered very important if the colleges you apply to are requiring them. When a top-tier school says it will superscore these days or only look at a student's highest numbers, it is being disingenuous. Superscoring, in general, is like asking a jury to make its decision on all the evidence presented after having been told by the judge to strike and forget what people just heard "because it is inadmissible in court." Top-tier schools are like elephants—they remember everything. So, sending in an initial low score with the hope that an admission committee will think only about your higher score will not help your case because top-tier schools weigh all aspects of your application. An example of an honest comment about standardized test score importance from Carnegie Mellon reads, "We're interested in the general pattern of your scores but will give the most weight to the highest score you've received on any of the exams." Clearly, Admissions wants to determine whether your much higher score on the SAT retake might be due to a few months of intensive tutoring ("… the general pattern of your scores") instead of your natural intelligence. Why give a college the chance to think that way about you? So, if you are applying to mostly top-tier or Ivy League schools, it's best to study as if you only had one chance to take the test and then actually take the test only once (twice, at most!) because you never know which school is going to request all scores to be sent. AP test scores during sophomore and junior years are still important to the top tier schools because so many students are opting out of taking SATs/ACTs (similarly, the IB exams are weighed heavily, if you take those).

- **Leadership commitment.** This does not mean being a member of five different in-school clubs. It means being the leader of one or two in-school projects or clubs and making impact through them, as well as being the founder and builder of two or three initiatives that make impact outside of school. Remember, you cannot do everything, and if you try, you'll end up like Buridan's ass from the famous parable notably conceptualized by Aristotle and later used to satirize the moral determinism of French philosopher Jean Buridan. The story goes like this: There's a donkey standing halfway between a pile of hay on the right and a bucket of water on the left. He is both starving and thirsty but doesn't know which to go to first. He turns right toward the hay, then left toward the water. Right, toward the hay, then left toward the water. Right, left, right, left. Eventually he collapses on the road from hunger and thirst. Students, if you have lots of ideas but think you must accomplish them all in the short term, you will collapse from exhaustion, and so will your ideas. If, however, you have foresight and perseverance and realize that eventually you will get to the most meaningful projects you have ideated (not everything is a "now" thing), **then** you can prioritize and spend the time you need on each.

Colleges care about how long and how deeply you have been committed to a few initiatives, and about what you have accomplished, not what you've dabbled in.

- **Letters of recommendation.** Choose only the two teachers who will glow about you. If you've grade grubbed in an AP History class and then decide to ask that teacher for a recommendation because you're an A student, think again. That grade grubbing will come back to bite you in the recommendation. Your high school AP teacher works hard and can be easily ticked off. Remember, you want to be an aggregator of attention in the Admissions office, not in the high school teacher's lounge. Never ask a teacher for a recommendation if you've battled them for grades. Here are some useful tips for ensuring that you get the glowing recommendation letter that you deserve:
  - Make the most of junior year by forming relationships with your favorite subject teachers. Hang out and chat after class. Ask for reading recommendations when you are interested in a particular curricular unit. Let your teachers know that you lead study sessions with classmates before tests or that you tutor students when asked. Provide your teachers with the anecdotes they can use to build powerful recommendations for you.
  - Participate and show interest in the books or concepts you are exploring in class. Ask thoughtful questions. Remember, every question you ask serves as a bet with yourself—that the question will be of interest to your teacher and of use to your classmates, and that any impression you make and information you gather that

does not seem to have immediate application might still become valuable in your future.

- Go to extra help to either receive help or give help to students who need it. Your teachers will show appreciation in the recommendations they write for you.
- Remember also to form a bond with your guidance/college counselors if you can. They send out recommendations and reports on you to your colleges of choice.
- Also important: stop by and say hi to your principal from time to time. Did you know, if you're a top student, you can ask your principal to make a call on your behalf to your first-choice school? Well, you can. But your principal has to know who you are first.

- **Your Common Application personal essay and supplementary essays:** I cannot accentuate enough how important these essays are. In fact, the application essays are so significant to the admissions process that I will devote an entire chapter to them in a section called "Writing Your Winning Application." The essays are your only personal shot (aside from your ResuMotiv) to show Admissions a side of you they can't see from the numbers on your transcript. You present yourself to Admissions by telling a story, something we, as humans, are biologically designed to hear and tell. How do we know this? Because chemicals like cortisol and oxytocin are released in the brain when we're listening to or reading a story. We make sense of the world and its inhabitants through stories. So, when Admissions asks you who you are, you don't give them an algebraic formula or a repetition of your résumé—you tell them a story.

- **Demonstrated interest.** Click on all emails that come in from your colleges of choice so your view is registered by the senders. Go on college visits when possible. Write to admissions officers every month or two with updates after you submit your Common Application. Do an exceptional interview. All these things show Admissions how much you want to attend that college. Of course, applying Early Decision (ED) can also help, but remember that ED is a self-selecting pool of the top students seeking admission to that college, so expect extraordinary competition. These are all the gateway factors that allow you to be considered at your top schools.

Finally, for those of you who have set your sights on the Ivy League and top tier and are looking for a little "college chiromancy," a formula to follow for more likely acceptance, I must tell you that there is no such formula. Sorry. In fact, if I tried to give you one, I am sure someone would exclaim, "But I know a student who got into Harvard with lower scores and fewer APs!" All I can do for you within the boundaries of this book is provide the following criteria that do tend to help give students a bump toward acceptance at our nation's most competitive institutions of learning: A 3.9–4.0 unweighted GPA in the most rigorous courses offered by your school plus high SAT (above 750 on each section) or ACT (above 34 on each section) scores plus high AP scores (mostly 5s). This is a start—only a start. Let's pause so that we can underscore the recent Admissions language surrounding standardized tests: when an Ivy League or top-tier university says it will be extending a test-optional admissions experience to applicants, that does not mean that you should decline sending in superior scores. Those scores are national data points and will be taken seriously by Admissions until the day that all standardized tests are discontinued.

Moving on with the "bump" formula, add compelling/interesting essays plus unique accomplishments outside of school that show passion and intellect over a significant period of time (such as winning national or international competitions, publishing, studying at a conservatory precollege program, having a solo concert career, creating an organization that produces major value that creates major value over a couple of years, or building an app that solves a weighty problem) plus glowing teacher recommendations plus demonstrated interest in that university.

Please take these observations seriously when you sit down to create your dream board. On your list, there should always be *REACH* schools; there just can't be UNREACHABLE schools.

The Ivies and all top-tier schools are picky about the above points because they want to accumulate a class of "world changers," future leaders in health, science, tech, industry, literature, and government, and a campus of students motivated to push each other to accomplish big things that benefit the school and humanity while they're at college and beyond. How do we know these points are true? Listen to the words of Harvard's Dean Emeritus William Fitzsimmons in a past *New York Times* interview: "We like to think that all of them [our students] have strong personal qualities and character, that they will educate and inspire their classmates over the four years of college, and that they will make a significant difference in the world after they leave Harvard."[3]

There's your sign. And how do they find their leaders? On your applications. Past success predicts future success.

3 William Fitzsimmons, "Guidance Office: Answers from Harvard's Dean, Part 3," September 14, 2009, https://thechoice.blogs.nytimes.com/2009/09/14/harvarddean-part3/.

What It Takes to Be an Exceptional Applicant

Can we talk for a moment about mindset?

Your success in high school, college, and life is profoundly influenced by the mindset you cultivate.

- If you spend your life online, you will be exposed to and constricted by echo chambers. Listening to people with the same opinions all the time prevents you from learning how to challenge opinions.
- If the friends you hang around with are naysayers (always shooting down your dreams) or exclusively followers (innovation does not happen if all you do is follow) or linear thinkers, you won't have the guts to build outside the lines.
- If all you see are problems, will you notice when there's an opportunity in front of you?
- If you look for the easy way out in high school (taking the courses that require less rather than more brainpower), will you be searching for gut classes taught by staff instead of eminent professors in college?
- If you believe that staring at the same college essay prompt or organizational challenge in the same way over a long period of time will eventually bring the most creative solution, then think again.
- If your only reason for picking up a book is to study for a test, you might not notice that books shape the way we think, not just the way we answer multiple choice questions.

- Different communities of people whisper different messages. Go out and listen. Think kaleidoscopically: your friend might walk down a street in NYC and hear noise, but you walk around and hear symphonies. This is what makes people with divergent talent and different cultural and educational backgrounds so interesting. Think about the rampant confirmation bias in society—you know it's there—the systematic decision to watch, listen to, and prefer any new information that confirms what we already believe. Be the student who is interested in all opinions: weigh them, turn them, research them, and then emerge with a decision that is yours for now with the understanding that it might change again if society, circumstances, or the people you meet change. Descartes (sixteenth-century mathematician and metaphysician) notes that the "diversity of our opinions arises not from the fact that some of us are more reasonable than others, but solely that we have different ways of directing our thoughts, and do not take into account the same things."[4]
- Make time for being fascinated—and not by your computer screen, please. You can't make high-level decisions in academics or in your personal life solely from internet articles, friends' assumptions, or cat memes. If you find that the things that fascinate you are different from those that occupy your friends, you will need to set aside time for each of those endeavors and extract novel experiences like the bee that purposefully heads from flower to flower to find its honey.
- Opportunity arises from the unexpected, so how will you know when to expect it or what it looks like if your default

4 René Descartes, *Discourse on Method and Meditations on First Philosophy* (Indianapolis, Indiana: Hackett Publishing Company, Inc., 1999).

mode is, "I never have luck or cool things happen to me," or "I live in such a small town, I'll have to leave before I find opportunities"? Please remember, you bring *yourself* opportunity. *You* make things happen. Keep your eyes open, try new things, say yes instead of no (because much of the time, *no* comes from a place of fear), meet new people any chance you get, listen to the older generation—the fact that they have lived a life makes them automatically "wisdom machines." As William Jennings Bryant noted, "Destiny is not a matter of chance; it is a matter of choice; it is not a thing to be waited for; it is a thing to be achieved."[5]

- Read. Those books on your shelves you've always been meaning to read cannot remain encased like memorabilia in a shadowbox—do not dust them off right before your college interviews just so that you have a favorite book to discuss. When I shop through my bookshelves for the right book to reread, I am always reminded of the beautiful statement by scientist, astronomer, and author Carl Sagan on the magic of books:

    > What an astonishing thing a book is! It's a flat object made from a tree with flexible parts on which are imprinted lots of funny dark squiggles. But one glance at it and you're inside the mind of another person, maybe somebody dead for thousands of years. Across the millennia, an author is speaking clearly and silently inside your head, directly to you. Writing is perhaps the greatest of human inventions, binding together people

5 William Jennings Bryan, "America's Mission", speech delivered at Washington, D.C., (22 February 1899), as published in *The Book of Public Speaking* (Vol. 2), http://www.forgottenbooks.com/readbook_text/The_Book_of_Public_Speaking_v2_1000538531/149, accessed June 2022.

> who never knew each other, citizens of distant epochs. Books break the shackles of time. A book is proof that humans are capable of working magic.[6]

Reading makes you a more capable and rigorous thinker. There will always be roadblocks on your high school path. Your superpower must be learning to jump the roadblocks. If you think you can handle an AP course but are unsure about whether you can receive an A, take the rigorous path, and push yourself to find out where your boundaries lie. Just maybe you can do it! If you never try taking that level of course, you will automatically be closing certain doors when college application time rolls around. For some, not choosing a very rigorous academic path might be a perfectly acceptable compromise for peace of mind, but for others of you, it might simply disguise your capabilities. You'd have to be an octopus to go through life without deliberating and doubting—embrace the fact that you are an intelligent, unique, creative being and, with that comes the "Spidey sense" to diagnose problems and notice opportunity. Choose to look for opportunity instead of problems. Saying *yes* to academic opportunity can create an exceptional applicant.

- Free up your mind. Whether you are trying to think of something new to say or how to say something old in a new way, or you're stuck on a design problem or working on an innovation within your field of knowledge but have hit a dead end and need inspiration from a muse, begin reading and learning across disciplines. Studying something totally foreign to you for an hour or two can spark an idea when you

6 *Cosmos*, episode 11, "The Persistence of Memory," Carl Sagan and Ann Druyan, aired December 7, 1980, on PBS.

return to your original problem. If you are an economist, read psychology; if you are a physicist, study fields like biology or immunology; if you are a computer scientist, study philosophy or literature to find out what makes humans (and, perhaps one day, technology) empathic. Outline the insights that you have assimilated from those other disciplines, and then apply them to your field. Since you bring to each of these foreign studies a unique point of view, you might not only generate differently beautiful questions for that field but also start looking at your own field through new lenses. Not everything has an "answer." Some problems just require a new way to observe. Friedrich von Stradonitz envisioned the round shape of the benzene ring after vividly dreaming of a snake biting its own tail. Nobel laureate Richard Feynman came up with his winning idea of quantum electrodynamics while observing the spinning medallion on a plate that a Cornell University student hurled into the air in the cafeteria. These and thousands of other "aha!" bursts came from mental time away from "the work," leaving room for the unexpected and synthesizing links between apparently disparate things. There are tons of stimuli out there just waiting to spark brand-new insights. Allow yourself the time and patience to wander, observe, and study "kaleidoscopically"; then, sit back and watch how inventive you become!

- Succeed on your own terms. Oh, this is a tough one. You are still rather young and dreamily determining what your future holds—be it medicine, engineering, law, education, literature, research, or creating in one art or many. Take the course, read the books, have the internships, learn from capable mentors, build the products that either reinforce your "first" future (because, dear student, you will have many) or turn your head in another direction. No one—not a friend, not a parent, not a neighbor, not a professor, not even Grandma—can make that choice or create that success for you. If you fail, it will be on your terms, and you will have the gumption to pick yourself up and rebuild. If you succeed, it will also be on your own terms, and you will know the pride that comes from choosing well. The world is built by flexible, imaginative, and highly motivated people. I was reading an unexpectedly interesting article on barnacles that someone recommended to me the other day, the first paragraph of which stopped me in my tracks. "The barnacle is confronted with an existential decision about where it's going to live. Once it decides, it spends the rest of its life with its head cemented to a rock."[7] As we've already discussed, your generation of students will not be expected to live linear lives; don't be a barnacle.

When to Think Like Alexander the Great and When to Think Like Chesterton

In his book *The Thing*, G. K. Chesterton discusses the wisdom of understanding policies and laws before just barreling in and deleting them when assuming they are no longer of use, as one might remove a seemingly extraneous fence on a piece of property.

The short lesson of Chesterton's fence is that one should always analyze and learn the reasoning behind the existing way of doing things before deciding to do those things differently. Think of Chesterton's random fence sitting on a property as a mental model. You

7 John W. Gardner, "Personal Renewal," speech given to McKinsey & Company, Phoenix, Arizona, November 10, 1990, *PBS*, https://www.pbs.org/johngardner/sections/writings_speech_1.html#:~:text=%22The%20barnacle%22%20the%20author%20explained,us%2C%20it%20comes%20to%20that.

might see no reason for the fence and find that it's an eyesore on the property. "Take it down!" you exclaim. However, if you pause and consider not only the immediate repercussions of your decision but the repercussions of those repercussions, you might determine the very good reasons that fence was constructed in the first place. There might be cattle over the hill that you can't see (they would have a fine time moseying over and dining on your grass if that fence were removed), or perhaps one day someone will buy that property over the hill and care for wild horses. Wild horses are beautiful to watch at a distance from a fence on your protected property! In other words, "Don't take down a fence until you know why it was put up."

Now, what could this possibly have to do with you, dear student?

Let's look at standardized tests as a fence. Although SATs and ACTs have been relegated to a lower position of importance at some universities and removed from the requirements of others (like the University of California system), those tests, along with AP scores, still appear to have tremendous value in the eyes of many top-tier and Ivy League universities. The dates for these tests sit before you like a fence. You could just decide not to take them. Why should you (asks your first-order thinking)? Maybe if enough students decline taking the exams, the requirement will fall out of favor. Not so fast! There are still valid reasons for the tests to be in place—if only because they provide national data points through which colleges can assess your mathematical and reading skills as compared with other college-ready students (and on many campuses, like MIT, for example, those skills must be at an exceptionally high level to ensure you make it through the first semester). Once you think about the advantages of attending your teachers' office hours, working through prep books, and studying intensively to do your best on these standardized tests, you might decide it's all worth the effort to show Admissions you were not worried about how you might score. That fence might be worth keeping.

Then there is the opposite mental mode: the Gordian knot.

Gordius, the king of Phrygia, tied a most intractable knot when he fastened the yoke of his wagon to a beam. As legend has it, anyone who could then untie the knot would become the ruler of Asia. Not to be outdone by any other warrior (or knot specialist), Alexander the Great tried very hard in ways both conventional and unconventional to untie the knot and finally assessed that the legend does not say what tools one could use to get the job done. So, taking out his trusty sword, Alexander swiped at the knot and cut it in half.

Legend or not, Alexander did wind up conquering parts of Asia in an extraordinarily fast and strategic fashion. However, for our purposes, what you need to know is that "cutting the Gordian knot" has become a way to describe a clean solution for an "apparently insurmountable difficulty."[8]

When can the simplest solution be the best?

An example of an annoying issue that enterprising students with ideas worth sharing come across is the difficulty or, in some cases, bureaucratic nightmare involved in getting their schools to create a TEDx: https://www.ted.com/participate/organize-a-local-tedx-event/before-you-start/tedx-rules.

To create your event, you *could* follow the standard rules found on the website: select your event format, determine if you need an adult co-organizer, create your event program, determine who your speakers will be, apply for a TEDx license, recruit your team of student volunteers, receive permission to use the venue/school of your choice, ensure your budget, gather your social media marketing team … Are we overwhelmed yet?

8 "Gordian knot." *Merriam-Webster.com Dictionary*, Merriam-Webster, https://www.merriam-webster.com/dictionary/Gordian%20knot. Accessed May 19, 2022.

Just reading through this standard operating procedure scares off most students from advocating for a TEDx club at their schools.

But not you! You can use the Gordian knot path and cut your work in half by just applying for a TEDx Studio license. You can now create a stand-alone event that can be either live or virtual. Students can apply online for a license that will be valid for one year from your approval date. As long as talks are under eighteen minutes, you will not be limited in the number of talks you can produce with a Studio license. The whole application simply involves you summarizing three fascinating ideas for talks by people you know will present (e.g., either exceptional student leaders, eminent artists, politicians, advocates, scientists, educators, etc., in your community) and submitting it.

Done! One Gordian knot slashed. One intellectually scintillating extra-curricular created!

I share all these mental models and pieces of unasked-for advice because I believe each one of you students is remarkable and represents possibility—the kind that shapes a world. No one said it better than the gifted cellist Pablo Casals:

I believe each one of you students is remarkable and represents possibility—the kind that shapes a world.

> "Each second we live in a new and unique moment of the universe, a moment that never was before and will never be again. And what do we teach our children in school? We teach them that two and two make four, and that Paris is the capital of France. When will we also teach them what they are? We should say to each of them: Do you know what you are? You are a marvel. You are unique. In all of the world there is no other child exactly like you. In the millions of

> years that have passed there has never been another child like you … You may become a Shakespeare, a Michelangelo, a Beethoven. You have the capacity for anything. Yes, you are a marvel. And when you grow up, can you then harm another who is like you, a marvel? You must cherish one another. You must work—we must all work—to make this world worthy of its children."[9]

We must all work to make this world worthy of you. We of the older generations are trying. But then: What will you do? Where will you take us? How will you get us there? Who will you be? These are the questions I hope you think about in between studying and racing from ballfield to performance stage to lab to job. These are the sacred questions.

What a Mouse and His Cheese Can Teach Us about the Path to College Acceptance

There are students who work at the highest level and attain the top grades because it is in their nature to do so—they are driven and achieve a sense of great pride in being rewarded those grades for their efforts. There are other very bright students who seek the grades with the belief that having top grades alone (and some scattered in-school leadership) will automatically bring acceptance into the Ivy League. Sadly, those students are let down when they are not admitted. Then, they feel taken advantage of by a system that was supposed to reward their devotion to excellence.

The good news is that many of you are resourceful and hungry young scholars who have learned how to learn, and this generation

9 Pablo Casals and Alfred E. Kahn, *Joys and Sorrows: Reflections by Pablo Casals* (New York: Simon & Schuster, 1970), 295.

prizes independent learners. The other good news is that if you can shift your thinking early enough in high school toward exploring more creative leadership, advocacy, or intellectual or entrepreneurial endeavors—the ones that *can* elevate you from the status of average bears with great grades to remarkable humans—you will also shift your college acceptance success.

Let's look at how being adaptable and fearless about taking new paths to possible success can lead you right to college acceptance at your dream schools! I am going to modify a story from one of the most famous business books of all time, *Who Moved My Cheese?*, by Spencer Johnson. The narrative tackles two things that you high schoolers deal with all the time: expectations and fear of change. In my adapted version of the story, the characters are all mice, and I use a fair bit of poetic license 😊.

I'll set the scene. Four little mice, Sniff and Scurry and Hem and Haw, are scampering around a maze, the place they spend most of their mouse time. They are in search of that one thing that will make them happy: for the mouse, it's cheese (for the high schooler, it's that dream school).

So, Sniff and Scurry wake up early every morning to be the first at Cheese Station A so they get the cheese before any of the other mice.

On the other side of the maze, Hem and Haw find Cheese Station B, and it seems to be loaded with cheese. Day after day Hem and Haw go to get their cheese from Station B. Soon, they become a little too comfortable with their cheese, thinking it will always be there, so they start waking up later and later, relaxing on the job.

One day, Sniff and Scurry notice the cheese at Cheese Station A is decreasing. Do they react and say, "Oh no, but our plan was to just follow the path to Cheese Station A forever?" No, they don't groan about it; they simply put their running shoes back on and pivot … smelling out a new path to a new cheese station … Cheese Station **B**. *Uh-oh!*

When Hem and Haw, who had always gone to Cheese Station B, arrive there the next day at their usual late hour, they are shocked. There is no cheese left. "What? No cheese! Who moved my cheese?! It's not fair!" They return the next day, hoping the cheese would magically return. It hadn't, but their hunger certainly had.

"We followed the best cheese path every day and deserve our cheese. It belongs to us!" say Hem and Haw. They are afraid of having to go back into the maze to find a *new* path to cheese. They had devoted time and effort to finding the best cheese path, after all. But successful paths to cheese, like successful paths to college, *change*.

It was fear of failure that made Hem and Haw worry about taking a different and creative path. Cheese Station B was their comfort zone—it's what they knew.

Well, Haw decided to stick it out on his linear path with the hope that cheese might still appear if he continued checking each day. That did not go so well for Haw.

Hem decided to take control. Facing the unknown of where to find new cheese without his friend, Hem began to visualize cheese success! He could do this! He set off on a new course. The sense of adventure began to energize him. Hem had learned a brand-new lesson: expect change and adapt to it quickly. What you're afraid of is never as bad as what you imagine.

Students, we can all take a lesson from Hem. There is no reason to continue down an outdated path of expectations. Find your curiosity and fascination *now*, and follow it toward a brand-new project, internship, or independent study *now*—something few others are exploring in school. If you realize the biggest inhibitor to change lies within yourself, you will be unstoppable.

Economist John Kenneth Galbraith had it right: "Faced with the choice between changing one's mind and proving that there is no need to do so, almost everyone gets busy on the proof."[10]

Your Four-Year High School Timetable: What You Need to Do and When

High school is important for so many reasons, the greatest of which is that this is when you embark upon a meaningful and qualitative period of self-discovery. Find what you love to learn. Embrace even those courses you don't love—because they are life experiences. Work as hard as you can to determine your path to college. If you're reading this book as a freshman, good for you! If your high school career is already underway, don't be tempted to skip through the sections here that are aimed at underclassmen; it's just possible that you might have missed a step in preparing for your college-admissions journey, and you need to be aware of that.

The admissions journey is as much a smart marketing endeavor for life as it is an academic endeavor. Finding *you* requires more than putting in the necessary hours to ace your subjects or join after-school activities that your friends have joined. Finding *you* requires a thoughtful, adventure that you should take as early as possible and in as many fields as are interesting to you to determine where your light will shine in high school.

Remember that the college-application bins in Admissions offices are crowded places. It requires something beyond your grades to stand out: it requires a special journey. Take the time you need

10 John Kenneth Galbraith, Economics, Peace and Laughter (New York: New American Library/Signet, 1972).

to find your extraordinary tilt during high school, and you will shine on your application!

Take the time you need to find your extraordinary tilt during high school, and you will shine on your application!

Look at your college application as an important painting. First you will apply broad brushstrokes by setting out a strategy for success beginning in freshman year—through scheduling the right courses and activities and exploring leadership opportunities inside and outside of school. By sophomore year your head should be seriously into your studies, and your after-school hours should be used to explore leadership positions, creative talents, technical skills, or business opportunities that you can turn the crank on in a big way. Begin to learn what you're made of. By junior year, you're ready to fill in the details: standardized exams, higher development of your talents, holding down a job, and founding or furthering your community project, organization, business, or political advocacy. If you're a STEM student, begin research at a lab or with a mentor, write a research paper, and position yourself for local or national competition. All of this will prepare you for an exciting and busy senior year of writing your college applications and demonstrating to yourself and Admissions that you are a dynamic person and a go-getter—someone who will be interesting in life and on campus.

Freshman Year

Choose the most rigorous courses offered at your school, but leave time for one fun elective to give your day a breather. There must be one class in your schedule where your grade is not based on two hours of homework and nightly studying. Schedule a meeting with your guidance counselor so that you can get to know each other. Be sure to talk about your strengths, weaknesses, and talents, along with special programs that exist through the high school or in connection with the high school. For example, some high schools have connections with city or neighborhood fine and performing arts schools. Are you the kind of student who must have an arts curriculum in order to flourish? See if you can arrange your course load so that you can leave school earlier each day to attend afternoon programs or classes at a local conservatory or arts school. Perhaps your high school will give you credit for those classes on your transcript.

Are you an athlete who is going for a county, state, or national title? Perhaps you need to finish early each day to practice with your tennis teacher or a coach. You get the idea. Freshman year is the time to talk about all your options. Most students fall into the trap of a standard curriculum when, in fact, they may not be standard students.

By January of freshman year, you should be investigating the summer programs that sound fascinating to you. Contact a college advisor for vetted and highly recommended programs that best fit your fields of interest (or find those programs within the pages of this book).

Sophomore Year

If you're not yet developing your own extraordinary tilt, get on it! You're only in high school once. Explore! Finding one's authentic self can take a lifetime for some and is certainly rare to come up with in a one-year period, so if you are reading this advice during sophomore year, please act on it. Why leave the discovering and developing of your talents and leadership skills until junior or senior year? Think about the stress! Junior year needs to be used for broadening your intellect, enhancing your talents, doing something expansive with your exceptional tilt, and, of course, studying for your standardized exams. You'll need to keep your GPA high because colleges scrutinize junior-year grades closely. Although you can develop yourself and make some extraordinary leadership happen during junior year, remember that the bulk of your time will be spent studying for AP and other advanced courses and preparing for and taking standardized exams. And senior year has its own demands. You're much better off taking the initiative and outlining interesting ideas for projects now.

THINGS TO KEEP IN MIND SOPHOMORE YEAR

Your grades are under a microscope now. Work your hardest to do well. This is the year when most schools allow students to begin taking honors and AP courses. If you think you'll be applying to top-rung colleges and Ivies, strive to achieve As. Hopefully, your freshman-year grades gave you a good start. Although top schools do like to see an upward trend in grades, make no mistake about it—they are used to seeing grades in the A range from freshman through senior year. That doesn't mean a couple of Bs along the way will keep you out. It just means that you might have to achieve more *outside* the boundaries of school (extracurricular leadership, a special academic project, competitive victories through one's talents, public service, etc.) to be competitive in that group.

Let me say a word about AP or IB courses at this point. I understand that the rigor of these courses and the stress placed upon the end-of-year standardized exams have gotten a bad rap recently. Yes, they will be tougher classes than your honors courses. Yes, you will have a hectic couple of months before exams. And yes, you have the freedom to choose not to take AP or IB courses. However, I hope you step up to the challenge. Look, AP and IB courses play a bigger role in your life than just showing Admissions your discipline and intellectual spunk. They also broaden your knowledge base, teach you how to think and write critically in ways you have never experienced, give you an idea of what college classes might be like (although regardless of what you've heard about the difficulty of AP classes or IB programs, they are in no way as difficult as top-tier college classes) and show you what you're made of. If you are afraid to take the intellectual plunge in high school, how much more frightening might freshman year of college be for you?

Part of life is learning how to balance the tough stuff, deal with stress, fail, pick yourself up, and then figure out how to succeed. Taking a challenging academic course of study in high school—whatever that may mean for your personal academic engine—is a wonderful beginning to understanding what it means to rise to challenges in life. There, I've said it: AP and IB courses are good for your intellectual and emotional growth.

The Difference between AP and IB

There are thirty-four possible AP courses (taught at a level *approximating* an introductory college course's difficulty), with associated exams administered during the month of May. The highest score one can achieve is a 5, and with that score usually comes college credit and/or the ability to skip introductory courses on campus. Students can pick and choose which AP courses to take and therefore can demonstrate their academic strengths by taking APs in their strongest fields.

Taking *more* than eight APs by end of senior year may not increase one's chances of getting into a top-tier university but certainly might increase one's interest and in-depth understanding of a subject area.

Many students now self-study certain APs online (like music theory, psychology, and computer science) and take the exams in the spring. The curriculum includes voluminous material to digest and memorize, along with training in textual analysis. AP students may be given a choice of whether to take the AP exams in May—so there is still the option of taking an extra AP course just for the joy of learning, without the necessity of an extra exam. Some high schools, however, have made it mandatory for students who take the class to take the corresponding exams by denying AP class credit for those who do not sit for the exam.

IB classes teach students to be critical thinkers and writers. With its inquiry-based approach, IB courses take a global and interdisciplinary look at topics. Students can choose to take individual IB courses or a full IB diploma—a program that runs for both junior and senior year and requires college-level classes in six academic subject areas. The six-course fields are mathematics, English language and literature, foreign language, a natural science, a social science, and a course in the arts or a second class in one of the core courses.

One of the major achievements of full IB diploma students (and one that prepares them well for college) is the writing of a four-thousand-word paper on an academic topic of interest. The project is undertaken with the mentorship and guidance of a faculty person.

Carolyn M. Callahan, chair of the Department of Leadership, Foundations, and Policy at the University of Virginia, explains, "The content of AP science and math courses often does not enable gifted students to achieve an in-depth understanding of the discipline … The IB program provides greater opportunity for in-depth pursuit of a topic." The takeaway is that a student cannot go wrong with experiencing either program.

Take the practice PSAT given in the fall of sophomore year. The score does not count, but it will give you a good idea about where you stand and what needs improvement in your math and critical reading skills. Then you can start working on those areas.

Begin using your vacation time to check out colleges online. See which has the environment that's best for you. You might already know that you want a "rah-rah" school, a big university, or a small liberal arts college. Students often have a clear idea about what sort of school appeals to them by sophomore year. However, do not close yourself off to other possibilities, because your grades and/or your interests may change over the next year, and so might your decision on the best college environment. Visit websites like Unigo (www.unigo.com) to read comments by students about their universities and YOUniversityTV (www.youniversitytv.com) to enjoy online tours of your college choices.

By December, start researching good summer programs in your fields of interest. Perhaps you want to audition for a well-known summer music/conservatory program, intern at a tech firm or law office, take an immersion course in an unusual language or one you already study, take an academic program abroad in courses not available at your high school, or do science research in a renowned program in the United States. All of these are wonderful ideas, but there are so many more options available to you.

Junior Year

Junior year is not for the faint of heart, that's true. It is a year replete with standardized testing, the stress of balancing a rigorous course load, leadership positions in full swing, plus additional visits to colleges. It's enough to drive any student to Starbucks! But resist the caffeine, or this could be you!

YOU SHOULD SWITCH TO DECAF IF:

- You've been on Wikipedia for twenty-three hours and still can't figure out why there was no Pope Sixtus VI in your AP Euro textbook.
- You've been studying calculus so long that the voices in your

head have bodies.

- You're writing code to circumvent the character limit on the Common App.
- You've spent more than forty-five minutes trying to figure out the difference between Chicago and Turabian citations.
- The idea of applying to fifteen colleges suddenly sounds good to you.
- You've found Waldo.
- You're annoyed with the Common App for not having an eleventh activity line for your expertise in miniature golf.
- Your English teacher assigns a ten-page paper, and you ask if it's okay if you're ten pages over.
- Your study break to Starbucks results in your request for something larger than a Trenta.
- Your guidance counselor sees you in the hall and asks how you're doing, and your response is, "Not now, I'm busy!"
- Your regional admissions officer has received twelve emails from you asking if he's gotten the previous fifteen.

Junior year is the year to keep your eye on the prize. Put every hour you can into your GPA but not to the exclusion of elevating your leadership profile *outside* of school. Continue the thread of leadership or talent that has brought you success so far, or create a novel leadership project or position that relates directly to the thread of interest you have followed until this year. Be careful about résumé padding—if you've never cared about joining the debate team, now would not be the time to start.

TAKE YOUR PSAT/NMSQT IN OCTOBER

Begin your PSAT studying by August and continue through to the exam date in October. It may seem unimportant to qualify as at least a commended student on the PSAT, but it does have its perks. Being a National Merit Semifinalist makes colleges sit up and take notice. It says several things about you, not the least of which is that you either have excellent natural intelligence or were focused enough to prepare in advance to succeed on this test. Either way, it's a win.

Start your search for scholarships and grants. Look for grants that are available through public service organizations, write for them, and begin a creative community outreach project if you haven't already developed a defining leadership activity outside of school. If you have a thread of service since freshman or sophomore year, now is the time to bring your work to some sort of climactic stage—whether it's organizing a major fundraiser, major media exposure, or winning a competition and networking with that competition's board to move your project to the next step. This is the year to make things happen in your leadership sector.

This is the year to make things happen in your leadership sector.

Are you concerned about being in a field like biology, which highly regards science fair victories, while you haven't won any to date? Here's an example of the kind of thing you can do to turn the tables in your favor during junior year: become founder of an archival journal of all research papers from your high school and hold fundraisers to fund its annual publication. Volunteer to create an online source for your high school science fair abstracts so that freshmen and sophomores can see the type of work that has been sent to national fairs. Interview the heads of research at all neighboring high schools to get the secrets of a winning project and offer the interviews in an online product to STEM students. Now you have an entrepreneurial project that reaches through the application and says, *Look at me!* This is a way to turn weakness into advantage. Colleges may be more impressed with your entrepreneurial attitude than they are with another person from your class who won a few awards.

Schedule a meeting in the spring with your parents and guidance counselor to discuss college options. Before the meeting, create an outline of the fifteen schools in which you are most interested. Also have a heart-to-heart discussion with your parents about finances. Is the college choice dependent upon scholarships?

Organize your SAT/ACT and AP exam dates. This bears repeating: remember that even if your chosen colleges suggest that you do not have to send SAT/ACT scores, they are certainly not saying that they do not want AP scores. You will self-report those on your Common Application, and they will be viewed as important pieces of evidence about your readiness for rigorous college courses. Taking AP tests shows a college that you are a hard worker, motivated, and a self-starter—all qualities needed on campus.

Now listen—regardless of how many friends are taking their spring breaks to visit colleges, you should plan to stay home and study for your AP exams. They come up fast and furious after spring break, and you'll need all the time you can get to feel like a master of your material and to keep your stress levels down. In the spring of senior year, you will spend a few overnights at your top-choice colleges—preview weekends—and that will allow you time to sit in on classes and test out the on-campus environment before making your ultimate choice.

THE FINAL STRETCH

Ask your two favorite teachers for recommendations by June. Hand them your résumé, and highlight any parts that you think will be valuable for them to know. Even your favorite teachers may not know that you intern at a law office during every vacation or that you run a business outside of school or that you write a political blog.

When it comes time to create your senior schedule, make sure it's the most rigorous one you can handle, within the most rigorous course load offered at your school. If you are hoping for a top-rung or Ivy League university, you must take AP-level English, math (at least Calculus AB, unless you are an engineering major, in which case you would be expected to take Calculus BC or even Multivariable), foreign language, history, and science.

There is nothing wrong with taking AP Statistics in school, as big data has created an information revolution and soaring interest in statistics and data science majors. However, if you are a strong mathematics student, I would advise taking AP Statistics in addition to AP Calculus, not *instead of* AP Calculus. If your high school does not offer one or both mathematics course, you can study them online through well-regarded online high school vehicles such as Brigham Young University, Stanford Online High School (OHS), Laurel Springs, or Johns Hopkins University–CTY. Why should you do this? Because although many top universities won't admit it, they have concerns about students who seem to take the easy way out of difficult courses. For some schools, not having AP Calculus (even if you have AP Statistics) is a showstopper.

TRUE STORY

An admissions officer from a particular Ivy League school was in a casual meeting with interested students at a top NYC high school guidance office (as is typical in the fall, when admissions officers visit high schools). During the Q&A section, a student raised his hand and said the following: "I have a 3.9 unweighted average (never got below an A– on anything), have 1580 SATs and six APs—all 5s—but I didn't sign up for AP Calculus in senior year because I want to go into law and thought AP Psychology would serve me better than calculus. Will that be a problem when I apply to your university?" Without missing a beat, the admissions officer replied, "You know, there are other very good schools you could apply to." What a burn! However, the lesson learned is to know which courses are expected at the colleges you apply to and, if in doubt, *always* take AP Calculus!

If you are not such a mathematics enthusiast, you can always study calculus in a stress-free environment online or through homeschooling. Such pushing of academic boundaries demonstrates to colleges that you care enough about the life of the mind (or the subject matter) to go for the extra challenge.

If there is a research paper that you have completed in any discipline and you are proud of it, make sure to keep it on file. Then send the paper either as a PDF or hard copy through snail mail to the department head in the university to which you're applying (as well as to Admissions).

It's Summer before Senior Year. *Buckle Up!*

It's Common Application time! Your personal statement, résumé, and activities form should be finished by early August. You'll be so thankful to have all that done once you see how many supplementary essays there are to conquer. If you can have your top five to six application supplements completed by the time you begin school in September, you will be a much calmer student senior year.

A way that your parents can really help you is to allot time to choose video segments and photos of your high school accomplishments for an elegant video-highlights presentation through ResuMotiv, the multimedia-generated résumé presenter. ResuMotiv takes your photos, videos, slides, audio, and research papers and creates a sophisticated and custom visual presentation of your high school successes, talents, and achievements. All my students, at home and abroad, use ResuMotiv to create a narrative arc of their high school careers. Top-tier schools love it. It's your one chance to meet admissions officers face to face and demonstrate your *why*, and that's very powerful.

Lastly, if you have noticed that you are simply not achieving the kinds of standardized test scores that reflect your intellectual ability, investigate colleges that do not require the SAT or ACT. Some of our best universities and colleges have removed those requirements: University of Chicago, the University of California system, George Washington University, Wake Forest, Bates, Bennington, Bowdoin, Colby, Connecticut College, and Franklin & Marshall College, among others. Additional schools are joining this list each year, accelerated by data from the admissions seasons during the pandemic, when colleges dropped requirements for standardized tests as testing centers closed around the country. As you are probably aware, even the Ivies are adjusting to test optional for the next few years as both a kindness and an experiment. However, most high-achieving students with competitive test scores will still be sending those scores as extra data points to be considered because *test optional* does not mean *test blind*, and the top schools always pay attention to students with high numbers.

Senior Year

TO-DO LIST FOR SEPTEMBER

- Meet with your guidance counselor to check over your first few college supplement essays and the Common Application personal statement, if you don't have a personal college advisor. Discuss any shifts that have occurred in your decisions to apply to certain universities—including which schools, if any, you have chosen for early admission. Discuss the wisdom of applying early for your specific set of circumstances: your grades, your finances, your scores, the pool of students from your high school against whom you'll be judged, and so on.
- Make sure that you have two safety schools and at least five target schools on your list, in addition to four to five reach schools. These days, it's wise to apply to ten to twelve schools if your GPA and scores put you on a competitive level for college admission.
- Scale up your leadership endeavor and get quantifiable results to put on your résumé from that leadership. For example, if you have built an app for the National Multiple Sclerosis Society (NMSS) that locates the specialists in MS across the country so that, during travel, if a patient has an episode, he or she can find a vetted and society-endorsed specialist, make sure to write the following on your résumé: (1) how many people in the country have MS (and therefore, the possible number of people your app can serve), (2) how many specialists there are, and (3) how many people are served by the NMSS in total. Another point that is significant to tell Admissions is if the NMSS *endorses* your app.

- Remind your two selected teachers about recommendation deadlines. Teachers can get overwhelmed during the fall.
- After all recommendations are sent, please be sure to give your recommenders a handwritten thank-you note. That's a lost art.

TO-DO LIST FOR OCTOBER

- Complete last-minute details on your early applications: whether Early Decision, Early Action, or Restricted Early Action. *Apply!*
- Have one more go at the SAT/ACT.
- If there are unusual circumstances to your schooling (for example, if you are homeschooled, schooled part time at a conservatory or film school, or attend school online), send a note to your admissions officer at each college and thoroughly explain your academic choices and reasons for pursuing them. That puts you on their radar, and that's a good thing.

TO-DO LIST FOR NOVEMBER

- Request supplementary recommendations from an additional teacher (in a different subject, if you want to show you're well rounded), your boss, lab mentor, or the Executive Director of an organization you serve.
- Love notes to Admissions: Toward the end of November, send an email to your regional admissions officer to show demonstrated interest (if you do not know who that officer is, ask your guidance counselor). This note should also act as an update on any new or continuing activities from the time that

you submitted the application. If you have won any meaningful awards, started a new project, or simply want to tell Admissions that X University remains your first choice and that you will attend if accepted, write those things in this note.

TO-DO LIST FOR DECEMBER

December is the month to complete Regular Decision applications, so ...

- Proofread before sending essays out into cyberspace. You'd be surprised how many rejections happen just because of a few typos. Admissions believes that if that's the kind of care you take on the most important piece of writing in your young lives, what kind of care will you take on your assignments once on campus?
- *Don't* wait till 11:55 p.m. to submit applications by deadline! Server crashes happen! That would be a devastating finale after all your hard work. Additionally, Admissions can see when you have sent in your application. Applying so late makes it look like that school was an afterthought.
- Make this month count by receiving top grades through the interim reports. Colleges take the first-semester senior-year grades very seriously. Those are some of the most important numbers that colleges see.

NOW LET'S TALK ABOUT DEFERRALS

If you've applied Early Decision (ED), Early Action (EA), or Restricted Early Action (REA), you might get accepted (yay!), you might get rejected (that school clearly doesn't know what it's missing), or you might get deferred. Deferrals cause the most frustration for seniors, so let's dig a bit deeper. What's going on when you are deferred from a college?

1. Sometimes the reason is as simple as the university being uncertain of the full candidate pool and wanting to wait for the Regular Decision (RD) round to see who might not have been admitted to their ED schools. That gives top-tier schools the opportunity to swoop in during the RD period and accept the students who are most competitive.

2. When a very high-level applicant is deferred from an EA school, the reason might be "yield protection." The committee would love to admit you but has made the assessment that, with your GPA, scores, and other qualifications, you are likely waiting for and will accept a school on an even higher rung than theirs (a perfect example is Tufts Syndrome—they reject you before you can reject them—or being deferred by U of Chicago because they believe that if you weren't awaiting a decision from the Ivies, MIT, or Stanford, you would have applied there with ED status, which is binding, instead of EA. There is some wisdom in that thinking).

3. Sometimes Admissions might feel that a student is a fine intellect but not an active leader or notable creative talent. Always interested in building a lively and diverse freshman class, Admissions might want to see if you develop leadership or passion projects during your senior year.

4. Sometimes Admissions has a question about a particular grade somewhere on your transcript and wants to see whether you have continued doing A-level work in all your AP classes or if you have chosen to further elevate your studies by taking an additional online course. This kind of deferral is a "let's wait and see" situation.

5. One reason you might not want to hear is that Admissions sees that you have the academic vigor and talents to succeed on their campus, but they have an overwhelming number of students who fit the bill from your state or even from your community, so they want to let you down gently. The inner narrative might go something like this: "We think very highly of you and believe you would do well here (hence the deferral and not a rejection), but our school has too many computer science majors," or "There are five other students applying from your school with the same credentials," or "Our school really needs tuba players this year, so please don't take it personally if we reassess you in the larger RD round."
6. Something to remember, when dealing with the top tier or Ivies, as much as 50 percent of an EA pool might be deferred. Staggering but true.

How to View Your Deferral

1. It is a chance to show that you have continued your academic excellence, as witnessed by your superb interim grade reports.
2. It is a chance to be viewed anew in an applicant pool that is not quite as brutally competitive as the early pool—typically considered self-selecting.
3. It is a chance to show that you pulled up your grades from the first quarter.
4. It is a chance to scale up your passion project—whether it be research oriented, entrepreneurial, advocacy, arts based, or technology related.

Once you have determined that you want to continue being considered for the school's RD round, you will either fill out a form sent by the school, write an email pledging your continued loyalty to that university as your first choice, or write a letter of continued interest.

How to Know What to Do

The only hard-and-fast rule is that if the university in question says in no uncertain terms that it does not want to receive any further updates, "why" essays, or letters from you, then please take that seriously. Most schools will give deferred students a chance to update with new materials or award notifications. If your preferred school mandates no additional information, then providing such information could endanger your acceptance to the university through RD.

If you decide to write a letter because the college in question encourages that, be sure to reaffirm why the school is an excellent fit for you (this can be a paragraph or a one-pager similar in content to a "why" essay), how you have used senior year to push academic and creative boundaries, and what new honors or awards you have received thus far. Ultimately, a university that is considering an applicant needs to know that the applicant cares enough to keep campaigning for admittance.

JUST DO IT!

1. **DO** complete your Common Application personal statement, résumé, honors and activities forms, and any college supplementary essays that drop early in July so that you're ready to hit the ground running on August 1, when the majority of college supplements open up! In this way, you might be able to complete six to seven essay supplements by the end of August. That's the way to walk into senior year with less stress.

2. **DO** clean up your social media; don't overshare! Students, can we talk? Approximately 40 percent of admissions officers uncover information on social media that negatively affects an applicant's chance of admission. Harvard's former dean of Admissions has noted that admissions officers "may have occasion to encounter an applicant's digital footprint ... which could be negative if it raises serious questions about character or judgment."[11] Hmmm ... they *may* see that accidental social media post? That *could* go poorly for you? Bottom line: make sure your social media accounts only show the best of who you are and the projects you've championed.

3. **DO** credentialize yourself by (1) taking advanced courses online through eminent programs like Johns Hopkins University–CTY or Stanford University OHS; (2) by taking summer courses at top-tier universities, getting certified transcripts, and sending them to your selected colleges (this shows them: "Of course I'll do well at your school! I've succeeded at a school just like yours this past summer!"); (3) by engaging

11 William Fitzsimmons, "Guidance Office: Answers from Harvard's Dean, Part 3," September 14, 2009, https://thechoice.blogs.nytimes.com/2009/09/14/harvarddean-part3/.

in science research; (4) by building apps, if that's your thing; or (5) by receiving advanced certifications in fields you care about (like the Laureate Certification in Advanced Science Research Writing[12]). Put those credentials to work in your life, not just on your college résumé!

4. **DO** contact your regional admissions officers every month or two after submitting applications to let them know about your latest endeavors or awards! Why? Because they want a reason to accept you, but they must see that you're scaling up your intellectual and leadership pursuits. Your note might go something like this: "Dear Admissions, I wanted to share some exciting news with you. I have just won X award." **OR** "I have just completed my independent research project on [title of your project and reason you're pursuing it]." End it with, "I look forward to sharing further updates throughout the year. Signed: *You!*"

5. **DO** click on every informative email that comes to you from a college you care about! Hover on the site for a few minutes so your view can be registered by the sender.

6. **DO** attend any casual meetings with admissions representatives from colleges you're considering! Wait till the end, go down front, hand them your business card (with name, intended major, and a link to your project's website), and ask a thoughtful, prerehearsed question. *Why?* So they'll remember you. **Does it matter?** Yes. It matters.

---

12 "Laureate Certification in Advanced Science Research Writing," laureatecert.org

7. This is the age of Big Data, and colleges are collecting your demonstrated interest. So, every time you click, every time you sign your name to a list, every time you take a college tour, every time you write a thank-you to the tour guide, every time you call Admissions with questions, every time you write to Admissions with an update—they're following you and your demonstrated interest.

TO-DO LIST FOR JANUARY, FEBRUARY, AND MARCH

The next three months are about waiting and updating but also interviewing.

In Alumni Interviews, Lead with Your Devotion to Intellectual Vigor

Ideas never come out quite the same way when we *think* them as when we *say* them. Memorize each major point on your résumé along with an accompanying anecdote and rehearse your answers aloud, just often enough to speak fluidly. Steer the conversation to whatever you want to concentrate on in the interview: your academics, your debate qualifications, your nonprofit, your business, your athletic prowess, your intellectual fervor, your musical talent, etc.

These days, alumni interviews are just as likely to happen over Zoom or Skype as they are in person. However, the etiquette does not change. Dress nicely, smile, and give off engaged energy from the moment you make eye contact (and do be sure to make eye contact—more difficult on Zoom, but keep your eyes on the lens!)

If you have an exceptional résumé, you can always ask your interviewers through email on the night before the meeting whether they would like to receive a copy. Some interviewers will tell you it is not necessary, while others will be happy to have the additional information.

Do you have any other physical products to show your interviewer? A book you've written, a magazine you've edited, or a short video of your company, nonprofit organization, or project? Anything visual is a bonus for the purposes of this interview. It will provide a jumping-off point for conversation.

Plan your segues from academic interest to academic interest, and rehearse those segues until they are fluid. If you are discussing your interest in certain subjects, no interviewer is going to stop you in the middle of a thought. A thread of academic passion is just what colleges are looking for. Then, seamlessly plan a bridge into how you will demonstrate your love for those academic interests on campus.

For example, if you're a history major, perhaps you will become a member of the debate society or run for student government. If you play the flute and have an intellectual interest in music composition, you might talk about auditioning for the college orchestra and taking a beginning composition class. If you're a writer, make sure you have researched all the publications on campus so that you can discuss your favorites. Once you fully present those thoughts, say something like, "Having accomplished X (a project, getting published, starting a business, concertizing) made me realize how important it would be to study Y at this university." Then, begin your monologue on the exciting courses in that area of study that you discovered by researching the university's departments and professors. Talk about the worth of each course to your planned academic concentration. Show that you have researched the work of a few professors, and explain what excites you about their research and how you might love to become involved as an assistant in that research. Show your dedication to both academic rigor and intellectual vigor. Students forget to do this during interviews, but it's important to remember that colleges will not accept you on your extracurricular prowess alone.

After you've presented the "intellectual you" to the interviewer, discuss the clubs, sports, and societies you hope to join. If you can come up with a way to communicate leadership or a new direction for one of those clubs, now would be the time to present that idea. Show the interviewer that you are a self-starter.

Show your dedication to both academic rigor and intellectual vigor.

Finally, prepare at least three interesting questions about the school for your interviewer (however, if the answers can be found easily online, the interviewer will know that). Have your answers prepared, and steer the conversation wherever you want it to go: to your academics, your debate qualifications, your nonprofit or business, your athletic prowess, your intellectual fervor, or your musical talent, etc.

Questions Your Interviewer Will Ask You

1. Tell me something about yourself. (This is your cue to talk about your biggest and most interesting accomplishments/experiences. A reminder: lead with an academic accomplishment such as research, if you can, and go into detail).

2. Why do you want to go to X University? Which courses of study or classes compel you to apply?

3. What would you like X University to know about you that cannot be found on your application?

4. What is the most interesting class you took in high school?

5. What is your least favorite class?
6. Tell me about a time you failed.
7. Tell me about a time you led.
8. How did you spend this past summer?
9. Which books have you read in the past year that were not assigned for school?
10. If you met the president today, what would you ask?
11. If you could have dinner with anyone—dead or alive—with whom would it be?
12. What was the biggest disappointment you've ever faced?
13. Which AP courses have you taken? What are your SAT/ACT scores? (These are questions that interviewers do not need to know to craft a written impression of you as a person and interesting addition to campus, but they sometimes ask anyway.)
14. Which other schools did you apply to, and which one is your top choice? (While they're not supposed to ask this, it does come up.) Let it be known to the interviewer if that school is your top choice or at the top of your list. Then, supply the name of one more school on the same tier and then a couple of schools that are a level down—thereby demonstrating that in fact, their college is probably the first choice, but there is one school that is close behind and giving them some competition.
15. If you say you have an interest in public policy or politics, beware, because depending upon how feisty the interviewer would like to get, you may be served questions about Facebook privacy issues, healthcare policy, international relations, etc. Be prepared with the latest news.

16. Again, if you can keep speaking about interesting things in your life and academic pursuits, you'll take up much of the interview time with those points. Remember to always tell the interviewer *why* you decided to take on the leadership, participation, or founding roles that you chose. The *why* is what impresses because it takes the interviewer into the core of who you are and will be as a student on their campus.

APRIL: AND THE LUCKY COLLEGE IS ...

Here it is! April 1, and you have been *accepted*! Now the tables are turned, and the colleges are courting *you*!

- Attend prefrosh overnights and "accepted students" weekends.
- While on campus, talk to as many people as possible. Talk to students and professors, sit in on classes, and talk to career services and Admissions! Can you see yourself both giving and receiving from this university?
- Talk with your parents about the financial aid offers. Did your second-choice college give you more aid than your first choice? Ask your parents to call the preferred school's financial aid office. See if they'll match the other college's offer. Sometimes, that works.
- If there is a waitlist in your future, then send a note that says you would like to remain on the school's waitlist.

However, it's almost impossible to get off the waitlist for a top-tier or Ivy League university, so my advice to you is this: fall in love with the college that fell in love with you. Remember, you were their first choice.

The Timeline and Reasons for College Application Prep

As you have probably noticed by now, it's doable but difficult to wait until the end of junior year before suddenly creating yourself. It's also not realistic to expect acceptance into top-tier schools with only high grades, some volunteer hours, and good test scores. There are no longer any admissions guarantees for the superb academic student. But there is one guarantee when you pursue fascinations beyond the standardized classroom—that you will create an interesting and valuable mind and will, undoubtedly, be a light in our world and a success in your own field.

Today's metrics for acceptance at the nation's top fifty universities and colleges are not as obvious as they might have seemed ten years ago. Students always had to have top grades, scores, and projects that made them stand out, but now they must also show adaptability, character, profound academic interest, and advocacy. You do not need to be an international speaker or run a program that saves thousands of lives, but you do need to uplift your community, your mind, your art, or your personal cause in thoughtful ways with an eye toward writing about how those experiences changed you.

Why Strive and Achieve for That Best-fit College?

Each school year in both mid-December and the end of March, I receive phone calls from happy, ebulliently shouting, newly admitted precollege students and home videos capturing cheering families, popping balloons, and overly excited dogs (the cats seem to take admission in their stride). These are students who have planned and studied and struggled and created and researched and pushed themselves beyond the common, both in school and out. They have given up some things and received other things because of dedication to their work, deployment of imagination and talents, and focus on what they believe is their destiny. I keep these recordings in a folder on my desktop to remind me each year what acceptance sounds like and how beautiful it is to strive and achieve.

Why do you do this? Why do you students put heart and soul into your high school career with the hope of attending that special university that will shape the next four years of your life? I have had the great joy and privilege of working with thousands of students privately over my thirty-plus years in the field and mentoring an additional five to ten thousand students annually during long-form conferences and admissions boot camps. So, the ardent and resolute pursuit of study at our nation's top colleges and universities is a vibrant part of my life.

The faculty of schools like Columbia University or University of Chicago, for example, believe that a great university should be selecting "the furniture" that is positioned in a student's mind. This concept was the core of the 1828 Yale Faculty Report, which suggested that a liberal arts education should not target specific professions but rather "lay the foundation which is common to all."[13] To be sure, as Jacob Bronowski asserted in *The Ascent of Man*, humans became "singular creature[s] ... not [merely] figures in a landscape,"[14] and the way we continue such an ascent is by studying the great minds, engineers, scientists, and strategists who came before us.

Perhaps having the time and mind space during college to study ancient civilization, literature, religion, politics, sciences, and math-

13 Report of the Course of Instruction in Yale College by a Committee of the Corporation and the Academical Faculty (New Haven: Yale College, 1828).

14 Jacob Bronowski, *The Ascent of Man* (Boston: Little, Brown and Company, 1973).

ematics shows you *how* to think by setting an academic table that tells you a little bit about *what* to think. And that's okay. Eventually, active student minds assimilate it all and begin creating their own connections and thoughts. I love this concept that college provides a student's first "apartment" full of intellectual furniture. Through the embrace of interdisciplinary majors and minors on campus and free rein on electives, regardless of departmental affiliation, a university provides the kind of student bonding and mosaic approach needed in professional careers and intelligent conversation. We should all be having open and interesting debate on the issue of what pieces should be assembled into a great college education (and not only because some universities, like Georgetown, will ask this very question in their supplementary essays) because those pieces will be different for everyone. The more debate on why we care so much about receiving the "right" kind of college education, the better!

There must be some reason our best and brightest students dream of studying amid a diverse and spirited community of scholars, regardless of the field they wish to pursue. Perhaps we have some understanding of the places we can go when exposed to multiple mental models, the stories of brilliant leaders and the obstacles they encountered, and the wisdom of history's keenest observers of the natural world. During the American Revolution, John Adams reminded the next generation of scholars, "I must study politics and war, that our sons [children] may have liberty to study mathematics and philosophy. Our sons [children] ought to study mathematics and philosophy … natural history [and] commerce … in order to give their children a right to study painting, poetry, and music."[15] Please feel free to fill in any area of technology and medicine in this snippet

15 L. H. Butterfield and Marc Friedlaender, eds. *Adams Family Correspondence*, vol. 3 (Cambridge, Massachusetts: Belknap Press of Harvard University Press, 1973).

of aspiration or change language to fit our more evolved place in history, but you get the idea.

So, why do we do this? Because we strive and hope. Because we think and invent. Because we disagree and then find places to converge. Because new remedies, cures, and technology are rarely the work of isolated geniuses from the same field. Because brain-computer interfaces mean that somehow scientists will have learned to decode thoughts (but not without the input of humanists and philosophers). Because the idea of relativity—that the same subject can be represented dependably and without compromise in a variety of ways—is central to physics and mathematics but should also be studied in relationship to journalism, religion, and politics. Because most of us spend our days problem-solving in our niche fields on our small patch of Earth; for us, that is where beautiful art, complicated emotions, and human strivings and failings all play out. Yet there are so many greater concepts and views to think about. Whether you are a STEM, humanities, or social science student, you can benefit from the writers, philosophers, and astronomers that study the universe and the human condition because there is bound to be syzygy in the questions you ask. At the very least, you might, as Elon Musk says, "expand the scope and scale of consciousness" (*Time* magazine).

At the most straightforward level, you strive for a fine liberal arts education to be surrounded by people who are equally or more talented than you and therefore will keep you hungry to do and be better.

You will learn how to tell stories and become an interesting interview subject by the time you are called for that first summer internship interview during the winter of freshman year. Yes, it all happens that quickly, and you do not want to come across as one dimensional. For example, if your skills and studied talents are only in technology or only in data analysis, the company's recruiter might believe that you do not have the breadth of educational experience to inspire a team creatively through multiple mental models. Remember that we live in a connected and competitive world—a global talent marketplace—where your skills can become billable hours for someone somewhere who will do the job as effectively and, possibly, for less money. Your generation will need to bring multidimensional talents to the table, and the best way to assimilate those is to attend a college that has strong faculty in every field, capable of engaging both your areas of specialty and the liberal arts through interpersonal skills, cross-disciplinary problem-solving, imagination, and communication of ideas.

Career acceleration is different today. Companies used to do internal training in business processes and human resources; there was a longer tail to their cultivation of an employee. Now, businesses want the ready-made employee because young people move on quickly from their first jobs. This is a generation of seekers. Therefore, students graduating from a top-tier school, whether public or private, have greater perceived value to employers because they have succeeded amid tremendous rigor of curriculum and have held their own among some of the nation's best minds.

In times past you'd make contacts in college, but you'd also have other opportunities after graduation: careers with face-to-face daily interaction through office culture. That is changing; the predominance of remote work means fewer opportunities for developing such work relationships. So, it's important to build those relationships during college with alumni that offer undergraduate internships, eminent faculty members, and those five peers you are surrounded by in your dormitory, at lunch, during coffee, or in the classroom who will push you to elevate yourself and stimulate big ideas.

So, there are many reasons for "why you do this"; i.e., strive to excel academically and adventure creatively both in and outside of school. The gifts you receive from taking a chance and going after an exceptional and interdisciplinary education become the foundations for the success you will build in the future.

PART TWO:

BECOMING A LEADER, A SCHOLAR, AND AN ALL-AROUND EXCEPTIONAL APPLICANT

You as Foxhog

How do you as high school students and future experts in your chosen fields use your minds and talents to benefit society and capture Admissions' attention for all you are and all you will be on their campus? How do you discover opportunity? You discover opportunity by doing, risk-taking, building networks, bringing together divergent interests to create that new product, organization or research ideas. After all, you learn who you are in practice, not in theory.

Because of that, I'm going to tell you about the fox and the hedgehog—because learning about the fox and the hedgehog will help you understand how to create yourself in practice, not in theory, during your own all-important pre-admissions period.

A fox evades his attackers in a number of exhausting but inventive ways. (He's a creative!) A hedgehog has only one tried-and-true strategy—he hunkers down and lets his spikes do the work (and that works for him!). So, as the Greek poet Archilochus notes, the fox knows many things, but the hedgehog knows one big thing.

In the same way, there are students and thinkers who look at the world through the lens of one particular idea; they believe in it and become expert in it—they're hedgehogs. And there are those students and thinkers who learn and act in the world through a variety of perspectives and mental models; they are open to outlier solutions—they're foxes. Steve Wozniak, cofounder of Apple, is a hedgehog; Steve Jobs was a fox.

So, which kind of student is best positioned for the future of top-tier college admissions and an impactful career? The student that is a hybrid of these two animals. You must know one or two big things in more depth and detail than your contemporaries to be respected, trusted, and move scholarship forward in your field. But to really ignite that knowledge, to make impact on campus, in the lab, in your future professional practice, you need to think, diagnose, and disrupt from a variety of mental models and perspectives—through positive risks you've taken, things you've built, platforms you've led—as early as high school.

To really ignite that knowledge, to make impact on campus, in the lab, in your future professional practice, you need to think, diagnose, and disrupt from a variety of mental models.

You need to become a new species: the foxhog. And you can evolve into a foxhog in so many ways through leadership, advocacy, rigorous research and entrepreneurship outside of school.

Let's explore some examples of how students merge their talents (art and STEM; business and psychology; music and invention, among others) and take on the attributes of foxhogs!

Greg: Bolts[16]

I'm going to walk you through a high schooler's case study: a quick mapping of how one of my students and I built his STEM high school journey so that you can see the actual path this young science researcher took to a fascinating academic and creative experience and to his dream college acceptances. This is Greg's journey:

Greg was an all-A student, he had a talent in art and design but hadn't taken art lessons since middle school. Greg determined that he would never use those skills: he was a STEM guy. Although Greg had a special academic proclivity for the sciences, he was not sure how to pursue them outside of school or how to make that interest pop off the pages of his application to Admissions. Here's how Greg differentiated himself:

- First, Greg applied to UC–Santa Barbara's summer research program; he was accepted because of his excellent application essays and grades, and he wound up studying the flow of non-Newtonian fluids at the Leal Lab of UC–Santa Barbara. As a result of his dedicated, critical work, Greg created an original research paper that he was, eventually, able to send to college department chairpersons a few years later.

16 All names of students and organizations or pursuits have been changed for anonymity.

- Next, Greg founded a science speaker series in his town—holding monthly sessions at the neighborhood bookstore (which also benefited the bookstore, giving them an uptick in new clients buying coffee and desserts during the speaker series—a win-win for everybody.) Greg lived on Long Island, and so he invited scientists from NYC and LI medical centers and from Cold Spring Harbor Lab on LI (one of the most famous biomedical research labs in the world, home to eight Nobel Prize winners). The speaker series pulled upward of fifty students each month and wound up sparking a rise in neighborhood high school research programs (so the high schools were motivated to notify students over the PA system about each of Greg's monthly speaker events).
- As someone who loved reading articles about his major area of interest—neuroscience—Greg read about and became fascinated by a neuroscientist who worked with stroke victims in rehabilitation at Johns Hopkins University (JHU). We decided, since Greg had a research paper and a speaker series to his credit, he should reach out to this scientist/physician at JHU. He did, and Greg gained an internship at the Human Brain Physiology and Stimulation Laboratory on campus.
- Over this summer internship, Greg created another original research paper on his project at JHU and presented it at the end of the summer before the lab director and postdocs—a presentation he videotaped for his college application. He put it on his ResuMotiv.
- While at the JHU lab, Greg found that he was passionate about the work they did and wanted to raise funds and visibility for the lab's latest project in stroke rehabilitation.

- In the fall, after his internship ended, Greg began sketching again and designed a beautiful and unique product: Bolts men's accessories (tie bars and cufflinks) that featured a lightning bolt (because that's the way Greg viewed the attack of a stroke on an individual).
- Greg spent weeks finding the right manufacturer, had the tie bars and cufflinks manufactured, and set up a donation link on the lab's website. After encouraging several local jewelry stores and designers to carry his product as well, Bolts went on sale that winter to a community of 1.75 million people.
- End of story: by the following summer, the summer in which Greg was writing his college applications, Bolts had raised $25,000 for the lab's research.
- Greg had a very good admissions acceptance year!

That's how you stairstep your way to getting noticed by Admissions.

Gabriel: Josué

If you're a premed student, have you participated in the kinds of human-to-human healthcare interactions at home or abroad that inspire you, proving that saving a life and developing empathy should be the cornerstones of your future medical pursuits? Summer of junior year is for having those kinds of interactions and experiences that can mold you, change your perspective, and inspire not only you but an exceptional college essay as well. Let me tell you a story that inspired a future physician:

My student Gabriel was on a mission trip to Honduras, doing triage, working in the pharmacy, and translating patient complaints from Spanish into English for the volunteer physicians. He talked about the lines of hundreds stretching from doorway to examination room, families that walked for many hours—now huddled into units of emotional support—sleeping on the floors overnight just to have their loved ones diagnosed. And there was little Josué, clinging to his mama with a fever that rose with every hour that ticked by. Finally, toward nightfall, Josué's mama knew she had to start the many-hour journey back home to her other children. She picked up the limp, feverish body of her boy and brought him to Gabriel, begging him through tears to make sure Josué saw the doctor and received medication. She gave Gabriel her address in case anyone needed to get a message to her. Then she went on her way.

The end of the story is that the doctors were able to diagnose Josué that evening and give him the medication he needed for recovery. At 11:00 that night, Gabriel and the lead physician hopped into a truck with Josué and began the journey to his village. The physician didn't want his mother to worry any longer than she had to. They saw Josué's mother walking along the road; they pulled over, gave her the good news that her son would soon be fine, and dropped both mother and son off at home.

Gabriel wrote on his college personal statement: "It was the kind of medical kindness one only reads about in novels, I thought. I was very aware that this moment was not just happening to me. It was happening to *us*—all of us who are young and dreaming of entering the field of medicine because: there is a chance of saving a family, not just a life; of saving potential, not just a child; of saving the future of a nation, not just one little, fighting spirit."

For those of you pursuing a premedical track, this is it, isn't it? The reason you have chosen the profession: to change the world with your medicine, your research, or your technological innovations?

However, until you have such experiences for yourself, you won't understand how they can change you too!

Gabriel is now a premedical student at Brown University's eight-year medical program, the Program in Liberal Medical Education (PLME).

Lena: DragonHorse Sneakers

Now, what about those of you who are entrepreneurial?

Well, it's one thing to talk about owning and running a business in the future and quite another to have started a business during high school. If you do move forward on your own projects, you will have a story of surpassing obstacles, managing volunteers, and changing perspective—topics Admissions loves to read about!

When Lena arrived in America to study from China, she found that, when learning a new language amid a new culture, doing a lot of talking is not the most effective move. So, she listened and watched: learning more through observation than she ever could have through broken conversations. Lena watched what people wore on their bodies and how they told a story by what they had on their feet. There was the hipster with Chukka boots, the sporty teen with impossibly white Keds, and the sneakerhead with a different pair of shoes for every day of the week.

It dawned on Lena that everyone notices each other's sneakers because shoes send a message about who that person is. Lena is an artist and entrepreneur, and her observations inspired her to use art to connect her generation of East-West scholars, innovators, and creatives through a globally conscious footwear line with a strong "global collaboration" theme.

DragonHorse was born. With sneaker designs that speak to issues of climate change, human rights, healthcare, world peace, global arts, and student collaboration in business, Lena's DragonHorse sneakers feature twelve designs and are worn by students in China, Hong Kong, India, Russia, Germany, and the United States. Lena proudly lists testimonials on her sneaker site, with students sporting designs of the generational issues that mean the most to them.

One of the coolest results of DragonHorse is that students are connecting with each other through Lena's website based on the sneaker designs they have purchased representing the issues they hold most dear. Many of these students from around the world are now activating social good projects *together* in their joint areas of interest: two young American artists are volunteering through Zoom for an art-therapy organization in China serving children orphaned by the pandemic, three have begun a recycling initiative in Hong Kong, two have collaborated on an app that connects food banks with student volunteers in India, and two Model UN students from Germany are developing a podcast featuring teen perspectives on pressing global issues. It is through these developing lenses that Lena is scaling up DragonHorse Sneakers with a socially responsible component: the unlocking of a charitable donation with the purchase of each pair of sneakers to support art-therapy organizations in China and the United States.

In this way, Lena's sneaker line is more than a product to sell; it is an emblem of transitional thinking in her generation: the transition from othering and isolating to connecting and collaborating.

Chris: WAVE Speakers

A maker deeply influenced by music, Chris wanted to create an immersive experience for other teens as well: a way to see the sound. WAVE is a kaleidoscopic music speaker by design, inspired by ferrofluid: a colloidal mixture composed of tiny nanoscale particles that become powerfully magnetized in the presence of a magnetic field. Chris sketched, designed, adjusted, prayed to be prototype ready, and failed on a bimonthly basis. Finally, in 2021, WAVE took shape in the factory as he had imagined it. Its unique shape and structure allow the speaker to reflect lights in a stratified way. When music plays, WAVE reads the soundwave of the rhythm, and then its software transmits the digital signals so that the Arduino board can understand. By recognizing the rhythm, the RGB light bar inside the speaker generates different colors of light and moving waves, corresponding to the feel and pulse of the rhythm, making music listening a multisensory experience.

Unlike other products on the market, such as the JBL Pulse, Chris's speaker is stationary, making it perfect for the dorm. Since Chris crafted the speaker to look like a traditional Japanese lantern, WAVE creates a calm, meditative state. Chris's love for design, music, and building have culminated in the creation of a product he is proud of and one which his peers now use in thirty-four international schools and colleges.

Bobby: Helping Hands, a Community Business

Bobby founded his business as a social enterprise in summer of 2021 to bring student service and affordable help with household jobs to his rural community. Working throughout his neighborhood, Bobby has the privilege of doing every odd job you can think of and conversing with every type of person: the farmer, the East Coast transplant, the community patriarch, the girl next door, and the cancer survivor. Bobby created business cards and developed community relationships the old-fashioned way: going door to door and handing out his number.

By founding and directing a small community business, Bobby learned not only management but collaboration—the kind of hands-on, focused work ethic that he believes is at the heart of all startups. Bobby's team has done stints as babysitters, painters, grocery deliverers, furniture movers, and drivers for the elderly. The people skills and heuristics required on the job informed Bobby's high school employees and inspired them to pursue undergraduate business programs.

After building his own small business, Bobby will clearly bring to campus the grit and enthusiasm of an entrepreneur. Having studied marketing online and solutions thinking in person, Bobby brings the eagerness of a business-development personality with a careful eye toward "overconfidence bias."

Bobby's Helping Hands donates 10 percent of all revenue to Seattle Animal Shelters.

What the Right Mentor or Advisor Can Mean for You

"Great things are done by a series of small things brought together."

—Vincent van Gogh

As students, you are all innovators in training by virtue of the technology you're learning and the extraordinary opportunities for convergence between that technology and medicine, law, policy, education, and the innate curiosity that you walk around your neighborhood with every day. So, you need to be asking very specific questions: "When I look at the

"Great things are done by a series of small things brought together." –Vincent van Gogh

world now, what's missing, and how can I fill it? What do I do when I don't have to? What books am I drawn to in a bookstore? Why do I come alive when watching sci-fi, doing robotics, solving complex mathematics problems, listening to medical podcasts, coding apps, creating algorithms that make abstract physics concepts easier for kids, reading Plato or Victorian literature, playing Beethoven, shadowing my internist, going on a mission trip?" What if you could incorporate those fascinations into a new piece of technology, a business, or a social project? Brainstorm, outline your idea, and determine which skills you might need to move that idea forward, and then find a mentor and/or subject experts and apprentice with them until you are ready to build your own impact.

Think about what is missing in your life with standardized tests, a standardized curriculum, and standardized extracurriculars. What's missing is time and space for you to develop your own unique skills, your own ideas, your creative talents, your audacious intellects.

So many parents tell me, "My child doesn't know what her passion is yet!" My response is always, "And she won't, either, if she doesn't start somewhere." Parents have a good sense of where their child's talents or proclivities might lie. So, begin your child's training in two of those areas, and enable their success with that training to the best of your ability (e.g., for a young musician, that might mean a lot of driving your child around town for lessons on the weekend or helping to schedule daily practices on the family calendar). If these pursuits wind up working for your child, great! If not, they might inspire a new pursuit. Remember, it's as important for students to find out what they don't want to do as it is to know what they do want to achieve. You don't get 100 percent of what you don't try for.

My hope is that this book gives you back something that has been lost—the path to finding out how remarkable you are. And one way to find that out is through mentorship or study with experts in fields you love or are curious about. Sometimes, all you need to turn the key on innovation or discover a great talent is to align with the right mentor or subject expert who will teach you the skills of the field, the right questions to ask, the way to elevate your talents to make impact on an audience, and the mindset to build yourself into a nonlinear thinker and world changer. It doesn't matter if your interests are in medicine, computer science, ML/AI, data analysis, music, dance, entrepreneurship, social good, or law. There are experts out there who will help you "become." And do you know what happens when you train and discover how exceptional you are? College Admissions notices.

Students, you are empathetic, passionate, vocal, stressed, and determined, and you don't know what you don't know. You want desperately to make impact! However, before you can be a thought leader, it helps to have a thought partner; mentors become the bridge, building student confidence, agency, and reflection.

Mentors, advisors, and subject experts have an investment in you and are, therefore, on your team. Monthly calls and action plans develop student savvy in discovering talents, creating a project, or learning team-management skills. Mentors and advisors help handle the "jazz" that is a part of your life. Your interest and abilities are not fixed; through curiosity and measurable action steps, they will keep evolving with you.

So, who are these mentors I'm talking about? They can be tutors, in-school teachers, college consultants, or family friends in fields of interest to you. Finding the right mentor at the right time has important implications for your development. When the right student meets the right advisor, that student will grow and try in profound and surprising ways, even reaching transformational success.

As a college advisor and life coach for high school students, I have the great joy and privilege of seeing the results of nurturing mentorship all the time. Initially, a student might *say* to me, "I don't really have a passion, or I just want to let you know that I'm an introvert, so 'leading' will probably not be my thing." What I *hear* is, "I have no idea how to build meaningful high-profile projects for my community without having five thousand followers on Instagram or winning the popularity contest required to become president of Student Council." What I *hear* is, "All my friends are super busy, so how can I gather enough classmates to collaborate on a new project?" What I *hear* is, "I'm terrified that developing my own organizations, research projects, apps, algorithms, or musical talents will take up so much time that my grades will drop (and isn't that what top-tier schools care about most?)." What I *hear* is, "I have tried to lead or start clubs and passion projects before, but because I did not succeed the first time, my inability as a leader must be a fixed asset—I've found my limitations."

Without experiencing the joys and frustrations of ideating, putting a foot down on the gas pedal, and starting a project, students stall in developing a growth mindset. Every idea, every progression into learning something new is equated with a test (because that is how success in school is measured for you). So you might enter college believing you do not have the skills to lead or design or build or help a community or mentor another.

The students who are accustomed to mentorship and advising view challenges and brainstorming as helping them become likely to learn instead of likely to fail. This is true of the math competitor, the creative coder, the performer, the writer, the TEDx speaker, the future entrepreneur, and the political activist. Skills are not permanent; they are constantly evolving, blossoming, and fading—at times relevant, at times outdated. Students are elastic engines of possibility, but they do not always realize it.

Let's Think about What Happens in a Student's Weekly Life

Monday: "Today's math test was a breeze. I'm awesome at math."

Also Monday: "How could I have missed handing in that English assignment? My grade is going to tank. I'm such an idiot!"

And again, Monday: "Wow, my principal is nominating me for a national leadership award. He must be really impressed with my community service!"

And finally, well, yes, Monday: "I only got three kids to sign up for my new club. I can't lead anything!"

Exhausting, no? And this is just Monday.

With such fluctuating assumptions hitting students throughout a single day, how can we expect you to locate your emerging talents, let alone define them? However, with mentors advocating for a growth mentality in their students, mixed messaging in school or clubs becomes data, not doom. Together, the student and advisor discover talents and cut away the detritus of after-school clubs that offer no ladder to valuable leadership or scholarship. Subject-specific advising that promotes a builder mentality contributes to the emergence of a student's uniqueness and provides permission for that student to try, fail, rebuild, and try again. It is priceless for a student to have a partner on that journey.

I have been incredibly lucky to work with talented and inspirational students from all over the world throughout my thirty years of advising. While I know that the following are only a few examples of ways young people can pursue engagement and meaning in high school, I believe there is value in sharing a handful of experiences that I helped my own students mold.[17] There will be important takeaways that inspire you to develop your authentic, remarkable passion projects either independently, with a team of friends, or with the help of your own advisor and subject mentors.

Creative Student Projects

World Coffee

Raj, a ninth-grade student from the United States, was feeling isolated when his family moved to Singapore for his father's business. During his time in Singapore, Raj discovered a love of debate and interest in international relations. These interests, combined with Raj's natural propensity for solutions thinking, led him to Model UN (MUN), where, after successfully advocating for his country's policy positions and becoming a respected and active listener, he rose to the position of Secretary General. Through MUN, Raj was meeting students from all over the world and learning their positions on climate, trade, peace, education, and diplomacy.

When Raj and I began working together, he had not yet built any passion project of his own and wanted to somehow reconnect with his friends from the United States in the process. I told Raj about the structure of the eighteenth-century coffeehouse in Europe, which helped catalyze the Enlightenment. Professionals and thinkers from all walks of life would gather at the coffeehouses and share new ideas and old concerns. This piece of history lit a fire under Raj, and he decided to develop a platform called World Coffee. Every Friday evening on Zoom, Raj's friends from the United States, Singapore,

17 Please note that both student names and organization names have been changed for anonymity.

Hong Kong, India, Australia, England, and Ireland got together for two hours to discuss a different focus problem in the world and to drink decaf coffee! As a result, Raj's World Coffee became an online hub for ideation sharing and accumulated a hundred-page book of solutions to small problems in each of these countries, complete with standard operating procedures for each solution. Not only that, but Raj found a meaningful way to reconnect with his friends from the United States who were like minded in their passions.

Raj's World Coffee book is now on the shelves of international school libraries in Singapore, Hong Kong, India, Australia, England, and Ireland.

Music Business: The Online Booking Manager

My student Jake followed music with empirical gusto and data-driven mapping. He evaluated the latest sounds, listened for changing trends, and researched artists, all without any goal in mind. Jake wanted to develop a project that demonstrated his zeal for a future in the music business but did not know where to begin.

After several conversations, we decided that Jake should map out a future business idea for the industry. In one discussion, we determined that by 2025, people will either recognize talent from unusual sources—for example, from YouTube or SoundCloud—or we can assume that the broadcast music industry will stay stagnant and pick up only the artists who follow formulaic structures of radio pop.

Jake believed that in 2025, we will continue to find artists globally through the new Patreons of the world. Patreon is the single largest source of independent funding for content creators on the internet; its monthly billing subscriptions for a few dollars makes it easy for people to explore new sounds. To Jake's mind, the Patreon model meant that more small record labels will need to support tours for their artists.

An aha moment! Jake and I continued brainstorming, which led to his journaling of a new venture that would involve a unified booking manager for global artists with every theater in its system. How do you onboard all those theaters onto a single platform so you can see where the vacancies are? That is the question he began tackling with a team of coders. He thought through the development of technological tools to create the platform: searchable by region; intuitive buttons with action words that do not create mental noise; clean user interface, connecting easily with every booking software. When Jake is done (and that will be soon), this platform will be a prime example of software as a service (SaaS).

The Creative Premed

When students are in high school thinking about preparing themselves for future applications as a premedical student or a biology or chemistry major on the premedical track, they often get so involved in the right courses to take, the preferred number of shadowing hours to complete, and the bench research to pursue that they forget themselves and their talents.

As one of my premedical students (let's call her Carrie) entered high school, time for her favorite pastime, sewing, was hard to find. "After all," Carrie thought, "how could I connect my love for sewing to a college application based around a future medical career?"

To achieve her volunteer hours for graduation, Carrie began volunteering as a tutor for elementary school children. Seeing a creative strategy by which Carrie could link her sewing and teaching, I explained that there was a way to be involved in the healing process years before she entered medical school: she could teach these children how to make a positive difference in the world by enabling them to heal other children in need through their creations. She founded Stuffers.

Carrie's nonprofit organization, which in 2020 donated over sixteen thousand teddy bears with accompanying face masks for COVID-19 protection, has a mission to teach children to use their innate empathy and artistry to heal others, one stitch at a time. On a daily basis, she teaches children as young as six years old how to sew teddy bears through weekly chapter meetings at elementary schools and community workshops. After they sew their teddy bears, she asks her young sewers to donate their new creations to their nonprofit partners who serve children of domestic abuse. By donating these handstitched bears, created with love, elementary school children who sew are empowered to be healers and advocates of kindness to other children in their communities.

After three years, Stuffers has reached over **thirty-three million people globally** through tons of young chapter leaders holding weekly chapter meetings, community workshops, and the magic of social media, like YouTube sewing-tutorial videos. Carrie has been featured on TV, published in over three hundred news outlets, honored through national awards and has won thousands of dollars in grants.

A Biannual Tech Zoo

I organized a group of my students from the same community to pool their talents and enthusiasm for technology and create a biannual Tech Zoo at the high school. I advised my student inventors to turn the school cafeteria into a place where kids can play with and control new tech built by other kids twice a year. Elementary and middle school students from the community would beta test and provide a feedback component on each invention.

At Tech Zoo's first event, there were induction coils and magnets that transformed a shaker flashlight into a device that strapped onto the leg, capturing enough energy to charge a phone while the wearer runs on the treadmill. There was a chore bot that mops floors (well, at least one part of the floor); a remote-controlled robot that can be deployed across hospitals to bring fresh masks, scrubs, and gloves down the hall, cutting down on wasting essential workers' time; an alarm app that turns your computer into a sound and light show on the due date of an assignment; and a serious-looking pen that turns into a can opener and flashlight at the touch of a button. Great fun was had by all (along with great admissions success for the inventors!).

Healthcare Policy Advocate

My student Gabriella's advocacy for STEM education and health-care policy led her to design a unique program for under-resourced schools in her city that brings together STEM-interested high school students and hospital faculty, technicians, and administrators at one of the city's busiest academic medical centers. Gabriella calls the program Health-Pathers, which has now expanded to serve 440 high schools in her state. Interested teens take part in an immersive, informational hospital tour of diverse departments: surgery, radiology, oncology, cardiology, research labs, and administration, among others; the students are then treated to lunch and Q&A sessions with various physicians, nurses, and hospital administrators.

This program is Gabriella's way of providing a path for students in her region who are underrepresented in the medical sciences to gain exposure to the many specialties of medicine, science research, technology, and healthcare careers—information and experience they do not receive at school. This past year, Gabriella created an offshoot of Health-Pathers through a two-week summer camp that provides half-day rotations shadowing physicians and hospital administrators—paid for by grants and hospital donations.

Because of Health-Pathers' success (reaching 270,000 students), the medical center is expanding its focus on the region's youth as tomorrow's frontline medical heroes. Pretty cool.

GlassTale: A Recycling Initiative for Hong Kong

Hong Kong is a city of 7.3 million people, and its landfills are dangerously approaching capacity. Of the sixteen landfills originally built, only three have additional capacity, but with 13,800 metric tons of waste added daily, this space will be used up in five years.

After moving to Hong Kong in ninth grade, Lucas, an environmentally conscious student who is active in class government, was looking for a way to use his advocacy skills to support pressing initiatives in his adopted home. One day, a lecturer from University of Hong Kong (HKU) came to speak to Lucas's class about the importance of recycling, as that was an initiative not yet embraced by the broad sector of families in the region. Upon becoming aware of the grave environmental issues facing Hong Kong, Lucas asked for the speaker's email address—determined that, if Hong Kong was to be his new home, he would set his mind and spirit toward engaging in solutions.

The lecturer kindly took Lucas under his wing and scheduled quarterly calls with him, encouraging Lucas to do three things: research, start small with his activism, and read several books, including Rebecca Skloot's *The Best American Science and Nature Writing* and *Ishmael*, by Daniel Quinn. A pivotal moment for Lucas came after completing *Ishmael*. Chapter by chapter, the book revealed how sad it is that humans have a fundamentally twisted and narcissistic relationship with the environment. Lucas understood that if we continue to see ourselves as conquerors instead of caretakers, the place we call home will soon no longer be able to sustain us.

I encouraged Lucas to do research on Hong Kong's landfills before jumping into a project. His exploration uncovered that 92.3 percent of glass, 374 metric tons per day, is added to the landfills, yet surprisingly, recycling remains a low priority to the government. Talk, instead, centers on incinerators. Young mothers are terrified about passing on dioxins released by such incinerators to their babies. Even parents of teens are frightened by their children's long-term exposure to pollutants like heavy metals and respirable suspended particulates. Lucas reported back to me and then to his mentor, the lecturer, that he believed a structured recycling program would at least buy Hong Kong more time. I encouraged Lucas to build a student organization that could address these issues of concern to him. Lucas founded GlassTales with three friends and a dumpster-size bin.

Lucas led this group of idealistic environmentalists through the bustling streets of Stanley Market every week. With clipboards, aprons, gloves, and a convincing attitude, they traveled from coffee shops to fine-dining establishments, meticulously checking off addresses, collecting glass with care, and hauling the precious cargo back to its storage area in under three hours. Over the semester, they recycled four thousand glass bottles from the sixteen restaurants and coffeehouses in the area. Although Lucas was making positive strides, we brainstormed how he might have even more impact.

The following year, Lucas set up a glass-recycling system at his school, with bins positioned strategically throughout campus. I suggested that Lucas make GlassTales an NGO. The team expanded to thirteen students and set up collection points across a network of six apartment buildings and complexes so that residents could routinely recycle their glass. It was Lucas's plan to create a continual network of environmentally responsible operations for years to come so a part of him could remain with Hong Kong even after returning to the United States for college.

Lucas began environmental research in the lab of his mentor at HKU during senior year and now continues his environmental science studies at Princeton, using his experience and talent to nurture the planet and reverse harm.

A Volunteer Student Marketing Corps for Community Vendors

After eighteen months of pandemic closures, mom-and-pop stores in towns across America began opening. They needed help in getting the word out about the new precautions they were taking to serve their customers: curbside pickup, home delivery, air purifiers in store, masked cashiers, etc.

One student, Mia, decided to help her community of vendors. An enthusiastic social media and marketing student who had received online certifications in the two fields, Mia realized that small businesses need help gaining visibility and differentiating themselves in a noisy marketplace. I suggested that Mia use her measurable leadership skills and natural advertising chops to create a nonprofit digital marketing service corps serving Forest Hills and Cue Gardens in Queens, New York. Within two months, Mia had her volunteer ad force organized: AdIt!

Along with "employing" social media-savvy students who manage the upkeep of Twitter, Instagram, and Facebook pages for neighborhood shops—posting safety updates, off-the-shelf items, sales, photos, and inspirational quotations—Mia doubled down on her coding study. I suggested that with a year of additional intensive study with a subject expert on Java and Swift, she would be able to build apps that would enhance the reach of AdIt. Mia got to work and created a marketing hub for all of Queens' restaurants and specialty food shops—advertising special events and menus. Since launching her app, a huge undertaking, Mia has reported that a majority of local restaurants and takeout shops have experienced a 25 percent uptick in patronage during a difficult time for shopkeepers. Exceptional.

Mia's success with her first apps encouraged her to continue studying with her programming teacher to create a variety of intuitive niche apps that, eventually, impressed Admissions at Carnegie Mellon when she applied and was excepted as a computer science major.

The Graffiti Grocer

Andrew had a talent for painting. He really could sketch anything: still life, landscape, portraiture, you name it. But his preferred artistic vehicle was graffiti art. Perhaps because graffiti art is a bit rebellious, like Andrew, or perhaps because it carries the intimation of social messaging, Andrew found it the most satisfying way to present his talent. Through graffiti art, Andrew felt a connection to issues of his generation that he had never experienced before. It was not only the control of the paint displayed by the artists that opened his mind to the range of techniques and skill proficiency required for this primitive art form but the range of commentary it enabled.

I suggested to Andrew that artists do not create in vacuums and that becoming more immersed in this genre by attending exhibitions would be helpful for his process and whatever project we would develop with his talent. So, Andrew began attending exhibitions of his favorite graffiti artists at local galleries. One of those artists took an interest in Andrew, began providing feedback on his latest work, and offered to introduce him around at the studio of a few accomplished arts contemporaries. This was a game-changer for Andrew.

Some of the artists displayed a political position, a social cause, or a generational journey. In art's ability to broadcast political and social protest, Andrew observed how graffiti art co-opts public spaces for the benefit of people who may not have the means to see art or engage with their own feelings about those societal pain points.

Along with his growing fascination with this art genre, Andrew had also become a dedicated advocate for fighting hunger in his community during the pandemic. He had valuable things to say with his art, but I suggested he tie those messages to his advocacy. We found a way. I suggested that Andrew use the spirit of graffiti art to create subliminal social good messaging on every exterior foodbank and pantry wall in Nashua. His work was beautiful and eye catching; why would a food bank manager not want to feature it?

As a public high school student in an urban environment, Andrew saw firsthand the racial and ethnic disparities between students of lower- and upper-class economic backgrounds. After contacting one of the local food banks he had run canned-good drives for, Andrew offered to create a mural on their large corner wall to capture attention, highlight their kind services, and build community pride by beautifying the space. The new visibility this wall of graffiti art and its hopeful messages gave the food bank led to an increase in activity of 50 percent in the winter of 2020. The manager of the food bank dubbed Andrew "the Graffiti Grocer" (now you know the title of *his* college essay). This was just the inspiration Andrew needed. To date, Andrew has painted the walls of fourteen food banks and pantries in his region and instilled social messaging that has catalyzed new food drive volunteers in six high schools.

Andrew's creative and social devotion caught the attention of every top-tier school to which he applied. Now, Andrew's artistic statements raise awareness about food inequality in his college town, inspiring other underclassmen and community members to lend support.

Enamored of Literature: The Big Book of Beloved Vocabulary

My student Dori did not want to build organizations; she is more of a quiet, imaginative girl and a passionate reader. As reading is her most time-consuming hobby and the thing that makes her most happy, Dori had no idea how to develop this hobby into a creative project that would both carry value for others and differentiate her in the eyes of Admissions.

I brainstormed a two-pronged project with Dori. When she reads, she keeps a diary close at hand. Upon finding and delighting in a new or very old, uncommonly used word, Dori would pause and write the word and its meaning in a glossary, complete with sample sentences using each word. Her glossary quickly grew to fifty pages in length. Dori imagined the glossary as the launchpad for a love letter she might one day write or a narrative she might one day limn. Dori named her glossary *The Big Book of Beloved Vocabulary* and donated it to the high school library (it was often first off the shelves when the AP English Literature class assigned monthly creative writing projects). Thrilled with her initial step toward creating something of value, Dori decided to scale up.

To put her impressive vocabulary to good use, Dori created an early childhood book series to instill a love of language at an early age. She called the series LitWrit. Each story fits on a page, uses at least two big, beautiful words (bolded with the definition at the bottom of the page), has an illustration on the right-hand side, and has a workbook section below the illustration for the child to write three different sentences with each new word. LitWrit became a favorite among third- through fifth-grade teachers throughout Dori's hometown and inspired her to move forward in self-publishing three short novels during high school. Dori was accepted to all her top-tier universities and is presently pursuing a writing career at Yale.

Devon's ShirtShip

Walking down West 45th Street with friends, Devon noticed a man and woman in threadbare clothing, billowy shelters on their backs, and cups rattling with tiny sums as they huddled into a unit of emotional support over the vent. The image was burned into his mind. His friends and he stopped for coffee and talked about school, but he saw *them.* The friends switched topics to summer plans, but he saw *them.* Finally, Devon excused himself, bought a ten-dollar Starbucks card, walked back down West 45th and stopped at the vent. He handed the card to the woman and removed the oversize college sweatshirt he wore over his T-shirt, then passed it to the man. "Selma and Sam," the man said as he gave Devon a nod. ShirtShip was born that day.

Nothing Devon did for Selma and Sam would change their lives, but it changed the way *he* thought about life. On our monthly advising call, we determined three needs in Devon's own community: people need basic necessities, small businesses need advertisement, and students need service opportunities. While others might have seen three distinct issues, all Devon saw was connection—one dynamic service organization expediting solutions. Devon called the organization ShirtShip. He did not know enough to calculate the obstacles ahead, so he leaped resolutely.

A perpetual clothing drive, ShirtShip creates a threefold symbiotic relationship: businesses donate shirts with their logos, volunteers wear those shirts during service to raise visibility for the business, and then the shirts are shipped to underserved families. Devon assembled his most ambitious friends onto a board of volunteers ready to wedge themselves into the fault lines of a pressing societal concern: clothing the needy. He imagined that businesses in his community would welcome the opportunity to increase their visibility, but Devon learned two things in those foundational days of ShirtShip: "We'll get back to you soon" means "Get lost," and a relentless spirit can jump-start positive change.

Devon anticipated dozens of responses as he sent out 220 email requests for shirts to local businesses. No offers arrived. Clearly this mission needed an advisor. We decided to solicit help from colleges so Devon wrote to the student directors of local university community service clubs. That was the move. The students set up calls between Devon and their club members, invited him to meetings, and allowed him to pitch. The club members became Devon's mentors. The first success arrived in a padded envelope three weeks later: two shirts emblazoned with the college name and logo. Understanding how to move forward now, Devon's board began emailing colleges. Campus service centers from Arizona to Maine responded—one to fifty shirts at a time. When local vendors noticed ShirtShip's volunteers sporting different donated college T-shirts during each of their community clothing drives, they began sending product with their company logo as well. Nothing succeeds like success. ShirtShip now serves a community of one thousand needy individuals from Philadelphia to NYC.

Success is a curious thing: it's not always the result of a carefully orchestrated progression of events—sometimes it's simply a response to the unanticipated things in life. Every leap in Devon's future, including his acceptance to Harvard, is in some way a nod back to Selma and Sam.

EcoComics

An environmentalist living in Cambodia for high school, Shreya started by getting her hands dirty through research at Teatown Summer Science Academy in the United States. She would be not only studying human impacts on the environment and the problems currently facing conservation biology but delving into the issue of invasive species as well. As one of twelve accepted research students at the academy, Shreya conducted an independent research study about Japanese barberry (*Berberis thunbergii*), a destructive invasive species that is commandeering forests all along the East Coast of the United States. Research was one part of Shreya's plan to raise awareness of pressing environmental issues. Shreya is also a talented cartoonist, and therefore, part of my plan for her was to determine a unique vehicle through which she could use her sparkling skill set. We landed on the idea of creating an online magazine devoted to the environment, present and evolving ecological issues, and endangered species.

After brainstorming, we came up with EcoComics: a magazine edited by students from around the world who are young scientists and journalists, creative writers, and illustrators devoted to the environment. EcoComics presents engaging heroic journeys of characters encountering endangered wildlife, invasive species, polluted waterways, and at-risk natural habitats around the world. For example, there is the story of Mayur, who devotes his weekends building new habitats for the sun bear, which is headed toward extinction in Cambodia. From the rapid deforestation of the bear's natural forest habitat to illegal hunting for traditional medicine, there are now fewer than one thousand sun bears. Attempting to care for this population means raising money for and re-creating bear bedding and food capsules. Shreya portrayed the story of Mayur and his sun bears in her magazine and created such precious illustrations for her "Save the Sun Bear" comic strip that donations from across Asia began pouring in from students who became fans of EcoComics.

Taking it a step further, Shreya coaxed her high school principal, a bit of an environmental advocate himself, into becoming a mentor and received permission for a "Save the Sun Bear" campaign at school. Shreya determined that by shredding their paper and creating a student volunteer team to bundle the material for transport to Free the Bears (a Cambodian nonprofit), her school could provide not only bedding for the bears but also biodegradable food capsules. In full-on *Shark Tank* mode, Shreya pitched the idea to the director of Free the Bears, complete with a tub of freshly preshredded paper. She explained that if her plan worked, it would cost the organization nothing but a weekly trip to pick up the tubs. The partnership was greenlit. EcoComics now has a readership of thousands in Vietnam, Cambodia, Hong Kong, Singapore, and India.

Add Your Missing X-Factors

The things that are missing from your story or application are as important as what is already in your application. Students tend to follow their peers into school clubs and out-of-school activities. There is nothing wrong with joining your peer group in activities, but if that's all you do outside of school, it makes for boring and repetitive applications from an Admissions standpoint. Taking other people's solutions and trying to insert them into your own life rarely works.

The things that are missing from your story or application are as important as what is already in your application.

So, for example, if you are pre-med and have taken all the requisite AP science courses and engage in Science Olympiad with your friends, please do not automatically think that's all you need to be an interesting premed major when you apply to college. You will find that you cannot import ready-made meaning from one student's life to another. What is fascinating to your friend might be a yawn to you. What is "enough" to your classmate might be just the beginning for you. Perhaps, in this race toward the "expected," you forgot to find your unique talent or narrative. Perhaps you did not push yourself to do research in a STEM field of interest (either independently through a science literature review and online study, which costs nothing but your time and devotion, or with a research advisor). Perhaps you did not develop a unique healthcare initiative or project in your community, or perhaps you did not have meaningful shadowing experiences or engage in mission trips that present you with opportunities for human-to-human interaction with patients. Admissions will notice what's missing and will make certain conclusions: "This student says she wants a future in medicine, but there are no research papers, credentials from free online courses, hands-on experience, or awards in STEM on her résumé. Let's see who else we have."

The same situation can happen if you are, for example, applying as a computer science major who has spent hours learning multiple programming languages (because that is what all your other "computer science friends" do) but has never built an application or algorithm or won the Congressional App Challenge. Admissions will always be weighing your application against students who have taken their interests a step further. So, examine your present résumé, and look for what's missing in the story you hope to put forth for college, and then see how to build yourself in those areas.

You might build or discover yourself through **creative** endeavors like writing a children's anthology, **intellectual** endeavors like developing a thesis, **competitive** STEM pursuits like science fairs, **founding a** small business, or **developing** a product (after plenty of failures). Or perhaps you prefer more leadership-oriented endeavors like creating an organization for a cause you care about or technical endeavors like building an app or an algorithm that is unique to your field of study.

Why should you do these things—differentiating yourself from all the other great achievers out there? Because Admissions can't wedge over 312,000 applicants into 17,000 (give or take) Ivy League seats. Even applying to our nation's top fifty schools has taken on a similar competitive pulse because there are so many intelligent, innovative, and practiced students graduating every year.

Differentiation means not getting pulled onto a hamster's wheel of the same courses, the same clubs, the same sports. It's the antidote to having the "common" application. Such conformity is more soul-sucking than the exceptionally high academic expectations placed on top students. Superintelligent students have been engaged in that academic-rigor struggle for years, and they've come out the other side fairly well. But the lack of creative pursuits, this standardization model of doing everything your friends think is cool or adequate, produces automatons instead of innovators and scholars. By the end of such a high school career, you might find the hamster wheel is still spinning, but the hamster is burnt out.

So, how do you differentiate? To start with, spend freshman year of high school trying out in-school clubs and out-of-school experiences such as journalism, community organizing, behavioral science research, computer programming, mathematics advancement and competitions, world literature courses, drama, music, fine art, dance, stand-up comedy, planning and starting a small business, sports, or woodworking. See what fits your talents and in which clubs you could likely climb the ladder to leadership while bringing value to that club. Then by sophomore year, begin cutting away the detritus—the time-wasting, less-than-fulfilling activities that will keep you from sparking or building the more unusual goals and ideas you have. If you really want to write a children's anthology about do-good robots and simultaneously conduct science research that will win in regional competitions, *and* study violin through your local conservatory's pre-college program on Saturdays, you should not be involved in after-school sports and the high school newspaper simultaneously. Simplifying your life does not mean making it any less artful; it means making success more likely!

Human beings are hardwired to add—we collect, consume, hoard (just think about the mad dash for toilet paper at the outset of the pandemic). We finish each other's sentences and build out scenarios from cliffhangers in movies as comfortably as we fill in our free time. Adding comes naturally to us, but it turns out that subtracting can be far more useful. When asked how he created one of the world's greatest artistic treasures, *David*, Michelangelo replied, "I simply cut away everything that wasn't David." When enhancing the value of a diamond, professionals subtract material from the stone, not add to it. When subtracted from, the diamond becomes a multi-faceted, brilliant, and polished gem.

So, take a page out of the great works of subtraction, and be merciless in cutting out anything from your schedule that does not scream "you." It's nice to remember that everything has its time, and if you must devote three months to test prep to reach a goal you've set, then there is no harm in subtracting another activity, because you can always return to it when the window opens.

Does Your Major Matter?

Admissions assumes that you will change your major and minor selections once or twice by the end of sophomore year in college, when you officially sign for your departments. That is why some applications will ask you to check a box asserting whether you're certain, somewhat certain, or uncertain about your major choices. They understand that perhaps you're a techie who enjoys grappling in the gray areas of ambiguity, so you might wind up majoring in philosophy at school; or perhaps you're a history devotee who discovers filmmaking on campus, changes your major to communications or media, and winds up writing for the History Channel; or perhaps you enter college as a data scientist who becomes captivated by a freshman neuroscience research internship that propels you toward going premed.

Embrace this nonlinearity. For example, if you know you want to study medicine, but at this moment in your high school career, the only awards you have come from the English Department and a national writing competition, list English or creative writing as a major on your college application and go in through that door. Once on campus, you can begin taking the courses you need for your success on the MCAT and background for your future in medicine, and even sign for an official major in the sciences. Additionally, get involved in your campus magazines and newspaper, because if you've been winning awards in writing, you ought to chase that trail a bit—you clearly possess talent!

The bottom line is that you should apply with the threads that speak most impressively for you *now*; that capture your attention *now*; that provide outlets for you to achieve distinction *now*. Know that some interests can be just for now, not forever.

You're a thinker. You're an "emoter."

You're a scientist. You're an artist.

You're driven. You're lazy.

You're curious. You're swayed by majority opinions.

You're old enough to make choices. You're old enough to take responsibility for bad ones.

You're a risk taker. You're cautious.

You're a detail person. You like to color outside the lines.

You're empowered. You're frightened.

"Do I contradict myself? Very well, then, I contradict myself. I am large. I contain multitudes."[18]

Be all things, and while you're being them, direct your attention to two or three you'll pursue with gusto and confidence during high school. You can always do other things in college. "You contain multitudes."

---

18 Walt Whitman, *Leaves of Grass* (Brooklyn, New York: Walt Whitman, 1855).

Nurturing Your Exceptional Tilt

It is helpful to develop what I call "exceptional tilt," a commitment to a personal quest, passion, or cause that's in line with your strengths and *your* ambitions (not someone else's version of your ambitions). This tilt isn't just something you put on, like a coat, to impress Admissions but an important piece of your journey of self-discovery, one that will serve you throughout life. The adventure and challenges in finding and nurturing that tilt give you a story worth telling and one that your college of choice will be interested to hear. For sure, a couple of your exceptional qualities and the right focused project taken together would certainly make a lovely college application package, but finding that rewarding and advantageous combination for each student is an art, not a checklist to fill out. Knowing the things you're good at doesn't make your journey a done deal, and the fact that you haven't explored a talent doesn't mean it is out of the question. Find the thing that fascinates you, and you will become fascinating. Your application will speak with a sophistication of thought and tone that we don't often see in applications of students who just follow the "right" activity path.

The adventure and challenges in finding and nurturing that tilt give you a story worth telling.

In high school, you're in the process of learning what your authentic self is. The extended process of self-exploration that we call "college" is there so that you can begin to climb out of childhood and step up to your talents, intellect, and leadership level. Everything you do in high school in an effort to improve yourselves for college is, in fact, improving you for *life*.

What does this mean to you, high school student and college hopeful? It's a fast-paced world, and you're coming up in it, so by high school, your individual exploration and creativity need to be pretty fast paced too. Remember, it's what you do beyond the walls of high school that makes the difference in your college application and prepares you for an interesting life. And you'll find a much easier trip if you travel this road as yourself.

That said, you still must be on top of your grades and your test scores—that hasn't changed. You still need to take the most rigorous courses that your school offers, otherwise admissions committees at your dream schools will assume you are afraid that you will not succeed in advanced-level academics. You do *not* want Admissions to think either of those things.

Suppose you're an activist out to change the world, and you've started your own public service organization or charity. This is terrific, as long as changing the world doesn't change your grades. Many young activists get so involved with their speaking and traveling calendars that they forget about their testing calendars. It's a simple rule: if your grades will suffer or your focused study for tests will be interrupted, then don't accept that public appearance. A hard fact: you're never so special that colleges don't think they can create the same great class without you. Never give a college a reason to reject you—be smart about balancing your talents, competitions, and engagements with your academic realities. If admissions officers think that your application and résumé demonstrate more emphasis on creating celebrity for yourself than on love of learning and classroom zeal, all that travel and those absences from class will add up to the impression that academics come last in your life. The process of engaging in scholarship is part of discovering and building your authentic self. If your GPA and standardized scores stay within the mid- to high range of your schools of choice, then you're doing things right.

People always ask me, "Will a 4.0 and 1600 get me into the Ivy League school of my dreams?" And I always say, "Well, it won't keep you *out*."

The problem is, there are tens of thousands of students with those numbers—as hard as that is to believe. Some come by them naturally, others through very hard independent work, and still others through weekly tutoring. Regardless of how they get there, they get there. The transcript will look the same for all of them. The things that will make the best stand out from the rest are their teachers' recommendations, their multiple college essays, and their uncommon, individual edge.

The truth in today's admissions market is that if you're aiming for a top-tier or Ivy League school, and you have SAT scores above 750 per section or ACTs at or above 34 per section and a GPA around 3.95 unweighted in an almost all-AP schedule, **you have the same shot as does a 4.0 valedictorian with 800 SAT scores *if* you have more interesting or compelling leadership, talents, or extra-curricular involvement *outside* of your school and/or on a national basis.** Additionally, if you have won any national awards for that talent or leadership, it puts you in a category above. Rejoice!

Admissions Lessons on Academic Rigor and Exceptional Tilt

1. Maria thought her 4.0 in all honors courses cleared the way to an acceptance at the Ivies. When I asked why she did not challenge herself with APs, Maria responded that she was afraid they would be too difficult, and she did not want her

GPA to fall. This is not an unusual decision by students, but it's a bad move and involves faulty logic. Top-tier schools must be sure, at the outset of the application, that the applicant has taken the most rigorous course of study available—not just at their own high schools but through other vehicles of education. It is true that some high schools do not offer AP or IB, but that is usually because the school is renowned for providing challenging courses that go far beyond the norm of a high school honors class. Stanford University OHS is like that. If that is your situation, then you do not have to be as concerned about the course designation you take because colleges are aware of your high school's profile. However, please know that even in those high schools, the top students often challenge themselves by taking a couple of AP-level courses online either through Johns Hopkins University–CTY, Laurel Springs, or Brigham Young University Online. Students do this because they want to differentiate themselves from the other students in their class. They also do this because it might enable them to gain 5s on AP tests in May, which, in turn, provides more data points by which colleges can judge them.

LESSON: A 4.0 in regular or honors courses from a typical high school is not perceived in the same way by Admissions as a 4.0 in an AP-heavy or IB curriculum with at least 3 HLs (high levels).

2. Karl spent hours each day on the erg. His 2K erg time (a reliable gauge of rowing potential) was typically mid 6:30s (which put him at tier 3). He was a valuable member of his school's crew team but not recruitable for the level of school he sought. Yet Karl truly loved crew and all the discipline it entailed. He had a 3.75 GPA in mostly honors courses

with two APs (because he did not have the study time to engage in more robust advanced courses with hours of crew practice). Karl would have likely maintained an even higher GPA with a more interesting high school career had he divided his time between more AP study and leadership in two or three additional activities while lightening up on his hours for crew. Once Karl noticed that he would not achieve the erg time for the kind of schools he wanted to attend, he could have pivoted in his activities. "I thought Admissions wants to see you follow your passions in high school," he said during our first meeting. "They do, Karl," I explained, "but your erg time does not signal how competitive you'll be in upper-level course work on campus, or how talented a writer or researcher you'll be, or how you'll give back to your school through leadership, or what kind of roommate you'll be. A nice erg score plus a strong GPA do not automatically translate into top-tier school admission." As you might expect, Karl and I got to work engaging interests he had long placed on the back burner: a workout gym for teens only and an organic doggy-treat business! Karl received acceptances to two of his dream schools.

LESSON: Explore two or three different talents or interests during high school, even if you wind up being a recruitable athlete. There is so much to learn about yourself and profound experiences to have that might relate to your sport of choice. Perhaps you organize a biannual race with members of your team, fundraising for the American Cancer Society. Perhaps you research the history of rowing and trace it all the way back to its use in transportation throughout ancient Egypt to its elevation as a sport in England with the Oxford–Cambridge 1828 university boat race. That would be a fun minithesis to read for admissions officers.

3. Charlotte did everything right. She took AP classes every year (including computer science), studied like mad to receive 5s on her tests, had an all-A average, and wanted to be an engineer. Her concern, however, was that other students would have far more engineering experience and actual projects by junior year because they could pay for extra courses or tutoring. I immediately disabused Charlotte of this thinking: within a few minutes, we had come up with a list of small but quirky building projects she could do by simply picking up the resources and tools for these projects in her dad's workshop. She signed up for HarvardX CS50 (which is free!) to "up" her programming game, and she applied to MITES and Beaver Works Summer Institute (free again!). Ultimately, Charlotte worked so hard and moved so quickly that she found a professional mentor in computer science and wound up having three engineering projects and five programming languages on her college résumé.

LESSON: There are opportunities online and in summer programs through which you can learn and excel free of charge. You must take the time to research them, apply, and do the work. I promise that the benefits will be worth your effort!

Who's a Leader? You're a Leader!

Are you a leader? And by "leader," I don't mean having run for student office and won; a lot of students have done that. I mean, have you been fascinated enough by something to have stepped out of your high school to make an impact in the lives of others? Have you started a business, organization, or project to provide for the community at home or abroad? Do you have a social or political platform about which you speak at schools, conferences, or TEDx? Are you a passionate science researcher and competitor? Have you written a novel or play or created a blog or website that has become popular? Have you founded your community's first Bollywood dance group or are you an award-winning ballroom dancer? Do you build apps that matter? If so, how many users do you have, and whom do those apps help? Have you led instead of joined? Top colleges are not as interested in members as they are in leaders.

Maybe your special tilt is toward the arts. Are you taking the initiative to nurture that talent? Do you attend a weekend conservatory program in music, art, dance, or theater? Do you have a portfolio or video reel to show? Have you worked in an arts field after school, and if so, what have you gained from this that can't be gained in a classroom? Is it the freedom of improvisation?

Pursuing a totally new project or adventure in high school requires improvisation. It's one of our core life forces. We all improvise. You've just received your driver's license, and you're driving down a neighborhood street. You don't expect traffic because it's always empty. But today there is a tailgater who won't allow you to drive the speed limit. Better think quickly, improvise, put on the blinker, and pull to the side so the tailgater can go on his merry way. Or perhaps you are babysitting a little girl who has difficulty reading, but by the end of the night, through song and dance, you were able to interest the girl in reading three books aloud with you. When the parents return home and marvel at their daughter's reading progress, they ask to employ you as a weekly reading teacher. But you've never taught professionally! You take a deep breath, believe that your present success predicts future success, and you say, "Yes." Suddenly, you are a teacher. Now that's a beautiful improvisation (and one that will grow into a fascinating and heartwarming college essay). Humans are meaning-making machines, and they make meaning by bringing all their capacities and talents to their interaction with life and other human beings. You as teens can have mind-blowing experiences as writers, student-mentors, activists, builders, hospital volunteers, researchers, and more by being more improvisatory in your high school careers. Put a little "jazz" into your life! Write about the unique adventures toward finding your exceptional tilt on your college application.

Perhaps you are a perennial student, and you take advantage of not being in a summer program or internship in person this summer by taking every free online course across the fields that interest you: philosophy, the classics, advanced science research writing, marketing, and mathematics. By the end of the summer, you have racked up three verified certificates for completion in three very different fields, showing that you are a Renaissance student. That's an interesting intellectual statement for Admissions to weigh.

Or maybe, along with being a talented STEM student, you are a ballet dancer who spends this summer choregraphing an original work that mixes modern dance and ballet on the theme of the pandemic. Then you write your college essay about how you wanted to portray, through movement, a period of time when people weren't allowed to move. You get the idea.

Can you show, through your high school career, in some way, that you have the gusto and curiosity to grab opportunities whenever and wherever they are presented to you? If so, your college admissions officers will see that you're the type of student who will make the most out of your classes, friendships, and clubs. Any way you can show this gusto will add points to your candidacy for admission.

Remember that admission is a holistic process at the top schools. Nobody looks for a straight-A student with no personality, gumption, or leadership. Nobody wants a student who is merely a member of every club and who has probably spent the last three and a half years studying in a room seven days a week. If you are an excellent student and develop outside passions that leap off the page and find a creative and illustrative way in which to present them, you will be able to compete with any valedictorian.

Defining Leadership

When you hear *leadership*, does it sound like something you could never do? Leadership is often viewed as one person's ability to command the support, efforts, and work of a group toward a specific goal. However, no one ever said leadership only referred to being the president of a school club, the founder of an organization, or the political force behind a new movement. Leadership is a state of being. Leadership means aspiring to be inspirational. It means moving on what you are passionate about or interested in to make something positive happen. Every person can create some positive change somewhere. The trick to becoming a leader is figuring out what specific cause or purpose fascinates you.

The trick to becoming a leader is figuring out what specific cause or purpose fascinates you.

A note about leadership: it's not enough to merely hold a position of leadership. You must *take* your idea or followers or project somewhere. This same definition applies to how you demonstrate leadership to admissions officers. Don't just write a title on your résumé. Explain to Admissions how you brought further success to the group, project, or club you lead. What they are looking for is regional, national, or international success; raising funds; or helping to create something of value in your school, town, or city through the group under your leadership. The best of all is out-of-school leadership that shows you followed your heart and founded an organization or social enterprise that, perhaps, serves education or the environment. The most impressive validation of your work would ideally come from having won some recognition for your organization or business or perhaps being invited to present at a TEDx event.

Admissions Officers Will Ask the Question, Where Is the Thread of Passion?

- Have you been consistently involved in the success and/or leadership of one or two clubs, organizations, or small business projects? What elements demonstrate that long-term interest? Awards? Grants from companies or social organizations recognizing your work and funding a particular project you are creating? Attending summer programs that will improve your knowledge base, leadership, or research skills?
- Have you engaged in high school club hopping (this has nothing to do with DJs and dance)—what I call *activity bombing*? Does it look like you engaged in résumé padding? Or is there long-term commitment to one or two projects/clubs?
- Word to the wise: Be sure to begin your involvement in these one or two organizations, clubs, or businesses as early in high school as possible (of course, freshman year would be awesome). If you don't, then Admissions can't see a thread of

passion or leadership skill over a long period of time. It's not *only* the title that you finally receive junior year as officer of a school club that will get you noticed—it's the "value add" you have to show for it. The students who have stories to tell are the ones who can write about taking an idea through brainstorming, failures, and successes. Those are the kind of passionate can-do undergraduates that admissions officers want on campus. Remember—the best guarantee of future success is past success.

- And … at least three days a week, get out of your school building after the bell rings and make something happen in your community! Opportunities are everywhere.

The Late Bloomers Can Win

Juniors! Do you believe there's no time left to do something during high school that will get you noticed by Admissions and blow their socks off?! Think again. For those of you reading this book during junior year, please take note of the many opportunities for leadership and new project development that still await you. Although the following students became builders and advocates later in high school, they still made remarkable impact on both the few and the many in their communities. That impact eventually led to acceptances at their dream schools.

1. Jerilyn was a superstar on her swim team. No one was a faster freestyler in the state of California than Jerilyn. So, it stood to reason that Jerilyn spent all her waking hours that were not devoted to in-school classes and homework on her swimming. At 5:00 a.m. every day, she was at

the pool, and on weekends, she was at practice or meets. Jerilyn knew that she wanted to be recruited for college but had no escape route if recruitment didn't work. At the start of junior year, when Jerilyn was most excited to prepare her swim reel for college, she suffered an accident that injured her rotator cuff. It turns out that the tear had been slowly worsening as her rotator cuff tendon degenerated during sophomore year's exertion and practice. It appears that Jerilyn decided to ignore some small shoulder pain during her summer coaching, and things went downhill from there. Jerilyn was unable to compete during the important junior year tournaments and therefore had no up-to-date video for the college coaches. Now what? With no leadership, research engagement, internship, or exceptional extracurricular accomplishments aside from her swimming, Jerilyn had, accidentally, created for herself a bit of a college admissions nightmare.

A competitor at heart, Jerilyn moved into next gear. If she could not exert herself through swimming, perhaps she could teach the joy and freedom associated with being in the water to children who are physically challenged. Jerilyn knew that she could teach because she used to instruct her little cousin on dives and strokes. So, Jerilyn contacted her local YMCA, found out when the city's special-ed classes for children on the autistic spectrum were held on site, and then offered to give the teachers some relief by taking one child at a time into the pool (with a lifeguard on duty) and acclimating the child to the water. So began her passion for teaching challenged children at the elementary school level. After two lessons, little Skye and Scott told Jerilyn that they were going to become great lifeguards when they grew up and then become champion swimmers, just like her. Inspired by her success at the YMCA, Jerilyn began a "Swim with Me" camp for children ages five to ten that summer as part of an ongoing morning program at her town pool, drawing children with mental and emotional challenges. Jerilyn recruited volunteer special education teachers as coaches and, effectively, became the CEO of her own popular program. The end of this story is that, even though social entrepreneurship started late in her high school career, Jerilyn got accepted to her top-tier schools, Duke and UCLA, and decided to pursue a career in education.

2. Alessandra is a young composer of color who writes prolifically, has her music performed by local orchestras, and studies composition and music theory at her city's precollege conservatory. Having spent most of high school concentrating on her solo composition career, Alessandra realized she wanted to inspire student composers of color throughout her city. She believed that without cultivated composition talents from multiple cultures, untold stories would be lost, and new musical ideas and insights would travel quietly and unseen. As a junior, Alessandra decided to do her part in redefining societally accepted definitions of what makes great music and great musicians. So, Alessandra began reaching out to local youth orchestras, precollege music programs, and orchestra teachers throughout her region, advertising a new after-school program in beginning composition and theory that she would run in the school cafeteria free of charge. She started small with five

students, a whiteboard, and electric keyboard that she rolled in from the auditorium. Through small weekly assignments, Alessandra was able to coach her students toward the completion of their first compositions, which were then played live by her school orchestra. By the spring semester, Alessandra had applications for her program pouring in from all over the city from students whose ancestral homelands were Argentina, Mexico, Kenya, Senegal, India, and China. Alessandra gathered seven other composition students from her precollege program and created multiple sections of her course, which was now called ComposedofUsAll. Soon, local and regional journalists began reporting on the program, and students' culturally significant compositions were being featured through online and in-person concerts. In a year, Alessandra managed to create a small but efficient movement, training and recognizing young composers of color to propel musicians of her generation into the next evolutionary step of enhancing and redefining music.

3. George is a Renaissance student: equally devoted to study in the sciences and mathematics as he is to literature and debate. George had never felt represented in the books assigned to his classes during elementary, middle, and high school. With a cultural background that is both Latinx and Taino Indian, George always wondered why there was so little indigenous literature in the curriculum. So, George gathered a group of four friends from his debate club and founded an organization that searches for indigenous novels and children's books and donates them to public schools throughout his city. George also spent his junior year lobbying for curriculum reform with school district admin-

istrators and met in person with a dozen principals and teachers. Happily, George's indigenous literature organization built fourteen public school indigenous literature mini-libraries and provided storybooks and public readings to over three thousand kindergarten through fifth-grade students by the time George graduated high school. Needless to say (but I will anyway), George's work impressed Admissions so much that he was accepted into three Ivies and received full-ride scholarships to two other top-tier universities. Equal to that admissions excitement for George was the fact that he actually had measurable influence on his community, teaching that every culture has a voice, values, and roots that need to be respected and learned about as early in life as possible for a child to become an accepting citizen of the world. In reading and analyzing stories of other cultures, students found out what makes their own cultures so distinctive.

4. Ashish was a supertalented math student who had already completed multivariable math by junior year and was on to advanced-level topics at his local university. A loner and puzzle enthusiast, Ashish had not yet found a way by junior year to demonstrate leadership or unique community impact. One day in October, Ashish's math teacher asked for his help in tutoring a high school student, Nelson, from Guatemala who had recently arrived and did not have much English. However, Ashish, luckily, had Spanish—AP Spanish, in fact. So, Ashish scheduled a tutoring session with Nelson at the library. To make a long story short, the session went so well that Ashish arranged to tutor Nelson, gratis, three times per week after school. From what Ashish shared with

me, Nelson never ceased to amaze him with how quickly he picked up advanced math, impressing upon Ashish the enduring potential of every student and the importance of safe, quiet learning environments. Apparently, Nelson could not work effectively in his apartment due to a boisterous and large family and an upper-floor neighbor who liked to play her music loudly enough for the whole neighborhood to hear. In the quiet of the library and under Ashish's calm and focused mentoring, Nelson's favorite subject became math. One month later, with the okay of Ashish, Nelson brought his two cousins, Murray and José, and older sister, Maya, to join the math group. Ashish had created his own tutoring center for at-risk kids, had made monumental impact on their future educations, and impressed Admissions with his kindness and skill. He did all that by end of junior year. As Ashish wrote at the end of his personal statement: "There's a phrase I often think of now: 'A stranger is just a friend you haven't met yet.'"

The Importance of the Local: Community Service

People think they must "go global" to make big impact, but the reality is that your local community needs you. You won't solve huge global problems like world hunger or an education crisis in Columbia or Senegal on your own or even with a small team, and perhaps there is hubris involved in thinking you can. But what *can* you do to make a difference? You can lobby your district to provide a science research advisor at your high school and engage the local medical community in petition writing and fundraising to bring ISEF to your town; you can gather groups of friends to paint the peeling classrooms in the nearest city or rural schoolhouse; you can mobilize a book brigade that collects books on indigenous literature to donate to local schools so that children in the earliest grades can learn about the stories and journeys of little-known cultures. All these small endeavors create big memories in the community and catalyze further engagement from students just like you. It all starts with one sentence: "I'm going to go do this today; do you guys want to help?"

Some Ideas

Identify opportunities unique to your city: become a liaison to the cultural food restaurants in the area and offer to sell their items at the local farmer's markets; do weekly cleanup of the docks in your area during spring and summer so that seagulls do not eat and choke on the lines and fragments fisherman leave behind; become a morel mushroom hunter in season if you live in areas that grow the mysterious commodity—you will be helping out the local farmers.

Some of you who are especially plugged into high school online leadership opportunities might know about the Making Caring Common Youth Advisory Board. This is a group of selected young people who work together online to address pressing ethical issues for teens and try to make school a kinder, more tolerant place. The youth board works with Harvard Graduate School of Education's Making Caring Common (MCC) Project, which provides resources and insights to educators and counselors on how to defeat bias and intolerance and promote equity in learning.

In 2016 and again in 2019, Harvard Graduate School of Education's MCC Project gathered admissions professionals and high school counselors and published a set of reports called "Turning the Tide: Inspiring Concern for Others and the Common Good through College Admissions." MCC is working with admissions professionals to implement recommendations for accepting a more socially responsible set of students to top universities.

Now, in no way does this report suggest accepting students who fall measurably below a university's average GPA or academic curricular rigor in high school. It would be difficult to call these schools the top tier if that were the case. Rather, its proponents are suggesting that Admissions implement recommendations for encouraging acts of social good and student contributions to community that demonstrate authentic investment of time and interest and result in meaningful contributions or deliverables at home and around the world.

The core message is that citizenship—who you are as a person—will be examined as closely as who you are as a mind.

With over fifty top-tier universities aligning themselves with MCC's messaging, you now have a wonderful excuse to branch out in your volunteering and innovating, serving a multiplicity of peoples and backgrounds.

For example, to my premedical students out there: Did a school health newsletter that you crafted and published for under-resourced schools in town inspire one child to encourage his mother to begin a daily "ten thousand steps" routine to improve her cardiovascular condition? Did your research on the new place of nutrition in preventive medical care set you on a path to receiving both a BS in biology and a master's in nutrition before attending medical school so that you could administer "healthcare" instead of "sick care"? Did the interviews you conducted with fitness professionals inspire you to lead a Saturday fitness routine with your whole family to keep their genetic high blood pressure in check?

These results would be as significant to Admissions as those of a student who runs 5Ks as fundraisers for breast cancer biannually.

The Power Is in Your Hands. What Do You Do When You Have the Power?

Let's look at additional ways to use your ingenuity and talents. Collect canned goods for the local food pantry, clean up the beach after a storm, or volunteer to shovel snow for the neighborhood's elderly. Start a volunteer student marketing corps to do social media posts for community restauranteurs and drive more traffic to establishments that had to shut down during the pandemic, or begin an "elder-car" service that picks up seniors' prescriptions and food items weekly for free in the community, or create a teen allowance fund that pools 10 percent of your socially conscious friends' allowances and uses the money to pay for repairs on local houses of worship, or build an after-school computer programming course for elementary school kids, or convince some orchestra members from your high school to give free-of-charge lessons in violin, viola, and cello every week at a school that lacks funding for music instruction. The opportunities in your own community are limitless.

The aggregation of marginal improvements will result in anything but marginal outcomes in your community.

The aggregation of marginal improvements will result in anything but marginal outcomes in your community.

In chapters to come, we'll discuss the ways that you can use the opportunities beyond the walls of your high school to create your personally meaningful journey—a journey that will set you apart not only in your future career and acts of citizenship but also to the gatekeepers in Admissions. That is a fact you can take to the bank.

I will introduce you to subject experts in the fields of music, computer science, mathematics, debate, artificial intelligence, machine learning, and leadership who will offer wisdom on how to excel in your chosen fields and use those skills for good. You will also read case studies and stories of smart and imaginative high school students who enriched their school careers, communities, and college applications in remarkable ways by fashioning a precollege adventure and kindness mindset. You have the potential to be so much more than any admissions officer could ever imagine.

Obstacles to Adaptability

If I were to set a project in front of you and say, "These twenty-five volunteers are your resources. We are opening up a farmer's market," you would be able to develop a plan using twenty-five volunteers. But if circumstances change and fifteen volunteers can no longer assist in the project, that plan needs to change with them. Being able to adapt in situations like this relies on removing certain preconceptions.

We think that the assets we assume to be available to us are controllable. Imagine you want to start a novel science magazine. You assume that because your school is friendly to student founders, you will have no problem founding this endeavor; however, when you bring it up to the department chairperson, you discover that the school cannot afford to pay another teacher to serve as a faculty mentor for such a work-intensive project. Do you scrap your idea?

Assets are not always provided, but they can exist outside the originally defined parameters (e.g., I may have provided you with twenty-five volunteers for the aforementioned farmer's market, but you have your own friend network to possibly ask. In the same way, you probably have friends who are STEM students interested in having their research published in a science magazine that is student run and published outside the school walls.) If you need a resource to build your passion project and that resource is not accessible to you, you can find ways to gain access to that resource either by trading a talent you have for a position or negotiating a way to apprentice with a professional by lending your hours to tasks that are too time consuming for that professional.

Building partnerships is a form of generating access to resources. If you are creating the community farmer's market and a friend of yours is a morel mushroom hunter and another is working on a soap company, then partnering with them provides new products for your market and a new venue for them to sell.

Even when it seems like you do not have much in the way of expertise to offer a professional, an organization, or a new club, it is up to you to make people see what you bring to the table.

Improvising through the Obstacles

Anytime you try to create or build a new project for social good, you will encounter obstacles or resistance. *But you can handle them. Watch!*

You can create something out of very little in any community. For example: You are a fast learner and a computer science enthusiast. You have just started learning a new coding language, but there's an internship in town that specifically requires competence in that language. The start date is two months out. When you apply and interview for the opportunity, the objection that will be raised is that you are new to the language and can't yet operate at the level they require. The way around this is to show examples of projects you created within two months of learning a different language. Demonstrating that you have a propensity for learning code quickly is a way to handle the objection that you do not yet know a particular skill. You're hired!

You are a politics enthusiast and decide to start an online magazine called *Global Voices from Gen Z* but need an editorial board. You discover that high school students are more difficult to organize than a kindle of kittens. Your friends want to know why they should get involved when they already belong to a host of in-school clubs that are popular. Do not even bother explaining that Admissions gets tired of seeing the same club commitments from applicants and are yearning to be surprised! Tune into your friends' favorite radio station, WIIFM (What's in It for Me?), and explain that you are creating an executive editorial board with titles. These titles will be handed out for a limited time only—on a first-come, first-serve basis. Once students understand they can have an editorial position on a national youth board for doing good work and being responsible leaders on behalf of your project, they will happily give up membership in less-fulfilling engagements in school. When students grasp that Admissions will one day see these leadership positions on their résumés—social proof that they are movers and shakers, writers, editors, and collaborators—they welcome the opportunities.

Getting into Science Research: A Walk-Through of How to Compete in Science Fairs

More than a century ago, Louis Pasteur said, "Luck favors only the prepared mind." He meant that sudden flashes of insight don't just happen—they're the products of preparation.

Sudden flashes of insight don't just happen—they're the products of preparation.

Preparation, therefore, is key to a successful and fulfilling scientific career and to admission into the best schools that nurture such a career!

Forward-thinking students who hope to pursue medicine, for example, will understand that the unique combination of patient interaction and science research is part and parcel of the same future—and having experience in both (through shadowing, volunteering, and bench, behavioral science, or biomedical research) can be pivotal to a student's early professional choices and acceptances to college. Exposure to research in high school provides background in the particular field and in the way researchers write and communicate, and those foundations are what enable students to win an internship at a lab—either in town during high school, at an eminent research university during summers, or on campus as a freshman, vying for the top research internships in the student's respective field. Students, you should not just focus on the bleeding edge of scientific research—that comes and goes. You must understand how to organize it, think about it, and write about it. That's why you do research.

Before the process of conducting research in high school, a highly respected credential to study for and achieve is the Laureate Certification in Advanced Science Research Writing. Perhaps you would like to learn to be a serious science communicator and engage in the well-known high school regional, national, or international competitions like Regeneron-ISEF, Regeneron Science Talent Search, or Genius Olympiad. Perhaps you want to broaden your foundation in science writing for lab internships during college so you can be an effective author on an article for publication. Where do you begin?

You as Science Researcher

My college advising practice, College Admission Central, serves a tremendous number of our nation's highest-achieving STEM students by connecting them with our ISEF-affiliated science research director and research coordinators. Working together, these students create sophisticated research presentations and papers for the regional, national, and international science fair circuit as well as for college admissions. If you consider yourself a young scientist or pre-med hopeful, then you will want to become involved in the extraordinary experience that is science research.

French philosopher Michel Foucault describes curiosity as "a passion for seizing what is happening now and what is disappearing; a lack of respect for the traditional hierarchies of what is important and fundamental." Such curiosity propels powerful fields of research in all sectors of academia.

Let's look at the most obvious benefits of engaging in research for an applicant to college. Admissions loves to see that you are pushing academic boundaries and going down "curiosity rabbit holes" through your independent research. If you want proof of that, just look at all the places on the Common Application where you can write about your research experiences. You can place your abstract in the "Additional Information" section; on applications to schools like Harvard, Yale, or Princeton, you can write an actual essay about your research as well as upload your paper. In shorter form, on the Stanford application, you can discuss, in 250 words, how your high school research project has inspired further curiosity in the field that you seek to address at Stanford. On the University of California application, there are four required essays of 350 words each, and if you are planning to major in any of the hard sciences, you should be *sure* to write one of those essays on your research. You can connect your research and curiosity to your Common Application personal statement or list your research on the Common Application activities form. You can also note any awards or honors you have received for that research on the "Academic Honors/Awards" section of the application. In addition to giving you the ability to carry out a college-level project, the process of engaging in independent science research will open doors to your collegiate future by impressing department chairpersons who receive copies of your research and regional admissions officers who see the proof of your focused, high-level work.

Shaping you into a more interesting interview subject or college-ready freshman, research experiences teach you organizational skills, persuasive communication, analytical and solutions thinking, adaptability (because research rarely goes according to your initial plans), and discipline. If your research is taking place in a lab, for example, you can add the benefit of learning collaborative skills.

So, what is a sensible and effective way to start?

For the first time in history, Nobel Prize winners are certifying dedicated high school and college STEM students in advanced science research writing through the Laureate Certification in Advanced Science Research Writing (see Sciencecert.com). After receiving the Laureate Certification, signed by a Nobel Prize winner in physiology or medicine, you have a distinct advantage when beginning your pursuit of competitions, research, and careers in STEM.

The Laureate Certification's intensive ten-week course is composed of self-paced modules covering all aspects of documenting a research project and creating a professional-grade research paper. Upon completion of this course, you will possess the skills and knowledge to author a paper that may be submitted to the most prestigious high school national and international STEM competitions.

The modules explored are "The Lab Notebook," "Title Page," "Table of Contents," "Abstract," "Introduction," "Methods and Materials," "Supporting Documentation and References," "Results and Analysis," "Discussion and Future Research," "Conclusion," and "Bibliography or Works Cited." Your course is delivered to you on demand via an industrial-strength LMS platform. You'll work at your own pace and on your own time and learn by the methods most comfortable to you: video, audio, or print. After receiving the Laureate Certification, contact your school's science research director or College Admission Central to speak with one of our science research coordinators who are Regeneron-ISEF affiliated judges and research directors, and map out ideas for STEM questions you would like to study. Then, begin your research!

After studying for and receiving the Laureate Certification, the hope is not just that you will become empowered to compete in the most important intellectually and financially rewarding science competitions during high school but also that you will leave high school as a confident, inspired, and technically capable research writer: the kind that will win those coveted and competitive research internships before and during college, bring value and fresh perspective to a lab director or mentor, and experience the pride of having his or her name included at the end of a newly published science paper. There should never be a situation where you are unable to procure a meaningful college research internship because you have not been taught how to engage in science research writing or competition during high school.

My college-advising team of research coordinators prepares and trains our STEM students for competitions in their chosen fields. Let's take a look at what goes into such preparation!

Our science research coordinator and a Grand Awards judge at the Florida State Science and Engineering Fair, Will Furiosi, sums up the high school research process: "The Society for Science established the International Science & Engineering Fair system with rules for conducting safe and ethical precollegiate research, while also providing opportunities for student competitions. The circuit entails increasingly challenging tiers of science fairs, including regional, state, and international levels, with many opportunities to qualify and compete at each tier. A student's research literature review, methodology, results, and conclusions are put on display as evidence of their work. At a fair, students present these scientific posters chronicling their research journey. A year's worth of research culminates in 10–15 minute-segments of discussion with the competition judges: professional researchers, industry experts, and pioneers in science. In the end, not only are students being evaluated on the quality of their research (which, at the international level, is highly sophisticated), but on the ability to communicate their work and its possible future impact on the sciences."

Different Areas of Science Research Projects

1. There are so many exciting areas of research that many students don't realize are possibilities. Students have carried out projects such as the following:

    - Understanding the genetic mechanisms behind muscle growth and decay
    - The impact of having a sibling with special needs
    - The effect of different seafloor material on the feeding habits of sharks
    - Determining if combining medications can increase their effectiveness on a cellular level
    - Using bamboo to create an emergency shelter for sustainable relief efforts
    - Forecasting and managing solar energy
    - Creating a new automated method of diagnosing colon cancer using digital image analysis

Your choice of research area should be interesting and important to you.

2. By far, the most successful students are not the ones who carried out a project for the sole purpose of winning a science fair (just as Nobel laureates are not the people who have simply read the most scientific journal articles over their careers).

The most successful students, year after year, are those who choose an area of research that is fascinating and important to them—a curiosity they have long held or recently noted or a behavioral or hard science issue they believe could use more data or a different approach.

This passion is what carries students throughout the challenging but rewarding process of science research, the ability to create a graduate level research paper, and their presentation during competition.

How to Choose a General Science Research Area and a Specific Topic

Some students choose a topic because they are talented in a certain field of science such as biology or chemistry; others choose an area because it has significance to them.

Some examples of student motivation for carrying out a project follow:

- A grandparent might have died of cancer, and the student wants to understand more about the disease
- The student visited a developing country and wants to create ways for people in that country to have a sustainable source of food
- The student is motivated by climate change and activism and wants to study the impact of invasive plants on the ecosystem
- The student loves building things or tinkering and wants to create a device that will help people with physical disabilities

How to Choose a Topic

1. Think about ideas that have interested you based on the following:
    - Something you learned in a science or social science class
    - A disease/disorder that has affected people you know
    - A topic in the news that you feel is important

- A hobby/activity that you are involved in
- A lack of information on a topic you think is important

2. Take a look at the categories list below.
3. Write down all areas that you may be interested in, even if you are not 100 percent familiar with the topic.

Visit the site listed to learn more about each topic: https://www.societyforscience.org/isef/categories-and-subcategories/all-categories/#BEHA

List subcategories and keywords from the areas of research that interest you.

Narrow down your overall list, but note the keywords for the specific areas you like.

Don't discount any area of research yet. Even if you don't think there is a professional researcher in your region working in that field of science, follow up with your science advisor. Many of these can be done at home or in any town, while others require the use of research facility.

Science Research Categories

The following twenty-one categories and subcategories are those that are typically used by the ISEF.

Animal Sciences (ANIM)
Behavioral and Social Sciences (BEHA)
Biochemistry (BCHM)
Biomedical and Health Sciences (BMED)
Biomedical Engineering (ENBM)
Cellular and Molecular Biology (CELL)
Chemistry (CHEM)
Computational Biology and Bioinformatics (CBIO)

Earth and Environmental Sciences (EAEV)
Embedded Systems (EBED)
Energy: Sustainable Materials and Design (EGSD)
Engineering Technology: Statics and Dynamics (ETSD)
Environmental Engineering (ENEV)
Materials Science (MATS)
Mathematics (MATH)
Microbiology (MCRO)
Physics and Astronomy (PHYS)
Plant Sciences (PLNT)
Robotics and Intelligent Machines (ROBO)
Systems Software (SOFT)
Translational Medical Science (TMED)

Suggested Timeline of Activities for a Successful Student Science Research Project

1. Build a strong understanding of the basic information related directly and indirectly. In most cases, you should expect to spend a few months building your foundation of understanding about all basic information and related research in your field of interest.

   You need to have a very deep understanding of all the background material, and related research is essential before you reach out to potential research mentors.

2. Here's an example of a good sequence to follow:

   - Read all information available using basic websites and printed material (such as the For Dummies guides).
   - Outline all information from general to specific.

- Create vocabulary lists of all words that are related directly or indirectly to your topic.
- Use the keywords that you have seen in the general information to find professional research and journal abstracts.
- A few tricks to finding research abstracts and articles:
    - Since most research articles are posted on-line in Adobe PDF format:
    - Go to Google, and type in your area of interest with a few specific keywords that you have learned.
    - Click on "Settings," then "Advanced Search."
    - In the field that says "file type," select "Adobe Acrobat PDF (.pdf)."
- Another option: In a general search engine such as Google, Bing, Ask.com, or Yahoo, type in "Research Journal Articles (the important keywords)."
- Google Scholar is also a great way to search for journal articles on the web.
- Highlight the key ideas and vocabulary in each of the abstracts.
- Keep a list of the following. This will be essential to refer to over the upcoming months.
    - Title of the research article/abstract
    - Primary researchers (authors) of the articles
    - Location of research
    - Year of research

- Next, you should formulate the details of the research project with your mentor. Remember, the specific details of a student research project usually do not evolve until after you meet and are accepted by a professional researcher who agrees to be your mentor. Together you decide on the specifics of a project suitable for a high school student.

Time Frame for Different Areas of Student Science Research Projects

Different types of projects have different time frames. You should consider some of the following, which will help you decide on the type of project you can do.

Are you available to work on a project with a research mentor …

- After school one day a week?
- After school a few days a week?
- On weekends?
- During school vacations?
- During summer vacation?

Think about whether you can have time after school to work with your mentor.

While most research students carry out the largest amount of their project during the summer and/or during their school breaks, being able to get a project started or learning all about the procedures you will be doing during the school year is a great advantage.

I had a student who visited an environmental testing facility after major rainstorms, a few times a year. While the project ended up having an engineering focus, the initial phase was to determine the erosion patterns on hillsides after torrential downpours.

There are also travel opportunities. For example, if you want to do some interesting marine biology research, you might decide to spend a summer in the Bahamas at one of their marine centers. For many projects, a lot of the research can be carried out during the school year as well as during the summer.

A Few Examples of Past Student Projects to Get You Thinking about Your Own

Behavioral/Psychology Surveys

One of our students contacted autism support groups around the nation via phone and email to see if they would help spread the word for his online survey-based research. He explained that he was interested in having feedback from parents who had a child on the autism spectrum. He wanted to determine if there was a trend among the families that had a strong parent-child relationship based on different parenting styles.

The autism support group leaders from around the country were so supportive that they were happy to pass his survey along to their members.

Computer, Math, Physics

One student told stories of how his parents wasted a lot of time while waiting for a subway train that they would take to work. When most of the trains opened their doors at the station, the cars were so packed with people that no one else could board the train. She was wondering if having alternating trains that stopped at alternating stations would help with this problem. She combined both her computer skills and her love for math to create a "skip-stop" system for addressing this problem. The system she created is currently being reviewed by the transit authority of a large city with the possibility of it being implemented soon.

Engineering

One student was an Eagle Scout who loved to camp, hike, and go kayaking. He was frustrated that he could not transport his kayak to remote rivers and streams. After some online research, he saw that there were only two viable options for a portable kayak. He noticed that one was so heavy it had to be transported by a cart with wheels, and the other was extremely expensive. Using a computer-assisted design software program at his school and assorted supplies he purchased in his town and then put together in his garage, he created a brand-new collapsible kayak that was lighter than any on the market and far less expensive. Not only did he win the top prize at a regional science fair, but he secured a patent on his kayak and won one of the top prizes at ISEF.

Brainstorming for your Research Project

Start Thinking about Project Ideas in Your Area of Interest

What are possible projects in your area of interest? So many students have an interest in an area of research but are not sure what possible projects a student could undertake.

As you do this, you might want to read about similar successful student projects from all over the world. One of the best ways to gain insight is to read about what numerous award-winning students have done.

The Society for Science and the Public runs the Regeneron Science Talent Search (STS) and the Regeneron-ISEF, and they have a website where you can read the abstracts from every student participant who has presented at ISEF since 2003.[19]

Here you can search entire categories of research or enter more specific keywords to find out what has been done within your specific area of interest.

As you read about previous projects, it is important to remember three things:

Don't just pursue a project because a student has successfully done it in the past. While we certainly don't want to limit your creativity, we do want to give you some direction for possible project areas. However, you should not pursue a research project category because a student in the past has done so and been successful at it.

Do carry out a project because you find it interesting and believe it is important to research that area. The most successful student research experiences are those where the student had a passion for an area of research, carried out a project in that area under the guidance of a professional, and was able to present their findings in multiple competitions and symposia. This is true whether or not the student won local or national acclaim.

Don't think that just because a project has been done that it cannot become a guide for a new project with a different focus.

Don't think that just because a project has been done that it cannot become a guide for a new project

"We see more and farther than our predecessors, not because we have keener vision or greater height, but because we are lifted up and borne aloft on their gigantic stature."

—Bernard of Chartres

19 You can read abstracts for past projects here: https://abstracts.societyforscience.org/.

The idea that we can do amazing things with new research because we are standing on the shoulders of giants is a common theme among scientists. Most research happens because someone was inspired by previous projects and wanted to learn more or test different variables.

Research Areas You'll Want to Avoid[20]

I want to make sure that you understand that these three items are on the list because of high school science fair restrictions. I wouldn't want you to carry out a project with the anticipation that you were going to present it in local and national competitions only to find out that these were not allowed.

1. Forensic science—most forensic scientists are biologists or chemists who have focused on the forensic aspect after years in the profession. The area of forensic science is often not allowed in local, national, and international science fairs, as it includes too many legal and/or ethical restrictions.
2. Behavioral studies involving topics such as depression, suicide, drug and alcohol use, or sex. The topics are not considered appropriate for a high school student to study at the level required for a science fair project.
3. Any project where you would have a high likelihood of endangering the lives of any vertebrate animal.

The fourth is a different type of caution. Some areas of research require that you have a facility available to carry out your research. If you don't live near or can't travel to such a place, then perhaps you should pursue a different area of research:

---

20 Numbers one, two, and three represent areas that are certainly interesting and worth studying; however, they may not be appropriate for most science research students.

4. Any field of study that would require you to travel to places that are unreachable for you. Some examples include the following:
    - You cannot carry out a marine biology project if you cannot spend time at a marine research facility (coastal states).
    - You cannot carry out a biology/medical-based laboratory project if you are unable to go to a laboratory site and spend multiple days a week for multiple consecutive weeks.

Finding a Research Mentor

Possible Sources of Research Mentors for Medical, Biological, Biochemical, and Microbiological Projects

1. Medical colleges
2. Pharmaceutical companies
3. Teaching hospitals
4. Doctors' offices
5. Biology or chemistry departments at local colleges

Some professionals may be excited to speak with you and very willing to help you carry out a project at their facility. Others may be willing to help but, because of restrictions, not sure where you would carry out the project. Others may not feel that they have enough time or space to allow you to carry out any project under their guidance.

Possible Sources of Research Mentors for Projects in Environmental Science, Plant Science (Botany), or Animal Science (Zoology)

ENVIRONMENTAL AND PLANT SCIENCE (BOTANY)

1. Environmental research or testing facilities
2. Environmental testing companies
3. Local Environmental Protection Agency or Department of Environmental Protection
4. Local environmental interest groups
5. Environmental sciences or botany department at local colleges

ANIMAL SCIENCE (ZOOLOGY)

1. Local veterinarian
2. Local Animal Control office
3. Local animal breeding or training facilities
4. Local farm
5. Veterinary department at a local college

Again, some professionals may be excited to speak with you and very willing to help you carry out a project but may not be as familiar with how to structure and carry out a student science research project.

The great part about many of these types of projects is that the mentor may be able to help guide you to carry out your research at home or in your town.

If you need the additional guidance or individual coaching and editing of your papers from our science research director at College

Admission Central, you can make arrangements for a session by writing to research@collegeadmissioncentral.

Possible Sources of Research Mentors for Engineering and Space Science (Astronomy) Projects

ENGINEERING

1. Local research facilities
2. Local engineering firms
3. Engineering department at local colleges
4. Local engineering interest groups
5. Local retired engineer

SPACE SCIENCE (ASTRONOMY)

1. Astronomy department of a local college
2. Astronomy interest groups
3. Planetariums

Most of the projects done in these areas may need either a research facility or a professional mentor who can meet with you. While some of the projects could be carried out with phone or online communication with your mentor, often face-to-face meetings are needed to both get the project going and to problem solve throughout the process.

Possible Sources of Research Mentors for Physics, Math, and Computer Science Projects

1. Local research facilities
2. Local companies that employ professionals with expertise/training

3. Physics, astronomy, math or computer science departments at local colleges
4. Local interest groups
5. Local computer programming / user groups

With these areas of research, a local mentor may not be needed, as a project can be guided by a professional at any location, local or distant.

POSSIBLE SOURCES OF RESEARCH MENTORS FOR BEHAVIORAL/PSYCHOLOGY PROJECTS

1. Local psychologist
2. Psychiatrist or social worker
3. Psychology teacher
4. Psychiatry or social work departments at local colleges

With these areas of research, a local mentor may not be needed, as a project can be guided by a professional at any location, local or distant.

It will be important that your professional mentor understands all the limitations on a student carrying out a research project.

Preparation for Reaching Out to a Potential Mentor

It's important to note that contacting a professional in your field of interest to possibly serve as a mentor is not advised until you have a very good understanding of these things:

- All vocabulary terms relevant to the area of research

- All typical equipment/tools typically involved in that field of research
- What projects the prospective mentor has worked on and what their goal was
- The amount of time you will have to spend after school and during the summer

You will also need to have these items already prepared before reaching out to a possible mentor:

- An email/letter already written and customized for the specific researcher you are reaching out to. Never send an email to more than one person at a time.
- A résumé / curriculum vitae listing the following:
    - Your contact information
    - The type of courses you have taken
    - What extracurricular activities you have been involved in
    - What your research interests are
    - Why you are interested in those areas
- An adult (other than a parent/guardian) who is willing to be a liaison (initial contact) between you and the potential mentor.

Professional researchers are usually more willing to consider allowing a student to carry out a project under their guidance if they know there is an adult other than the parent/guardian who is willing to assume some of the responsibility for keeping things on track.

Extra Special Tips and Hints to Amaze the Competition Judges

- Before you present:
    - Write out possible "typical" questions that you will be asked, and prepare answers.
    - Write out possible "tough" questions that you might be asked, and prepare answers.
    - Some great sources for possible questions that may be brought up would come from your mentor or science teacher really grilling you on typical and tough questions.
    - If you are homeschooled or do not have a research director at your high school, that's where College Admission Central's subject experts in science research come in: you can make an appointment with our science research director for critique, practice, and grilling on the typical and strategic questions from various science fairs across the country!
- When answering questions:
    - Pause briefly before answering, then rephrase at least part of the question in your answer.
    - If someone asked, "What would be the impact if the temperature were raised in your experiment?" you could respond "If the temperature were raised, it would …"
    - Answer it, then verify that you answered it and that your answer was understood.
    - Don't forget to end your presentation with, "Thank you for letting me share my research with you."

In general, students, if you can create a mentoring relationship in science research with your teachers in your subject of interest, then that is wonderful, and you should go for it! If you cannot locate mentors in your school for the areas mentioned above, but you believe your talents and interests lie in these fields, you now know where to find some of the nation's top research experts, ISEF-affiliated judges, and coaches. Give College Admission Central a call, and we will be happy to connect you!

STEM Research Competitions and Certificates

Whether you are thinking about a future in medical school, science research, or engineering, a high school research experience is intellectually stimulating, powerful on a college résumé, and personally rewarding.

One of the most exciting parts of the science research process is having the chance to present your research to others. Sometimes this will be in the form of a science fair, and other times it may be in the form of a national symposium.

Both are equally rewarding; however, let's take a moment to focus on the different science competitions a student science researcher may enter.

Science competitions are presented here in the order based on the typical school calendar:

- Regeneron Science Talent Search (Regeneron-STS)
- Junior Science and Humanities Symposium (JSHS)
- Regeneron International Science and Engineering Fair (ISEF)
- The BioGENEius Challenge
- The Sigma Xi Student Research Conference and Showcase
- Arizona State University Sustainability Solutions Science Fair

- The Laureate Certification in Advanced Science Research Writing
- The Columbia Junior Science Journal

Regeneron Science Talent Search

The Regeneron STS competition is "the nation's premiere science research competition for high school students," open to citizens or permanent residents of the United States in their senior year. Each year, nearly 1,900 students enter the Regeneron STS competition, submitting original research in pressing scientific fields. Students submitting an individual project must be seniors.

This is a sophisticated research-paper-based competition. Core components of the application include personal essays, short-answer responses, activity and basic information, scientific research report (maximum twenty-page research paper about entrant's original research project), recommendations and transcripts submitted by adults, and test scores (optional).

Big money can come from being a Regeneron winner, so it's worth investigating.

Each of the three hundred students named a scholar in the Regeneron STS will receive a $2,000 award for their outstanding science research. Forty finalists will receive a minimum award of $25,000 upon completion of Finals Week. The top ten award winners will win from $40,000 to $250,000.

For more information:

www.societyforscience.org/regeneron-sts/

Junior Science and Humanities Symposium

JSHS is for individual projects in any area of research.

Age/grade varies based on the region. Most of the regional/state fairs are held in February or March. Students who present via PowerPoint

and win can progress onto the next level. Five projects from each state advance onto the National JSHS. The top three projects win $2,000, $1,500 and $1,000 respectively. The top two of these compete at the national level. A research paper written in accordance with the regional symposium guidelines is required to compete.
For more information: www.jshs.org

How to apply: Contact your regional/state JSHS competition at http://jshs.org/regions.html

The BioGENEius Challenge

This is for high school students with individual biotechnology-based projects. Different formats exist at the regional, state, and "at-large" competition.

For more information:

http://www.biotechinstitute.org/go.cfm?do=Page.View&pid=89

Where to find your regional affiliated BioGENEius Challenge:

http://www.biotechinstitute.org/go.cfm?do=Page.View&pid=12

If there is no BioGENEius Challenge in your state, you can apply to the at-large BioGENEius Challenge:

http://www.biotechinstitute.org/go.cfm?do=Page.View&pid=13

Princeton Plasma Physics Internship for Seniors

This high school semester-long internship or summer internship at Princeton Plasma Physics Laboratory is a highly competitive and sought-after honor for young scientists.
For more information: https://www.pppl.gov/high-school-semester-long-internship-high-school-summer-internship

Regeneron International Science and Engineering Fair

Regeneron-ISEF is "the world's largest international pre-college science competition," with more than 1,700 high school students from over seventy countries, regions, and territories who showcase their independent research and compete for more than $5 million in prizes.

- To win a spot at the Regeneron-ISEF, you must be a finalist at your regional/state ISEF-affiliated fair.
- Most of the regional/state fairs are held in February or March.
- Competition is via poster board and oral presentation. A fully refined research paper is required (and is the same paper you can use for applying to the Regeneron STS competition during fall of senior year).

For more information: https://societyforscience.org/isef/

The Sigma Xi Student Research Conference and Showcase

This conference gathers high school, undergraduate, and graduate students across disciplines to share their research through poster and oral presentations and connect with professional science researchers and like-minded peers. Top presenters receive a monetary award and invitation to join Sigma Xi for a year. Students interested in being selected for oral presentations must typically submit abstracts by the end of August. Members of Sigma Xi include Nobel laureates, National Medal of Science winners, and presidential science advisors.

Conference application deadlines (deadlines change each year; please check the website annually) can be found here: https://www.sigmaxi.org/meetings-events/student-research-showcase

More info on the competition timeline can be found here:

https://www.sigmaxi.org/meetings-events/student-research-showcase/competition-timeline

Arizona State University Sustainability Solutions Science Fair

The Sustainability Solutions Science Fair is a virtual competition for high school researchers, innovators, and engineers from age twelve to eighteen, internationally. Arizona State University, in partnership with Wells Fargo Foundation and the Rob and Melanie Walton Foundation, seek projects that drive positive change. Awards reach up to $2,500.

More information can be found here:

https://sustainabilityinnovation.asu.edu/sustainabilitysolutions/programs/solutionsfestival/sustainabilityfair/

The Laureate Certification in Advanced Science Research Writing

The Laureate Certification (see Sciencecert.com) is a ten-week online course of study that enables students around the world with little to no access to STEM research to gain the methodology and training in writing a high-level science research paper. For Admissions to see that you have the intellect and will to study for and receive the Laureate Certification, an official certificate in Advanced Science Research Writing signed by a Nobel Prize winner, is a game changer!

The Laureate Certification helps you have yet another unique essay topic for your application. You can talk about how the certification changed the way you look at nature or human life or how you think scientifically about process and procedure, natural habitats, oncogenes, viruses, big data, or marketing. Every young scientist should have at least one essay on their science study.

The *Columbia Junior Science Journal*

If you are dreaming of publication, the *Columbia Junior Science Journal* might be your ticket. The journal accepts and reviews one- to two-page original research papers or two- to five-page review articles in the fields of natural sciences, physical sciences, engineering, and social sciences. All published papers are peer reviewed by the journal's Editorial Review Board.

More information can be found here: http://cjsjournal.org/

These journals and competitions help answer the question of "Now what?" After you complete your Laureate Certification and move on to your actual research projects, you now have a couple of worthy platforms through which to try out your new research chops!

Mathematics and Computer Science Competitions

THE AMERICAN MATHEMATICS COMPETITIONS

This American Mathematics Competitions (AMC) is a series of examinations and curricular materials that build creative problem-solving skills in middle and high school students. AMC 8 is for middle schoolers; the AMC 10 is for tenth graders and is composed of difficult multiple-choice questions. The AMC 12 is an intuitively demanding test covering the entire high school curriculum excluding calculus. The AMC 10 and AMC 12 open the door to a series of competitions leading to the international mathematical Olympiad.

More information can be found here:

https://www.maa.org/math-competitions/amc-1012

And here:

https://www.maa.org/math-competitions

USACO

USACO provides teams from the United States to the International Olympiad in Informatics (IOI), the most prestigious international computing contest at the high school level. The USACO holds web-based contests during the academic year and in the late spring conducts the US Open, their "national championship" exam. You can expect for contests to run for three to five continuous hours in length. USACO does a great deal to help talented student coders, providing hours of free online resources that students can use to train their programming and computational skills.

For a free online training guide, go to https://usaco.guide/. Students can place Bronze, Silver, Gold, or Platinum for the most advanced.

CONGRESSIONAL APP CHALLENGE

This is the most prestigious prize in student computer science and has transformed the way Congress views computer science education and innovation. High school or middle school students talented in coding can use any programming language and any platform for their innovative app project. There are no limits to the topic you choose to develop. Students compete in either the district they reside in or the district in which they attend school. Preregistration typically opens in May.

More information can be found here:

https://www.congressionalappchallenge.us/

Advocacy, Tech, and Leadership Programs and Honors

HARVARD UNDERGRADUATE INTERNATIONAL RELATIONS SCHOLARS PROGRAM (HUIRSP)

The Harvard Undergraduate International Relations Scholars Program is the most prestigious and unique international relations program for high school students. This three-day, competitive, application-only, virtual program engages the nation's brightest high schoolers in discussion with Harvard professors, policy makers, and eminent government officials. Students learn how world leaders are addressing real-world challenges from all sides of international relations.

More information can be found here:

https://www.harvardforeignpolicy.org/harvardirscholarsprogram

GLORIA BARRON PRIZE FOR YOUNG HEROES

The Barron Prize honors twenty-five inspiring young people who have made a significant positive difference to people and our planet. The top ten winners each receive a $5,000 cash award to support their service work or higher education.

More information can be found here:
http://barronprize.org/

MILTON FISHER SCHOLARSHIP FOR INNOVATION AND CREATIVITY

Not that many families know about this creative and generous award. Up to $20,000 ($5,000 per year for four years of college) is granted to exceptionally innovative and creative high school juniors, seniors, and college freshmen who may demonstrate their talents in any number of ways. Students must be from Connecticut or the New York City metro area and plan to attend college anywhere in the United States or be from any part of the United States and plan to attend college in Connecticut or New York City.

More information can be found here:
http://mfscholarship.org/

THREE DOT DASH GLOBAL TEEN LEADERS

Although the number of young leaders changes annually, in 2022, 33 Global Teen Leaders from 22 countries on 5 continents were selected to be mentored in their field of social action and to attend the Just Peace Summit in NYC.

More information can be found here:
https://www.wearefamilyfoundation.org/three-dot-dash-apply

MAKING CARING COMMON

This high school youth advisory board is selected from students across the nation to ideate and create solutions that will make schools more caring and respectful places. The MCC board takes on such pressing social challenges as bullying and exclusion.

More information can be found here:
https://mcc.gse.harvard.edu/research-initiatives/youth-advisory-board

THE DIANA AWARD

The Diana Award is one of the world's most prestigious awards for humanitarian and social action work. The award was established in memory of Diana, Princess of Wales, with the mission of inspiring positive change in young people up to age twenty-five. Students must have carried out their activities for a minimum of twelve months.

More information can be found here:
https://diana-award.org.uk/

MIT SOLV[ED] YOUTH INNOVATION CHALLENGE

This is a chance for students to submit their tech-based solutions that intend to (a) improve learning opportunities from early childhood on, (b) support economic opportunities for all, (c) reduce healthcare disparities and accelerate access and d) combat climate change. The ten top solutions will share $200,000 in funding and receive mentorship from members of the MIT community.

Solv[ED] is open to solutions at all stages of development and defines tech-based solutions as those that apply science and evidence-based knowledge to humanity's practical aims.

More information can be found here:

https://solve.mit.edu/challenges/solv-ed-youth-innovation-challenge#challenge-subnav-offset

And here: MIT Solve | Prizes:

https://solve.mit.edu/challenges/solv-ed-youth-innovation-challenge/custom/prizes

Advocacy, Social Science and Humanities Awards and Competitive Programs

Scholarships exist in every field you can imagine, so if you can help it, do not wait until the end of junior year to begin your search. These scholarship competitions require thoughtful essays that can take a good deal of time to get into shape. Ideally, you will want to schedule a meeting with your guidance counselor to learn how to construct these strategic essays. There can be a lot on the line. Some merit and service-oriented scholarships provide enough funding to pay for a year of college, so they are worth the effort!

Now, for some of the most sought-after merit scholarships, honors, and programs that can open doors for you when Admissions sees them on your application.

EQUITABLE EXCELLENCE SCHOLARSHIP

Exceptional young minds and leaders are awarded for outstanding achievement in school or community. "Equitable will provide 100 $5,000 annual scholarships that will be renewed to award recipients each academic year for four years, for a total of $20,000 per recipient. The company will also award 100 one-time $2,500 scholarships that can help students to underwrite immediate costs associated with higher education such as tuition, books or room and board. Students who have made an outstanding achievement related to reducing risk in areas such as financial, environment, health and/or emergency preparedness or an achievement around empowering society to better face risk, are encouraged to apply."

More information here:

https://equitable.com/foundation/equitable-excellence-scholarship

COCA-COLA SCHOLARS FOUNDATION

Some of the nation's greatest young minds and leaders are chosen for this scholarship. It is highly competitive, with thousands applying each year. Students complete an application that details their grades, research, and significant community service and leadership inside and outside of school. The 150 selected Coca-Cola Scholars attend Scholars Weekend in April and are awarded $20,000 in scholarship funds.

More information here:

http://www.coca-colascholarsfoundation.org/applicants/#faq

TELLURIDE ASSOCIATION SUMMER SEMINARS

Although it doesn't involve a cash award, being accepted into Telluride Association Summer Seminars (TASS) tells Admissions something about your intellect. Students are selected through a competitive application process. TASS participants attend a seminar led by university scholars and participate in varied academic (learning for learning's sake) and social activities. TASS students are brought together for a summer of intellectual challenge amid a diverse community of curious minds. It's an honor to be selected.

More information here:

https://www.tellurideassociation.org/our-programs/high-school-students/

THE ANSON L. CLARK SCHOLAR PROGRAM

This is an intensive seven-week summer research program for twelve of the most qualified high school juniors and seniors. This is an eminent hands-on research experience for selected students of at least seventeen years of age to do research in their field of choice: humanities, social sciences, or the sciences. Essays, transcripts, test scores, and teacher recommendations are required. For deadlines, please visit https://www.depts.ttu.edu/honors/academicsandenrichment/affiliatedandhighschool/clarks/.

THE *CONCORD REVIEW*

The *Concord Review* recognizes and publishes sophisticated, college-level history essays by high school students. Students send their published research papers to Admissions, along with their applications, and these academic works are often pivotal to top-college acceptances.

More information here:
https://tcr.org/submit

RESEARCH SCIENCE INSTITUTE

From June through August annually, eighty of the world's most accomplished high school STEM students attend Massachusetts Institute of Technology for the Research Science Institute (RSI). Determined through a highly competitive application process, RSI is the most renowned cost-free summer science and engineering program—combining "on-campus course work in scientific theory with off-campus work in science and technology research."

More information here:
https://www.cee.org/programs/apply-rsi

HIGH SCHOOL HONORS SCIENCE, MATH, AND ENGINEERING PROGRAM

This renowned, highly competitive, intensive, seven-week research program is hosted at Michigan State for some of our nation's brightest rising high school seniors. Research opportunities exist in all areas of science, rigorous engineering, and mathematics through this summer residential experience. The application is extensive, requiring two long-form essays, two teacher recommendations, a transcript, and a list of rigorous courses taken and books you've read.

More information here:

https://education.msu.edu/hshsp/

PRINCETON PLASMA PHYSICS INTERNSHIP FOR SENIORS

This is an extraordinary opportunity for outstanding students of physics and mathematics within commuting distance of Princeton University. A limited number of internship positions for high school seniors are available throughout the school year and the summer, postgraduation. All internships take place during the school day, so special provisions must be made with the student's high school.

More information here:

https://www.pppl.gov/high-school-semester-long-internship-high-school-summer-internship

PROMYS

PROMYS is a six-week summer program in mathematics for eighty of the strongest and most motivated high school math minds from around the world, held on the campus of Boston University. The deadline is typically in mid-March, by which time the program must receive all required application components: solutions to a challenging problem set, letter of recommendation, high school transcript, and an application form, which includes short answers.

More information here:

https://promys.org/programs/promys/for-students/

Although it's difficult to say which awards or honors make the ultimate difference in a top-tier acceptance, any of the above will enrich your lives, grab the attention of Admissions, and move the dial several steps closer.

Emerging Fields (Who Knew?)

HARVARD UNDERGRADUATE INTERNATIONAL RELATIONS SCHOLARSHIP PROGRAM

In its short time of accepting applications from high school students, the Harvard Undergraduate International Relations Scholarship Program (HUIRSP) has become very popular, following the recent uptick in interest among high schoolers in law, diplomacy, and international relations.

For young people thinking about a career in law, politics, diplomacy, nonprofits, or international business, it becomes essential to understand various people's communication styles, thinking, mannerisms, habits, philosophies, languages, and national political messaging. HUIRSP workshops bring admitted students together for conversations with national and international policy makers and government officials. Students might even be invited to write an essay for publication on the HUIRSP site. Such academic and experiential background will help you think, act, negotiate and make pivotal decisions according to what you know about the students and eventual professional colleagues before you. The best way to prepare for such a broadly intellectual field is to study international relations in college.

However, in a world that becomes smaller and smaller through virtual meetings and education, there is wisdom in having all students, regardless of field, gain some background in additional languages and intercultural communication during high school. The success of your interactions with the world depends upon the quality of your knowledge.

Students begin such global education early these days through debate club, examining global social and political issues, or through Model UN, where students dramatize the role of UN delegates as they replicate the workings of UN committees. This activity teaches students about key international issues through research, public speaking, analysis, writing, and leadership. The best delegate in each committee receives a gavel.

Many of my students enjoy short, intensive international relations programs such as HUIRSP or writing policy papers through Georgetown's online courses in International Relations: How the World Works or their summer college credit classes in international relations, comparative political systems, and US political systems, studying the complicated and important role of democracy. As James Madison said, "If men were angels, no government would be necessary."[21]

Another Emerging Field of Interest for Writers and Technologists Alike: Magic Systems

You know how we have spent a good deal of time talking about the importance of storytelling in the college application? Well, my students over the years who are writers, gamers, and "world builders" (on boards and screens, anyway) have taught me multitudes about how nonacademic endeavors like gaming and game design have honed their writing and storytelling skill.

---

21 Federalist paper #51 (http://www.constitution.org/fed/federa51.htm), accessed June 7, 2022.

For those of you with no particular love for fantasy, gaming, or science fiction, please feel free to skip this section. However, for those students who enjoy actively cultivating creativity and exploring non-document-based writing, engagement in world building and game design can be the avenue to do just that.

Here is what my students have taught me: When authors create the setting for stories of high fantasy or science fiction, they rely on a set of rules that they establish at the outset. In the case of settings where magic is prevalent, books like Chris Paolini's *Inheritance Cycle* (high fantasy novels) or Tolkien's *Silmarillion*, his collection of mythopoeic stories, the authors must decide the rules of that magic: Is it empowered by emotion, drawn from ancient knowledge, or gained from some other source, finite or infinite? There are myriad questions that can be answered, and with each answer the author moves closer to a hard magic system.

The defining characteristic of a hard magic system is that there is a consistent and repeatable connection between a resource or an input and its output. Think of hard magic systems as closest to Clarke's law,[22] which states that magic is technology we do not yet understand. What this means is that in a hard magic system, the same action taken will always produce the same result. So, if I say *fireball* in my story, a ball of fire would be created. In a hard magic system, there is an understandable and replicable method by which the fireball is created. The explanation could be any number of things: from controlling the kinetic energy of the air to make it hot enough for explosion to magical spirits causing fires to erupt. Fun!

22 Arthur C. Clarke, an English futurist, undersea explorer, and science fiction writer, author of *2001: A Space Odyssey*, wrote three laws: (1) When a distinguished scientist states that something is possible, they are almost certainly right. When they state that something is impossible, they are very probably wrong. (2) The only way of discovering the limits of the possible is to venture a little way past them into the impossible. (3) Any sufficiently advanced technology is indistinguishable from magic.

In a soft magic system, such as found in *Avatar: The Last Airbender*, there is no repeatable explanation provided for the resulting phenomena. For example, characters in moments of need may create entirely new forms of magic or adapt what they know to solve their current predicament (you engineers do it using rules; the writer uses fancy words). The "magic" is reliant on intangibles like the user's emotional state, imagination, or anything considered a deus ex machina at that moment to activate the power, potency, or existence of the magic.

You could see how this kind of creative fascination could lead to works like Isaac Asimov's Foundation series of science fiction (hard magic disguised as science) as well as *The Wizard of Oz* or *Lord of the Rings* because of how undefined its magical restrictions are.

GAMING

For students who have a fascination with writing and world building, it is not a far leap to go from words on a page to interactive systems.

A game, by definition, is a form of play or sport—a mental competition with a pre-established set of rules to which all participants agree.[23] Gaming itself can be further subdivided into game design, game balance, and game play. A game designer establishes the field of play, the conditions by which the game should be won or lost, and the requirements of play. Someone focused on game balance takes the conditions of victory or failure and weighs them against one another to preserve the fairness and fun of the game system. Finally, the players are those who engage in the alacrity of competition. This all sounds so much more impressive than "I play games with my friends" because it is, and admissions committees now understand that.

23 Merriam-Webster, "game," accessed June 7, 2022, merriam-webster.com/dictionary/game.

By depicting your gaming hobby and experience in these terms you can make admissions officers recognize that the time you spend creating worlds and playing within them is an intellectual exercise that grants you a perspective that your competitors in the college admissions game may not have.

Let's talk about the strategic mindset you have developed over and above some of your classmates. How quickly do you learn a new game? And by that, I mean how easily do you understand and absorb a new set of rules or new information about the task before you? That demonstrates adaptability, which, by the way, is what Admissions and employers are looking for today. In the case of a game that you design with your friends—for example a tabletop role-playing game—how often do you outsmart the situations into which you are placed either through mastery of the mechanics or quick thought and careful words to resolve the scenario in which the players have been placed? (Typically, there are five to six people sitting at a table playing a game. One person is the director of the story and controls all the nonplayer characters and directs the pace and action of the game. The other players are working together or against one another.) The takeaway is that gamers can exercise and improve their ability to lead fellow players or practice their skills in conflict resolution (and there are plenty of conflicts in gaming). Such tactics of negotiation, leadership, and finessed communication are some of the most prized abilities a successful student and young professional can acquire.

Gaming and the math mind: When you are dealing with games that require the rolling of dice or calculation of results from randomized variables, you naturally get faster at mental math and averages of probability. In a game that includes a finite number of resources or outcomes, being able to calculate the probability of you landing on

New York Avenue before anyone else is beneficial (did you know that the most commonly rolled number in Monopoly is seven?).

Gaming and social entrepreneurship: I have students who use gaming to raise money for charitable causes that matter to them. The friends get together every weekend and put part of their allowance into a charitable fund before beginning each gaming session. At the end of each school semester, they tally the total and send their donation as a group. What a fun way to simultaneously play and give back!

There are several charities that use Gaming Livestreams to raise money—the same way charities use 5K races. Two of the most famous charities in this space are Games Done Quick and Extra Life. Both charities host marathon video game livestreams where influencers and speed runners (people who complete games as quickly as possible in various categories) provide entertainment for viewers, who give donations directly to the charity for the enjoyment of watching. Students can participate. If you love gaming and you want to make impact in charitable pursuits, find out how to get involved.

You would be amazed by how many universities have on-campus clubs and courses dedicated to these very same endeavors. There are collegiate e-sports leagues, card game clubs, and game design communities (and if there aren't, you can establish them).

NYU offers a game design BFA, a minor, and even a game center through the Tisch School of the Arts, where students can study game programming and design, as well as the mathematics and psychology of game rules. Northeastern University's BFA in game design prepares students to develop creative games across broad platforms while recognizing emerging trends. Worcester Polytechnic Institute focuses on design skills and programming in its game and interactive media design major, while Rensselaer Polytechnic Institute offers a BS degree in games and simulation arts and science. At USC, you can receive a BS in computer science with an emphasis in games from Viterbi School of Engineering or a minor in video game design and management or video game programming.

All of this is to let you know, students, that if game design, play, and storytelling are what make your heart sing, then there are programs at many of our nation's top schools to nurture and address those interests.

PART THREE:

WRITING YOUR WINNING APPLICATION

The Art of the Essay

As college acceptance rates plunge and résumés explode with diverse intellectual and extracurricular morsels, the personal statement and your supplementary essays enable you to make a unique appeal to Admissions by demonstrating the exact story you want them to know about you.

Often, guiding voices will tell you that there is likely one main story that stands out in your high school career, and you should write that. I disagree. You have many stories and numerous noble attributes. Make a list of your top five stories—you will likely use them all because of the many supplemental essays colleges ask you to write. Pick the narrative for your personal statement prompt that excites you the most, that makes your personality pop off the page, and that describes your finest attribute, intellectual work, inspiration, or passion project in the most visual way. Show that story with clear and beautiful language, take us on a journey from point A through a development or pivot that brings us to point B, and then close by hearkening back to your opening paragraph. The essay needs tension and to keep the reader asking, What are the things we don't know about you that you are going to demonstrate? How did you change? What did you learn about yourself? Why does it matter enough for you to write about that thing in the most important essay of your young life?

Remember, you don't need to exploit exotic experiences (not everyone has those!); you need to explore and execute your topic through anecdotes and self-reflection. As you move through your points and scenes, keep asking the question, Am I propelling my thesis forward and answering the prompt? Will Admissions care about my takeaway by the end of the essay, or will they say, "So what?"

Above all, please be creative in your opening paragraph! Can you imagine how easy it is for admissions officers or readers to zone out at 2:00 a.m. after reading dozens and dozens of applications? Something must make them remember you. Some story or description or inspirational quote needs to surprise them and keep them reading even though they were only moments away from turning in for the night.

If you find yourself at the computer with a blank page in front of you and no original thoughts, pick up a new book you've been waiting until summer to read, hold it in your hands, and open your mind to the language, tone, and point of view—let yourself be surprised by it. Dog-ear it, annotate it, argue with it, find a new truth. Then return to your keyboard and that blinking cursor of possibility. You might find you have sudden inspiration!

Or try the Charles Darwin experiment and completely change up your immediate environment. Charles Darwin had this great ritual at his estate in London where he did all the work on the *Origin of Species*. He had a path built through his property that he called the sand walk. He would complete a certain number of circuits on this sand walk at the same time every day right before he sat down to write. He found that moving away from his work environment would free his thoughts.[24]

Many exceptional ideas and writings are birthed when the author is caught off guard by nature or by other human beings. Nobel laureate Richard Feynman came up with his Nobel Prize–winning idea of electrodynamics while watching the medallion spin around on a plate tossed into the air by a Cornell University student in the cafeteria. J. K. Rowling crafted the outline for the entire Harry Potter series while riding on a train from Manchester to London, even though she had been unable to even frame the narrative while working rigorously on it every day at her favorite coffee shop. So, go out and take a walk and give yourself a chance to synthesize connections between all the wonderful fragments of stories you are considering for your personal statement. Your aha! moment will arrive.

Do not approach your personal statement as if it were a five-paragraph English essay for school. You will need to explore events, inspirations, and attributes until you come up with the core for an answer that not only responds to one of the Common Application prompts but also to this question: How do you want to be perceived?

When you're determining the basis of your personal statement, there are so many ways to run with it, but whether you choose to write about an attribute, event, academic passion, or a pivotal decision,

24 Damon Young, "Charles Darwin's Daily Walks," *Psychology Today*, January 12, 2015, (https://www.psychologytoday.com/us/blog/how-think-about-exercise/201501/charles-darwins-daily-walks)

start with a blank piece of paper, and begin to list turning points in your life. You might remember a time when you had to choose between very different alternatives, a time when someone chose for you, a time you fought for what you believed in, a time you were too afraid to fight, a burgeoning love of the arts or sciences and lessons you learned from these disciplines, an internship, a job, a moment that thrust you into the spotlight, or a time that you were pushed into the background. Investigate your memories and the stories they hold and divulge the reason you made the choices you made and how you have grown from those events and choices. When you organize your thoughts along a timeline from childhood to the present, you'll unearth fascinating narratives that you might have catalogued deep in your memory bank, not readily accessible.

Create a bond with your admissions readers by allowing some vulnerability to be laid bare on the page. It seems counterintuitive to let down your guard and tell a personal story to a committee of people who have never met you. I know. However, the way human beings relate to each other is through stories and sharing of accumulated life experiences. Presenting a meaningful moment in your life at the opening of your essay will enable the admissions officers to relate to you and care about your story. If they care about you, they will fight to admit you.

Create a bond with your admissions readers by allowing some vulnerability to be laid bare on the page.

When you decide on an anecdote for the beginning of your personal or supplementary essays, you will need to set the scene for your reader. Start by jotting down everything you saw, heard, or felt. Describe the weather, the colors, the smells, and the sounds surrounding that anecdote. Speak onto the page, and do not worry about the sophistication of your language. That comes later.

Then take the next paragraph to develop your story. Steer clear of tangents! For example, if you are describing your recipe for vegetable soup, it makes sense to include potatoes, onions, tomatoes, and zucchini; however, if you suddenly add chicken, you no longer have a vegetable soup, and you spoil the recipe. In the same way, if you are talking about your experiences shadowing a master physician who inspired you to study medicine by the humanistic way he diagnosed and communicated with his patients, do not suddenly add sentences about your award-winning neuroscience research at JSHS and then return to your shadowing experience in the office. You will have lost your reader within the first sentence about your poster board.

Stay lean when you tell a story. If there are sentences that could be deleted without anyone noticing, then they should not be in your narrative. Every sentence must help explain your motivations and move your story forward.

After you have the story in front of you, add the extra color, anecdotes, lovely language (admissions readers love artful language), and emotion that will reel in the readers and make them remember you. There are good words, and there are better words. Better words give the readers an immersive visual experience. It is so much nicer to read that you worked in a room full of computers pulsing and thrumming than it is to read that you worked in an office with forty-five computer scientists and their screens. Big words are not necessarily beautiful words—use your online thesaurus and discover a world of language you might never have used before but surely will in the future.

When you engage in rewriting a particular paragraph, it helps to highlight the new and improved material in a color. My students know to expect my multicolored edits and annotations—it helps them zero in on the important suggestions and makes them excited about progressing with their own colorful second or third drafts.

A Few Literary Devices to Use

An unexpected opening seizes our interest with something dynamic, humorous, or suspenseful. It can even involve dialogue if it sets the tone and draws us in—keeping us a little off kilter until the end of the first paragraph so we are compelled to read on.

Examples:

- "I knew it was love the moment she appeared in those yellow stripes." Well, that got my attention! I thought I was going to read about someone's first love, but not till the end of the first paragraph did I find out that the author was a dedicated marine biology student who had a passion for Caribbean fish—and went to Saint Croix every summer to study them. Now, had he started his essay, "The Caribbean parrotfish is one of the most beautiful fish in the world," neither you nor I might have been predisposed to have read it. But because he packaged the opening in a colorful and teasing way, the reader is impressed and compelled to read on. *Essays like these make us understand how great packaging affects our choices in everyday life.*
- Another example: A mother goes into a candy store to buy her kids a treat. There on the shelf are two containers of candy. One says "Gummy Worms" and the other says "Dinosaur Food." Which does she pick? Dinosaur food, of course! When she takes it home and her kids open it up, what's inside? Gummy worms. This is just like Admissions!

An admissions officer has two applications open on his desk, and they both have the same "gummy worms"—uh, scores, GPA, in-school activities—but one has uniquely packaged essays and compellingly thought-through extracurricular pursuits; which application does he accept? The *dinosaur food*! This is a life lesson. Find your original message! As a student, you will be constantly marketing yourself: on campus, when you explain to a lab director why you should be seriously considered for one of her internships; when you meet the head of the charitable organization you want to serve, and you have thirty seconds to pitch the reason you want to form a student council to brainstorm and activate new ideas for that organization; when you ask out that special someone, and you're not even sure that they know you're alive; when you're convincing Mom and Dad that getting a puppy is a great way to teach you responsibility! There is no difference when it comes to marketing yourself on a college application.

- Let's look at another opening: "That night, I sat down on our front stoop, picked up the pebbles in the surrounding garden bed and hurled them in angry succession at the sky." I am equally engaged by this opening, as I would be in any opening of a film that gave me a hint of the protagonist's vulnerability. Clearly, this is an "overcoming obstacles" essay, and it will not be cookie cutter.

Openings that grab us and pull us into the student's life are demonstrations of strong writing ability. As NYU's former dean of admissions Shawn Abbott notes, "You'd be hard-pressed to find too many universities that aren't compelled by students who are strong writers, even if they are studying math or science."[25] Lesson: take your essays very seriously.

Writing Your College Essays

You know how you think you should wait until inspiration strikes before digging into your college essay? *Don't.* Make inspiration happen. As William Butler Yeats said, "Do not wait to strike till the iron is hot; but make it hot by striking." Finding that one focused thought, that special characteristic you possess that makes you an interesting human being or a memorable roommate, that thread of passion, that course or teacher for whom you're excited to wake up in the morning—that is a journey traveled via stories. Telling a story on your college application that reflects well on you without coming off as "bigheaded" requires a light touch we call artful bragging.

Writing creates visuals. It's painting in layers. It can use descriptive or florid passages that run like musical notes through events of your life or heighten emotion and tension by changing your message from a rambling screed into an impressive salvo of fiery opinion.

As I've mentioned earlier, chemicals like cortisol and oxytocin are released in the brain when we listen to stories, alerting us that we are biologically programmed to tell them and embrace them. When I ask students to tell me about themselves, they do not begin by offering me an equation. They tell me stories: about their brothers, sisters, parents, or grandparents and about themselves, taking me through their academic interests and talents, their dreams and the obstacles or victories they've encountered in pursuit of those dreams, their family's struggle to give them those dreams, and their own concerns about choosing a meaningful path that, through rigor and creativity,

25 David Kirby, "The College Entry Essay: Tips from Admissions Officers at Leading Schools," Huffpost, updated November 30, 2013, https://www.huffpost.com/entry/the-colllege-entry-essay-_b_4013010.

will lead to acquiring those dreams. Through our years of work and adventure together, we tease out the most meaningful stories from the students' journeys, and those stories are the ones animating their college applications.

The Personal Statement: What Admissions Officers Say They Want and What They Really Want

Admissions officers say they look for the student's unique voice in each essay, but you had also better send sophisticated writing on nontrite subjects. Remember, you're writing on a college level now, not to your friend from camp. So …

- No contractions.
- No trite essay topics like "How I Scored the Winning Touchdown" or "How I Saved the World through My Community Service Trip."
- No colloquial speech—your writing must pass muster in a top-college classroom. If it's too cutesy or informal, it may not bring you an acceptance letter.

Stephen Farmer, vice provost for enrollment and undergraduate admissions at the University of North Carolina–Chapel Hill said, "What we want for students is the feeling that they're looking for the next great thing they need to know. We like to see a sense of joy and curiosity."[26]

You may say you're just a regular kid who hasn't traveled, founded an organization, built a robot, won national competitions, or held an

26 Linda Kulman, "The Right Way to Pitch Yourself to a School," *U.S. News*, August 16, 2010, https://www.usnews.com/education/best-colleges/applying/articles/2010/08/16/the-right-way-to-pitch-yourself-to-a-school.

internship in Silicon Valley. Okay, but drill down to find out what makes you tick. Do you love visiting with your grandparents on the weekend? Why? Tell us in detail. What does that say about you? Do you feel strongly about making your own money and that's why you have a job after school? Why? Where will that attitude take you in life? It doesn't matter if that job is at a New York law firm, a Los Angeles film-editing company, or your corner drugstore. The reason for doing that job every day and taking pride in having it is a story itself.

- Are your parents immigrants? How has that affected what you want from life? What do they expect from you, and what do you want for yourself? How will this make you different from others on campus? Why is that part of the fabric of who you are?
- Have you ever engaged in an activity that changed your point of view?
- Do you read the paper each day? If so, why is that important, and what does it say about you?
- Have you always wanted to do something but haven't yet? What has stopped you? Are you planning on doing it? What do you expect to get out of that experience? Why do you want it?
- Are you a sports enthusiast who always attends your friend's piano recitals? Why is that important to you? Do you see both sports and music as performance? What does it say about the kind of friend you are or your intellectual curiosity?

Thoughtful, well-crafted answers to any of these questions will paint a picture of you and the kind of student you'll be on campus.

Don't worry that you don't have the proper tools or interesting experiences needed to tell your own story. You've got plenty!

> "Most of the basic material a writer works with is
> acquired before the age of fifteen."
> —Willa Cather

Many art forms follow similar rules—they use a combination of the subtractive method and the additive method to end up with a piece that has both great clarity and imaginative messaging. Photographers use a subtractive process through which they remove all but the desired colors by passing the illuminating light through *subtractive* filters. In this way, the photographer can allow just the right suggestions and hues they intended and leave the ultimate interpretation or associations of the work to the audience.[27] And let's not forget how Michelangelo cut away "everything that was not the David" to make *David.*

"Most of the basic material a writer works with is acquired before the age of fifteen." —Willa Cather

When answering one of the seven Common Application prompts, you have so many options and so many ideas that pop into your mind. Some of you think, Why not use all of them? So, you write down all the clues and facts that lead to your story: where you are, what you are doing, which awards and accolades you have won, and what your major will be in college—all in the first two paragraphs. Where's the mystery? To an admissions reader, what should read like a creative narrative winds up reading like a résumé. You add and add and add, leaving no room for the imagination to run wild. That's demotivating for the reader!

27 Chris Corradino, "Composition Is a Process of Subtraction," New York Institute of Photography, July 28, 2015, https://www.nyip.edu/photo-articles/photography-tutorials/composition-is-a-process-of-subtraction.

Your idea for responding to a prompt can change dramatically depending on how you express it. From the moment the light bulb goes on in your head through the time that you unpack the idea, your communication of that idea goes through several iterations before you type or write the first line. So, do create a meaningful, lusciously descriptive scene in your first paragraph, but do not *tell* us all the important points you are about to unravel in the rest of the essay. Let these points reveal themselves. This kind of essay writing requires a subtractive process in the beginning and then, as you move through the body of the essay, a more detailed, "additive" explanation of who you have become and why. Character and scene development, style and clarity are more important than you think—even in 650 words.

Essay Excerpts: Examples of the Subtractive Method

Garbed in a black leotard with black sheer pinstripe tights and a metal cage skirt, she arose from the park bench. Tossing a messy beehive bun weaved with black feathers and twigs, her curly blackish-blue hair mirrored a bird's nest and created a useful diversion on the streets as she conducted a fleet of jet-black crows in choreographed routines, secretly picking the pockets of walkers-by. Anything might set her off. (That was my stage direction, and I was sticking to it.)

I created Crow Lady while studying at XYZ Summer Theater Program. Until that summer, I had been a Shakespearean actor—studying Shakespeare, performing in youth Shakespearean ensembles, and eventually, gaining small roles in

Shakespearean touring companies. Not only did I always know every word I was about to utter, but my audience knew my lines as well. I was terrified of improvisation. But on a sunny summer morning in London, my ensemble director tasked the class with creating our own divas inspired by "Moulin Rouge" and Toulouse-Lautrec's "Stars of Paris"—all in one weekend. Our divas needed to be larger than life, rant about how they were wronged, and capture the audience's imagination. I would need to improvise and unleash Crow Lady on the students before me.

After a weekend of frenzied costume-creation, I arose from my seat. Summoning courage and the unpredictability of my new character through a slow, awkward, and ridiculous strut, I approached the stage and hoped for divine intervention. Students and coaches began laughing ebulliently. So far so good. I had birthed Crow Lady's physicality and eccentricity. I fed off the audience's mounting giggles by speaking in an indescribable mix of accents. I teased the audience, "What are you snickering at? If I find out you were the one who plucked my pretty bird away, I will flog you with my flock!" I have no idea where those words came from, but I had discovered my inner-improviser and she carried my ranting diva to the finish line.

There are gaps at the beginning of the essay that require the reading audience to fill in pieces with their imagination. Is this student having a dream, seeing a play, in a play? Is *she* Crow Lady? Giving us our definitive bearings in the first paragraph would be tantamount to giving us boundaries as well. We would be less interested in reading through the entire narrative because the narrative would now seem common. Starting with a quirky description and then giving us a clue at the end of the first paragraph compels us to read on.

Some of our most renowned authors understood and used the idea of gaps and "less is more" in their own writing. Author of *The Little Prince* (*Le Petit Prince*), Antoine de Saint-Exupéry, noted that "perfection is achieved not when there is nothing more to add, but when there is nothing left to take away." Award-winning novelist Italo Calvino also observed the value of economical writing: "Above all, I have tried to remove weight from the structure of stories and language."

Remember to employ purposeful gaps and just enough description to create a vibrant visual and the desire to read more. The missing information will engage your reader (read: admissions officer) and inspire further reading to close the information gap. The intensity of a reader's curiosity about a piece of missing information in an opening paragraph is dependent on whether we believe we will be able to close that gap by the end of the essay. Of course, every 650-word personal statement must end by sating the reader's curiosity and closing that gap, so Admissions knows that if the essay's opening is compelling, it will be worth sticking around to discover the close.

In fact, the rest of this 650-word essay from which the above segment is excerpted provided a clear exploration of who this student is as an actor and artist—in and out of class.

Let's look at one more lengthy excerpt from a personal statement that uses gaps and the subtractive method artfully:

Night and Day

"Shall I compare thee to another?" I can't. You're not like the other ones. I don't usually get anxious before encounters, but this time was different. Would you still love me or had my lapse of attention driven you away? I had told you I would be back in a week. It had been three. My research had kept me pinned to my desk. Now, as I made my final preparations before going under, I thought, "How am I going to explain this to you?"

Loyal and alluring, you had sought me out every day, when I was at my most vulnerable. Why then and why only me? There were at least fifty others you could have chosen—plenty of local guys. Yet when you approached me with those dusky eyes that beckoned and teased with unyielding curiosity, I no longer needed to know the "why"; I just knew that I was the lucky one.

At our first introduction I did not know how to act. An awkward and muffled "Hello" was all I could muster. Yet you continued to dance around me with carefully calculated spins and twirls, as if wanting me to notice what you were wearing. With each movement closer, your flaxen yellow top caught the light. I tried to avoid eye contact and turned aside, attempting to appear uninterested. I even took off in another direction, but you followed close behind. I finally gave in and allowed you to welcome me into your world.

Our initial interactions were limited to darting eye contact and casual acknowledgement. But I was hooked. I allured you with delicacies of wheat and seaweed. You took them tenderly from my hand. Over the next few weeks, I began to sense a connection. The day had no light without our encounters. You became my guide and I, your protector. Swimming together among the coral heads, you pointed out the easily missed Hawksbill Turtle and I kept the threatening lionfish at bay. At the *Swirling Reef of Death* we would seek out the unseen and share the amazement of new discovery. We were happy together.

So, you can imagine my concern and distress about seeing you again after breaking my promise. I moved towards our usual meeting place. I put out my hand towards you, but this time you kept your distance. I advanced in your direction, yet you strayed further from me. I felt lost. Trying to appear strong and unaffected, I sought out another. She was beautiful in appearance and so much like you ... so much, yet aloof, distant, and easily diverted. I thought about what a relationship with her would be like but knew it would never be right. You and she—night and day.

There was no other Wrasse like you. As I stripped off my mask and fins and climbed back on the boat, I looked out onto the waves and watched as you darted through the haze, turning left at the Old Spanish Anchor and out towards the southwestern tip of the island ... We'd pick it back up next June.

Admissions readers are enticed to read on and on in this playful, well-written essay because neither the student's activity nor his location is made evident until four paragraphs into the narrative. In this risky but descriptively written piece, there is "subtraction" everywhere through which we can let our imaginations run wild and fill in the blanks. This student is a devoted marine biologist who artfully hinted about his academic passion for marine life (and wrasses in particular) within the constraints of this personal statement. There was just enough for Admissions to see how the applicant connects his academic passions and free imagination to his practice of snorkeling.

An opening paragraph description that reels in the reader:

It is 6 a.m. Girls are spray-tanning in the ballroom under the long, grand crystal stalactites of chandeliers. I begin the ritual removal of the layers: first comes the coat, the sweater, and the heavy woolen scarf, finally revealing the costume and its pungent smell of glue, fresh from the fastening of jewels to the bodice. I remove the fuzzy slippers, my last reminder of comfort for the next several hours and begin the bandaging. Wrapping the toes first with toe tape, I visualize success. My feet are cramping now as I slip them into the sweaty, warm shoes, wet from the prior night's practice. I hear my heels clicking against the floor and watch the girl in the mirror with a blindingly neon yellow costume that wears her. I cross to position. My hair is pulled so tightly it is the only thing keeping my eyes open. I do a final check on my garment and pull apart the beads that are still stuck together. The rattling announces the beginning of competition season. I am dancing now, filled in a way few things in life fill me as I revel in the exchange of mutual energy between judges, audience, and artist—an exchange as natural to me as awakening with the sunrise.

Do you notice how the rich description in this opening allows you to visualize the scene and feel for the author?

How to Move through Your Opening Paragraph

"Fill your paper with the breathings of your heart."

—William Wordsworth

Always start with a novel idea, and then inject the familiar into the essay (anecdotes, real-life examples, explanations of what your unique opening insinuates). Definitely do not begin your essay with commonplace telling (e.g., "I leave the house every Saturday at 6:00 a.m. and take a one-hour bus ride to my internship at ABC Hospital. There, I help with scribing and get to meet the patients." This is an example of how not to write). "Telling" instead of "showing" makes your essay common and safe as opposed to visual and intriguing. Use suspense or any vehicle that will create curiosity, and then develop your experience through the lens of a bildungsroman—a hero's journey. (Now, you might equivocate about my not using *bildungsroman* in the most literal sense here, but please know that *bump* was not a word in English until Shakespeare decided it was.)

"Fill your paper with the breathings of your heart." —William Wordsworth

Use a Little Humor to Encourage the Likeability Factor (If You Enjoy Writing with Humor)

Let's look at a complete personal statement. I'm going to ask you to take notes while you read, jotting down the literary devices that make this essay successful. The essay might be helpful to students because it's not written by an applicant who is an international award winner or someone who had a larger-than-life high school career. This essay holds value because it's written by a typical intelligent student who just wanted to tell the story of earning her black belt because it was pivotal for her.

I led a double life; STEM student by day, self-defense artist by night. From the age of four, discipline and I understood each other. By elementary school, I practiced my moves every evening after homework, and rehearsed the commands in my blue "Runaway Bunny" pajamas. Kiotsuke—I stood up straight. Otagai ni rei—I bowed deeply in front of the mirror. Kawate—On guard!

I dreaded waking up every Sunday morning for karate classes, (and spending my Wednesday afternoons there did not thrill me either). However, my mother swore to me that I would find something of great value in it one day, as she had as a child; so off I went. The Shotokan division of karate was not for the weak of heart, and as far as I could tell at four, it was not for me either.

By Middle School, I campaigned against karate through active and frequent polemics staged at the kitchen table. "It's all so random, mom!" I would blurt out. Breathing, posing, moving—performing hits that seemed to land more out of luck than from technique. "Why should I stick with this?" I harangued my mother. "If I spent 35% of my karate practice time on debate, I would win every mock trial in school; and with the remaining 65% of my practice time devoted to chess, maybe I would be a grandmaster one day."

"Karate is purposeful, not random," my mother would answer. "This will empower you as a young woman and as a mind. One day you will see. I promise—you will see."

By high school, Sensei began to speak in physical terms that I easily synthesized and believed. My work on the floor mat with that piece of wood before me was all about leverage, he explained—not only how to extend force against it, but to know where the wood was weakest. I positioned my legs a shoulder's width apart, with the left leg adjusted to one- and one-half shoulder's width—pointing 30 degrees forward. Now, with 70% of my weight directed to the front leg, I was in position to make the strongest impact. That square of wood did not have a chance. The tiny mass that was my 14-year-old fist combined with just the right level of acceleration created the momentum to push through a solid, seemingly unyielding object. Atemi: Strike! It was not luck when I broke that square. It was math and physics. Newton's third law had come to life for me. F=MA. The mass of the fist multiplied by the acceleration enabled by my posture equals the force imparted to the wood, rendering it into splinters. Karate was my new obsession.

I spent time after school researching formulas that would help me understand the purpose of each punch (zuki) and the results of different amounts of energy propelled through each punch; then I would recite those formulas on the way to class: (ET = EP + EK + ER). I was going to be a blackbelt.

Everything changed the day Sensei used math and physics to explain each move. I never uttered another complaint about attending class; and powered through each test until I won my blackbelt. Here, for me, was purpose; here were real world calculations and explanations that my sys-

> tematic mind could be excited by and accept. My love for mathematics and physics will always be entwined with the purpose and empowerment I found in Karate. Thank you, mom. I finally **see**.

Now, what was great about that essay?! If you noted the use of realism and genuineness (through her actual physics formulas and arguments with her mom); humor (which, if done disarmingly, creates likeability); and loads of action words (which keep you excited about reading on), you have had a great start in understanding how to craft a creative, personal essay.

A Final Word on Devising Your Personal Statement

In painting theory, there is something called the primal mark: it's the first bit of content that you create for an idea—that first mark on the canvas. Instead of limitless possibilities, the artist, then, becomes constrained by that first mark such that the rest of the composition must come from or lead to it.

Seniors, I understand it is difficult to create the first personal statement, so try this concept from painting theory. Brainstorm that first big idea that you would love to talk about, put the "strokes" of it onto the page, outlining beginning anecdotes, bullet points that organize the story, a lesson learned or pivot that occurred in your life because of the story; then begin working through the constraints of that story, and watch your thesis evolve. Developing and then sticking to that primal mark can encourage you to trust your instincts while forcing you to be ever mindful of your main point—your *why*—in writing the essay. Not that the first idea is always the right one for a college essay, but it certainly gives you the confidence to write down the next one.

The Why Essay: Closing the Deal with Admissions Officers

When colleges or universities ask why you want to attend, they expect detailed answers. In fact, your "Why X University" essay can make or break your chance for admittance.

- Don't include generic paragraphs that could be switched out for another school.
- Don't take entire essays and simply change names of departments and courses that you'd like to take.
- Don't discuss climate or the beauty of the campus.
- Do speak about specific professors with whom you'd like to study or do research.
- Do speak about what you intend to study (it's okay; admissions officers know that this can change during college) and what you hope to take from and give to that campus, both academically and in your extracurricular pursuits.

Admissions can tell when their school's "why" essay has been put together with broadly worded pieces from other schools' "why" essays. Your job is to make every college feel loved and special—not generic. Prove, point for point, how X University will fulfill your collegiate academic and extracurricular vision. Do not just say that X University has a good major in politics. Explain why the school's particular major is well suited to you. Which courses are you excited about taking? Is there an interdisciplinary spirit to the department that fits your broad way of looking at the world? Is there a professor with whom you'd like to do research? Why? Who are the professors whose classes you're excited about taking? Which clubs or publications do you wish to become involved with and why?

Nailing the "Why"

Here's an example of a weak "why" essay:

I am interested in many subjects, and I know I will be happy academically at Tulane University because it has a broad selection of courses. I can major in business and still take English and history. This is important to me because I am still deciding on my major. I have been inspired to study courses across many disciplines and have become active in lots of school activities like the newspaper and Key Club. I expect to be involved in many activities at Tulane as well, and in that way, give back to my school.

Well meaning, but unacceptable. The first problem with this "why" paragraph is that it doesn't tell us *why* anything! Additionally, almost every sentence starts with *I*. Repetition of the same word or pronoun from sentence to sentence makes the writing uninteresting and repetitive. Another flaw is the general and weak substantiation of points. This essay, above all, must provide the details of what makes the particular university the right fit for you—according to the high school courses you've taken and loved, according to the opinions you hold about political or social matters, according to the career path you hope to pursue, according to the talents you wish to develop, and so on. Details, details, details. Show how much due diligence you put into your research for every university to which you apply. Not only aren't there specific courses or professors provided in the paragraph above, but we are not at all sure that this applicant has written the "why" paragraph for this specific university. Replace Tulane with the name of another university and see if it fits just as well. Unfortunately for this student, it does.

AN EXAMPLE OF AN EXCELLENT AND CREATIVE "WHY" ESSAY FOR CORNELL'S DYSON SCHOOL OF APPLIED ECONOMICS AND MANAGEMENT (650 WORDS)

Driving through the beautiful Bitterroot Valley can be a bit of a dichotomous experience. One is confronted by endlessly beautiful wilderness and natural life. Deer flit through the woods, hawks soar regally, and trout leap frantically. However, one is also met by decades of human poverty: meadows full of rusted-out automobiles, groves of forest smothered by deprecated settlement, and the charred remnants of mobile-home lots, left to collapse.

In 2011, after moving to Montana from the desert oasis of Las Vegas, Nevada, I had little perception of the poverty which engulfed my neighbors. I was too busy being enthralled by farm animals and bluegrass fiddle. However, I gradually learned about the unfortunate results of logging and industry growth in Montana: deforestation, soil erosion, and destruction of animal habitat. While loggers and ranchers are concerned with the preservation of their livelihood, conservationists are concerned with protecting valuable resources from possible depletion—limiting peoples' ability to survive in an otherwise economically depressed region.

I am passionate about intelligently answering the question of how society can preserve both the livelihoods and culture of a state, while also conserving and managing the ever-lessening natural beauty with which it has been blessed. Both intentions carry serious negative consequences: sheep ranchers are either run off of federal lands or into bankruptcy by conservationist lawsuits, while poorly-regulated logging companies mow down vast swathes of invaluable forest cover or carelessly start forest fires.

My interest in applied economics has driven me to seek effective resolutions. I hope to work towards encouraging beef ranchers in the Bitterroot to focus more on specific breeds of cattle that finish better on grass than grain, allowing them to be raised without costly and destructive feedlots. Additionally, I believe that a local farm based on the community-assisted agriculture model will make progress in spreading environmentally safe practices.

After researching the most forward-thinking programs that explore the science of economics with the intention of benefiting humanity by investigating models that both boost our markets and preserve our world, I have found the peerless Applied Economics Management degree at Dyson with a concentration in Environmental, Energy, and Resource Economics. It is evident from reviewing courses and faculty that the economics of natural resources, sustainability in resource-oriented markets, and stable food policies for developing nations are at the forefront of the Dyson model and philosophy.

Taking Environmental Economics and Resource Economics will help me focus on tools to explore current and future policies related to incentivizing reduced pollution and protecting nonrenewable resources. Sustainability Marketing focuses on the second half of my drive—preserving struggling markets along with the environment. I am compelled by the course's exploration into the identification of environmental issues, and its further investigation into how to sustain the environment while making profit.

Having followed the work of Professor Wayne Knoblauch, I am inspired by his mission outside of the classroom to create programs to assist individuals in the business of agriculture, creating networks to provide vital resources. Furthermore, Professor Prabhu Pingali remains singularly distinguished in my search, with his extensive experience in the world of agricultural development, specifically in emerging markets. He has used his expertise to seek "a way forward in the transition towards nutrition security" in application to India. I would seek out a research internship with Professor Pingali because nutrition security is of concern in rural America as well and there are innovations waiting for the right solutions-thinking. These pioneers in agribusiness are the kinds of mentors that can provide multiple mental models from which I might devise solutions for pressing problems.

If I am to be a voice in resolving problems evident in markets like Montana's, I need the divergent lessons of Environmental, Energy, and Resource Economics to craft my intellectual foundation. Such a focus at Dyson would be invaluable in taking this 18-year-old with vision and building me into a professional with tools to promote a sustainable future.

A WELL-CRAFTED "WHY" ESSAY FOR NYU STERN

I come from a world that believes in "hiring different." Students determine their value propositions: finance, business development, or technology, and then play to their strengths throughout their careers. However, I am eager to formally develop the interdisciplinary business education that NYU–Stern's philosophy and faculty provide, allowing me to make future business decisions based on a web of intelligences learned from models in economics, finance, entrepreneurship, and the entire spectrum of the entertainment industry.

As I develop the scholarship and savvy for a future in the music industry, I believe that the underlying principles of economics and finance will help me cultivate a more sophisticated hybrid mind. My musical endeavors, product design, and business development pursuits with manufacturers in China is what has allowed me to be in a state of fascinated creation and stimulation throughout high school. I exuberantly engage in CAD drawing and 3D printing; PCB (printed circuit board) designing and manual soldering; keyboard playing, and DJing; visual designing and model building. However, Stern's unique EMT major, Finance minor, and freedom to take coursework in economics would provide a formal framework for my curiosity and love of invention. Additionally, I have witnessed the value of studying amongst students of like passions, on streets that make music 24 hours a day this past summer by having been selected for the Clive Davis Institute which opened up an entirely new way to listen, innovate, and discuss music.

Through classes such as The Art of Listening and Topics in 20th Century Music, I can hone my music appreciation and analysis. Stern's courses in Topics in Entrepreneurial Finance and Chinese Financial markets, which address the question of whether China must accelerate financial innovation, are vital from the perspective of a student who expects to work in both the East and West. Additionally, courses through EMT such as Deal Making in the Entertainment Industry and Globalization of the Entertainment Industry offer unique value for my prospective professional future.

I would also love to join the board of NYU–Stern/Tisch Entertainment Business Association, doing outreach, hosting panels, and coordinating mentorships. Outreach to workshop mentors would come naturally to me as I must engage in international outreach for my podcast, East-West Notes.

In NYU Stern's unique undergraduate programs, I will gain both the field-specific scholarship and accessibility to a city that moves to the beat of business and music.

PART FOUR:

ADVICE FROM YOUR MENTORS

You are beginning to see how intuitive college advising and subject-specific mentorship can change the shape of your high school career and your college application. Advisors and mentors are valuable for the questions they ask, which activate curiosity and energize talents, developing those talents into tools for elevating thoughtful and entrepreneurial behavior.

The following segments will introduce you to a diverse range of exceptional mentors. These subject matter experts have shared their philosophies, anecdotes, and road maps to success in each of their fields—it is their way of giving back and mentoring you. Read carefully as they explain the opportunities that exist in their fields for differentiating intelligent high school students and future college applicants. Pick up your highlighter and Post-it Notes as you learn from some of the nation's most respected specialists in the fields of mathematics, leadership, business, technology, music, debate, and scientific research.

Introduction to Higher Mathematics Study and Competition

Students work and play amid a world of constraints. We spoke earlier about the constraints necessary to observe when writing a successful college personal statement. In mathematics, there are rules to follow and formulas to apply, but also ways to turn problems on their sides for surprising solutions. In computer science, there are debugging procedures and algorithm structures to follow, but also ways to break down problems and learn how machines develop solutions and sequences—imagining and reckoning computationally. In music study and performance, there is written sheet music and a strict meter to follow, but also space for improvisation and interpretation once you develop facility and begin to perform. In the fields of business, leadership, and debate, there are similar technical rules and regulations that act as frames for the imaginative and innovative thinking you possess. Being trained and mentored in these fields teaches you to respect those constraints and recognize that there are times to work within them and times to innovate outside of them.

YOUR MENTOR:

WES CARROLL

(MIT), One of the Nation's Top Mathematics Competition Coaches

Would You Like to Succeed?

They say there's no such thing as a dumb question, but this one might be an exception: **of course** you want to succeed, no matter what "success" means for you. And I'd like to help you define it.

What is success? Well, at this moment, success mostly looks like getting into a great college. Okay, let's go with that for now.

You want to accomplish this because there's a long history of college functioning as a great stepping-stone to a great job, a great career, and even a great life. And you're working hard at it because the best colleges admit only a very small number of the many people who apply, and you want to be one of them.

So, I will now add my voice to the mentors in *The Exceptional Applicant* and tell you what I know will boost your college application and change your life: *math.*

How Is Math Useful?

If you ask around, it's not hard to get an adult to say something like "Math is important," "You ought to do well in math," or "Math will help you get the jobs of the future." What you don't get is answers to these questions: **Why** is it important? **How** do I get good at it? Those are the questions that I'm going to try to answer for you.

Normally, this would be the part where the mathematician tells you how awesome math is in general.

But instead, let's talk about how math is awesome for particular purposes. For example, here's what theoretical computer scientist and professor at UT-Austin Scott Aaronson has to say:

The career paths with the highest potential for growth require more and deeper mathematical preparation than ever before. Calculus and other mathematical foundations are not important because they are admission requirements for colleges, or because they are relics of the "Sputnik era." They are important because they provide fundamental knowledge and ways of thinking that are necessary for success in these fast growing and in-demand fields.

Neither Scott nor I were mathematics majors. Personally, I was trained at MIT as an engineer with a specialty in computers.

Also, because of the times we live in, no human knows even a tiny fraction of the math that actually exists. (Some of it isn't even readable by humans; it was developed by computers.)

So, I am not here to tell you how awesome math is. That isn't my point. It's just a tool. I'm no more excited about math than I am about hammers or Wi-Fi. Just a tool.

But here's the crucial insight: the stuff that math is a good tool for is really important given how fast things have been changing in our society.

What Even Is Math?

Math is the language of patterns, patterns are the keys to technology, and technology is how and why our culture and economy are both growing so fast. Being good at math puts you in the place where the change is happening, where the money is being earned, and where the decisions are being made.

But it also goes deeper than that. Math is also the language of abstraction. That's a fancy way of saying that math gives you a concrete way of talking and thinking about things that do not and cannot exist in the physical universe. You cannot hold a "five"; you will never see a truly perfect triangle in real life; some aspects of integrals can perhaps be visualized, but the thing itself is purely an idea without a physical representation.

> **Being good at math puts you in the place ... where the decisions are being made.**

Sets, groups, operations. Proofs, axioms, propositions. These are ways to connect, discuss, and refine *ideas*. It's what math was designed to do. It's *all* math does. And as long as ideas are an important part of our world, math will be an important part of what you need to know in order to live and thrive here.

Once you're good at it, math also becomes **the study of studying things**. If all else fails, then math will tell you what questions to ask to figure things out, and it'll tell you how to start answering them.

Are you starting to see how powerful this can be? William Paul Thurston said it well:

Mathematics is not about numbers, equations, computations, or algorithms: it is about understanding.

So ... Why Don't I See It Everywhere?

Okay, fine, math is important for your future. So, then, surely adults must do a lot of it, right?

But that doesn't seem right. After all, when was the last time you saw an adult solving an integral? When was the last time you heard the word *cosine* come out of the mouth of a grown-up who wasn't your teacher? For that matter, when did you last witness an adult solve an algebra or geometry problem of any kind? I'm gonna bet on "never, not once in your life." Why not? If math is so important, then why don't I see it everywhere?

The main reason people don't see adults doing math in everyday life is pretty simple: most people have too narrow a definition of what mathematical thinking *is*—because it's happening all around you, all the time. Don't just think of numbers—think of analysis and judgment; think of weighing options; think of "thinking outside the box." Those are the skills and habits you get from math training.

When someone's deciding on a job offer, that's math. When they're deciding whether to buy that house: math. When they're solving some tricky problem for work: math. The harder the problem, the more impossible it seems, the more math matters.

Because that's what math is supposed to teach you: **what to do when you don't know what you're doing.**

Some people do this reflexively and without much reflection on how they do it (or on how they could improve that natural skill). For some people, that's enough. But in my view, the smarter strategy is to focus explicitly on how that skill works so that you can improve it over time. That will give you a natural advantage when you don't really know what you're doing.

That's critical, because "not knowing what you're doing" has been a bigger and bigger part of each generation's experience for a good long time now, and it's only getting worse from here.

If that sounds right to you, then I recommend that you start now: get good at figuring out *what to do when you don't know what you're doing*. It's the only skill that will be necessary for both surviving and thriving. And math is at its core.

Then Why Doesn't Math Class Look like That?

You've heard me say that math is about learning what to do when you don't know what you're doing. But you've also noticed that what you do in math class doesn't seem to be about that. **Why not?**

I'll answer your question with a question: Have you ever seen a pro athlete just run in circles during a game? Of course not. And yet there's a running track at most high schools, and there are treadmills in most gyms.

Put another way: running around a quarter-mile track doesn't only make you good at running around quarter-mile tracks. It makes you good at running in general. Heck, it makes you good at exerting yourself in general. The important part of a track isn't its shape or its size. The important part of a track is just that *it gets people to run*.

And there's another benefit to a track: if you're running around in ovals at a steady pace where an expert can watch you and time you, then the expert can critique and improve your running form and your decisions about when to speed up and when to conserve.

So, it's a funny thing: we want to get better at running for some purpose—like, for example, recreational cross-country jaunts—and yet when we want to be better cross-country runners, we sometimes run on a track instead of running a "real" course.

That's the thing about improving a skill: sometimes you need to break the skill down into subskills and practice each of those individually, and sometimes you need to practice the whole skill as a unit, with all subskills contributing appropriately.

What does this have to do with math? Everything. Math is the "running track" of **structured thinking**. It's how you can build the mental muscles you need for later intellectual challenges and also the way in which expert coaches can critique and improve your thinking "form" as you practice.

What's funny is that most people—even most math teachers—don't really understand this. And if you don't believe me, ask your math teacher why you have to learn math. Chances are you won't get an answer anything like mine.

Students ask this question all the time in classrooms across the world, and it almost never really gets answered. Because no one wants to admit (to their students or to themselves) that we don't really know what you're going to need to know in life; it's just that math is one of our *best guesses* for what you'll need. It's the tool that has empowered us to navigate all the changes of the past fifty years and more, and it isn't showing any signs of going stale.

So it's time for you to get good at it. Here's **the right way to proceed**, from the very beginning.

HOW EARLY SHOULD A GIFTED MATH STUDENT BEGIN EXPLORING THE FIELD?

Immediately! After all, exploring is what gifted students have been doing all along.

How do you explore? Read about what's interesting to you. Solve puzzles that are challenging and alluring. Talk about puzzles with others who are interested. Enter contests, join activities, listen as people explain concepts, and then explain them to others yourself.

The sweet spot is to find something you're interested in, think about it until you're stuck, read about it until you're bored, and talk about it until it gives you an idea.

What about Classes?

In particular, don't be in a giant rush to learn multivariable calculus or whatever. I mean, sure, read about whatever you like, even if it's superadvanced, but don't be in a huge rush about it. Math isn't a collection of badges; it's a way of thinking. It takes time to acquire the mindset. What works best is to try to think carefully about what you're studying, asking questions and trying things out as you go.

The big mistake here is trying to finish the curriculum as soon as you can. That leads to only kinda-sorta knowing a lot of math, which, it turns out, is pretty much worthless. First, handle your classes.

As a high school mathematician interested in leveraging your love of math for college-admissions advantage, your first priority should be learning the math offered by your high school, in depth. In most cases, this means earning a 5 on the AP Calculus AB exam or a 4 or 5 on the AP Calculus BC exam, by the end of your senior year. Your goal is to **learn this basic material well**, not to maximize the material you cover.

Next, Address Admissions Tests

Your next step depends on the advice of your college counselor. If they say that you need to maximize your admissions test scores, then get that done as your next priority.

This is tricky because the math required for the ACT and SAT is actually pretty easy. The hard part is staying calm yet alert for three or four hours straight so that you can avoid avoidable mistakes. This is best accomplished through the right kinds of practice. Learn more about this at **wescarroll.com/admission-tests**, or get in touch with me at **wescarroll.com/start** if you'd like to ask me some questions directly.

Finally, Pursue an Extracurricular

After you have your coursework figured out and you have an admissions test prep game plan, your next target should be **extracurricular math**.

This can take a lot of different forms, and you don't have to do them all. For most, one is plenty: just dive deeply into that one.

The most straightforward extracurricular math path is to participate in (and win) **math competitions**. These are opportunities to show off your interest in math and creative problem-solving, all while solving interesting and elegant puzzles dreamed up for you by some of the world's best.

And—perhaps most importantly for the moment—the results of these competitions are watched and well understood by the admissions committees of the top schools.

The most prestigious and well known of the competitions is the AMC 12. It's held in November and takes place during the school day. **Your school must register** for the competition, so you should tell your math department to sign up well in advance. The top scorers are invited to compete in a higher-level exam called the American Invitational Math Exam (AIME); just being invited is something of an admissions golden ticket.

If you are especially prone to anxiety or have other difficulty with timed tests, you might consider the USAMTS, another highly regarded competition with a very different format; where the AMC takes place on one day, with a seventy-five-minute time limit, the USAMTS takes place over the course of several months in the fall, with practically no time limit at all. The AMC encourages quick thinking backed up by deep training; the USAMTS encourages deep thinking and perseverance.

If competitions aren't your path, then two other good options include summer math camps and research opportunities.

Some math camps are more focused on math competitions (i.e., creative problem-solving, especially under a deadline), and others are more focused on the exploration of various advanced topics with no agenda other than enjoyment and understanding.

Finally, there are opportunities to do real research with professors and other academics; this can result in credit as a contributor to a published work.

An AMC Prep Road Map

Assuming you pick the AMC as your extracurricular, here's **what you should be doing when**.

Students who are just getting started should try a few different math competitions and read a few books intended to help you do well at the competitions. Visit some of the websites and forums that are great for this purpose, including the Art of Problem Solving (AoPS) and brilliant.org. Check out some YouTube channels: Vi Hart and 3blue1brown are just a few of the great options out there.

Expect to *spend time* on these things.

But, to be clear: the results of these competitions matter much less than the thinking that you have to do in order to prepare for them. That matters a lot. Plus, if you participate, you'll meet other people with whom you can talk about math. That's a huge bonus.

As much as possible, you should be increasingly "owning" your own learning and thinking about how you learn best. Don't learn something just because it'll be on the test, and don't try to learn it just well enough to do well on the test. Find your own interest in the subject, and learn it for that reason. Learn it your way. Research it your way. Experiment with what works best for you. Master it.

Also, if you get to pick classes, then pick classes with teachers you like best. That's more important than taking certain subjects, because what you know is less important than how you think. Teachers you like will usually help you think better. (That's why you like them.)

By your last two years of high school, math competitions like the AMC and the USAMTS will be some of the best ways to get exposed to math that you otherwise would completely miss.

Summer math camps are also a great resource. Canada/USA Mathcamp (mathcamp.org) is my favorite, and there are many other great options out there. Most of them require you to pass an entrance exam in order to attend, and this is where your previous practice and exploration will really pay off, because the camps aren't looking for people who can ace the SAT; they're looking for people who are curious and who have followed their curiosity in the past into learning new things and discovering new ways of thinking for themselves.

Throughout, your overarching goal is to stay in the **zone of proximal development**, which for our purposes means that you should be doing stuff that's hard for you but still doable. That's how people learn best and fastest.

Now, let's get into some more step-by-step detail.

BEFORE PRECALCULUS

- If you are not yet in high school, compete in the AMC 8 each February. Prepare during the fall.
- If you are in high school but are not yet in a precalculus class, compete in the AMC 10 in November. Prepare during the summer.

Preparing for these exams can include taking a preparation class. These vary in quality; everyone will get value from the best of them, and the best students will get value out of even a poor class. So, pay attention and get what you can.

There are several excellent books out there; I recommend finding and working through some if that sounds like your wheelhouse.

Here are a few of my favorites:

- How to Solve It (Pólya)
- First Steps for Math Olympians (Faires)
- *AoPS vol. 1 and 2* (Lehoczky and Rusczyk)
- The Art and Craft of Problem Solving (Zeitz)
- *Mindset* (Dweck)
- Study Is Hard Work (Armstrong)
- The Power of Habit (Duhigg)

Note that the first half of this list is focused on technical AMC skills, and the second half is focused on the practices of champions in any field.

Finally, there is nothing like sitting down and taking a past year's exam for the purpose of seeing what happens. Critically analyzing your performance after the fact is hands down **the best way** to determine what you most need in order to improve. It's also the hardest way to proceed, both technically and emotionally, which is why this work is usually done with a coach.

DURING AND AFTER PRECALCULUS

- If you are in precalculus or have already completed precalculus, compete in the AMC 12 in November. Prepare throughout the year.

Your preparation calendar should look something like this:

March through May

During this time, you're going to be busy with classwork, especially junior year. So your AMC prep during this time should be structured to be effective without taking a lot of time or energy. **Memorization** is well suited to these constraints. My AMC prep course is made for this purpose, as are a number of great books and other available resources. The big-picture goal here is to spend just a few minutes each day adding to your mental library of tools and techniques. By the end of the spring, you should have considerably more ways to solve problems than you did during the previous winter holiday.

June through August

The summer is the time for intensive prep. Dedicated prep programs are a good option; this includes competition-focused math camps, online and in-person prep courses, good old-fashioned reading and practicing, and skilled coaching.

The goal during the summer is to get practiced at **using** everything you learned during the spring. There's a big difference between having a lot of knowledge and being able to use it under pressure. Summer is a great time for integrating and expanding all that knowledge in a way that will pay off in the fall.

September and October

Your schoolwork will be keeping you plenty busy. This is a time for maintaining the gains you made over the summer. If you have a light course load, then continuing to build your skills and abilities during this time will be very helpful. But it's important to not overdo it. Just keep your head in the game through the fall, staying comfortably on top of all your commitments.

November

This is game time: your goal is to take the AMC in a well-rested, prepared, and confident state. Only 5 percent of competitors will make it to the next round. But you've been building up advantages for yourself for months and months so that you can be one of those top few.

December and January

You are now preparing for the AIME, which you hope to have qualified for. You will be getting the invitation in December or January.

February

This is AIME month. Time to show off all your great preparation a second time—this time for even higher stakes! But don't worry: you've already gotten a huge boost to your college admissions prospects just by making it this far. Anything beyond this is just bonus.

FAQ

How does working within the constraints of mathematics create more imaginative thinkers in any field? You know how pearls are made? Basically, pearls are made of oyster snot. If you want a pearl, you put a grain of sand inside a certain kind of oyster. That oyster, annoyed by the sand, will basically cover it in layers and layers of oyster snot. That's what a pearl is. A grain of sand and a bunch of oyster snot.

The constraints of math are the grain of sand. And you, my friend, are the oyster: your attempts to grapple with the rules of math will lead, over time, to your getting good at figuring out solutions to annoying problems. In other words, you'll get to be a snotty oyster. And guess what? Everyone wants to be close to people who are good at making pearls out of sand. Whether it's money you want or popularity or respect, there's a path to get there through math.

Which college majors become possibilities for the successful mathematics student? Math leads into anything and everything. A good mathematician is good at learning and good at analysis. That covers all majors. Sure, engineering, science, and pure math departments are the obvious choices, and indeed they work well. And the finance folks have figured out that math is where it's at too. But the other majors figure it out real fast once you show up.

Which career paths? Math is not necessarily good for pro sports. But other than that, the sky's the limit.

What tangible benefit does math give me? In a word, creativity. Math gives you creativity. What about music? I hear you ask. Art? Dance? Those sound more creative than math. And in one sense, they are. But here's the thing. Math teaches you how to *create* creativity. Because at its core, the practice of math is the practice of looking carefully at what you believe, considering different ways of mixing those beliefs together, and examining what gets created as a result. In other words, math is a road map for creating something out of pretty much nothing.

Yeah, I know this is awfully abstract. But consider this: many more mathematicians are also musicians (and vice versa) than random chance would predict. (I'm one of them.) All my life, people have suggested that that's because math and music have rules in common. And all my life, I've known that those people are wrong, wrong, wrong. Mathematicians and musicians both know that the rules of the game are just the starting point and that the real fun

You'll find your own great path, provided you pay attention to where you're trying to go.

comes from mixing the rules together. Productive creativity that comes from a few simple rules: **that's** what music and math have in common.

The Starting Line

I hope I've inspired you just a little more toward curiosity in mathematics, abstract thinking, and competitive opportunities.

You'll find your own great path, provided you pay attention to where you're trying to go.

The Rest of the Journey

I interview for MIT. Here's the thing: MIT knows it can train smart kids in almost anything it wants to. It also knows the two things it can't train: curiosity and passion.

Following a thoughtful approach to learning math checks both boxes: it kindles your curiosity, and it demonstrates passion.

And as I've been saying, it's not about MIT anyhow: I can tell in about five minutes whether the person I'm talking to can think mathematically. So can any decent interviewer (whether for a college or for a job). Given ten more minutes, I can discover whether they're actually any good at it. The people who are good at it are the ones I prefer to work with, to create with, to play with. It's part of my recipe for a happy life.

If it's yours, too, then I'll see you along the way.

You can get in touch with me by visiting wescarroll.com. I look forward to hearing from you and to helping you in any way I can.

—Wes Carroll

A Crash Course Introduction on Leadership

Leadership doesn't always seem coachable, but the strategies and tactics that top-level entrepreneurs and professionals in all fields use are eminently teachable. High school students can learn them as well. In fact, even if you don't see yourself leading a team, an understanding of these techniques will make you a stronger member of any team you join.

What's the difference between how the student *leader* feels and how the student *member* of a club feels? Nothing. The difference is in how they act. They might both feel scared of asking for help or overwhelmed by all the action steps involved in making impact. The leader simply toughs it out and takes one action step at a time, refusing to think about the whole project. That would cause analysis paralysis. The leader exhibits discipline as he or she moves each block into place, eventually building a tower—a project or organization or app or piece of research that will change the game for someone or some group in the local community or even the world. No one will ever be able to see how this leader feels about the challenge of writing, building, or leading. It's the act of moving that people will see. So, it's not how you feel. It's what you do.

Let's look at why some students might fear leading: typically, it is because they do not believe they will succeed. Here's a secret: plenty of great leaders don't succeed 100 percent of the time. When there is success, it is often a result of practiced organizational skills, belief in self, and visualization of either accomplishment or possible obstacles that might arise and be circumvented.

A Few Techniques of Leadership

- *Visualization* means preempting the concerns that can be raised and obstacles that can be put in your path and predetermining solutions and points at which you can pivot your project. Let's say you're putting together furniture for your dorm room with your roommate; amid all the pieces, screws, and Allen wrenches, something is bound to go missing, and you will have put in precious hours before you even notice the missing piece. You can let that stop you in your tracks: "Oh no, now we'll never have our comfy couch!" or you can preemptively design a framework before any of the pieces leave the floor. Organize the pieces with your roommate by size and category. Approach the building process by first determining whether there **are** missing components, and only put in the hours to build if you have the appropriate number of parts according to the instructions. If you see there's a missing piece, no problem: you and your roommate will return the furniture and build from a new box of materials instead. In other words, you visualize a plan, execute that plan, and have a preset detour toward success in case there is an obstacle you cannot surmount—the missing piece.
- Perhaps the most discussed form of visualization is how musicians use it backstage before a performance. You know you've practiced the notes as a technician, you've rehearsed them as an artist, and now you breathe and envision the excitement and drama of playing that fast and breathless third movement: you see your violin bow whip into the air at the final note and the audience rise to its feet, clapping and shouting, "Bravo!" You are pumped! Now, as you wait in the wings, you hear your introduction, breathe deeply again, put

a smile on your face, and head out onto the stage, believing that you are going to give that audience a beautiful performance that will end with a standing ovation.

- *Active listening* is being in a conversation, hearing the objections and concerns raised, and staying engaged with the person who is speaking rather than responding by parroting back the same material you have already spoken. Great leaders engage in active listening to understand fully what their community, audience, or contingent needs. Listening is not defined by thinking about what your next comment is going to be or how to reframe the point you just made in different words. It's hearing a concern openly and empathetically and then addressing that concern specifically, allowing the others to feel that they have been heard. The best discussion of active listening can be found in Julian Treasure's TED Talk from 2011: "5 Ways to Listen Better." Julian, who is a consultant to worldwide organizations and businesses on the use of sound, underscores four elements of active listening: receive, appreciate, summarize, and ask.
- *Empathy.* Simply stated, remember you are working with your team or classmates as opposed to being an external force that is lording over them. Learn when to collaborate as a leader and when to take the helm in making a decision, and always base your decisions on the helpful input of your peers.

You will now learn from Bo Eason, a leader on and off the field. Bo has been a professional football player (NFL safety for the Houston Oilers), an actor and playwright, and a management and leadership trainer for Fortune 500 companies. His first book, *There's No Plan B for Your A-Game*, is an eight-time best seller.

YOUR MENTOR:

BO EASON

Former NFL Safety, Houston Oilers

Every morning my dad woke my brother Tony and me by saying, "Keep moving, partner. You're the best in there, darn it. You're the best."

You're the best. He massaged that message into our brains everywhere we went, from the Little League baseball field to getting on the school bus to the time we went on a double date with the Tomasini sisters in high school. Every morning, every evening, for twenty years he continued. He saw greatness in us that we just couldn't see for ourselves. My brother and I were embarrassed that he would say it right in front of our friends and teammates and dates. And then one day, years later, we thought, "Well, maybe he's right. Maybe we are the best." My brother and I surrendered to what he saw in us, and we lived into our own greatness. He spoke us into existence.

Ever since my childhood, I've been obsessed with what makes people great, what makes them the best, what makes them great leaders. And because of that obsession, I inherited my dad's best quality: the ability to see greatness in people and speak it into existence. I can show anyone who has the guts to commit—anyone who will choose the pain of discipline over the pain of regret—how to become a top performer. It takes commitment, and it takes focus, and it takes the willingness to drop anything that does not serve your mission as a leader.

Here are a few other beliefs I picked up along the way around leadership:

1: Leaders Model the Best

While I was being wheeled off the field after my career-ending knee injury playing with the San Francisco 49ers, I decided I'd go to New York City and work with acting coaches. I moved to New York and found the best acting and movement coaches available. I took every class I could find.

I asked all the people in classes with me, "Who's the greatest stage performer of all time?" and they all said, "Al Pacino."

I ultimately got introduced to Al Pacino (that's a great story that I'll leave for my book *There's No Plan B for Your A-Game*), and I asked him how I could learn to be the best stage actor of our time.

Al Pacino told me I had to get onstage—any stage, anywhere, as often as I could. He helped me lay out a fifteen-year road map for my success (I thrive with long timelines!).

2: Leaders Live the Plan ... and Say Yes to Nearly Everything in the Name of Becoming the Best

I took to heart what Al Pacino said and worked to spend more time on a stage than anyone else in the world. I spent the next fifteen years acting anywhere I could get a role, starting with a children's play in Sacramento, California.

I went from competing against and playing with the top athletes in the world to acting in a kids' play, *The Shoemaker and the Elves.* I was the mayor of the town, and I wore this big silly hat, and I was acting with a bunch of kids. I'd gone from signing autographs in NFL stadiums to standing in front of a hundred noisy kids who were not even looking at me.

At one point during the play, I looked out into the audience and saw my brother, Tony, and my friend and ex-roommate Kenny O'Brien sitting there. They'd showed up to support me, which was great.

So you have to picture this: These guys were both NFL quarterbacks. Tony had just taken the New England Patriots to the Super Bowl, and Kenny was the starting quarterback of the New York Jets. They were huge guys sitting in these kid-size seats, and they were looking at me like they were just totally in shock. Like they were thinking, *Good job with the mayor's hat, Bo, but what the hell are you doing and why?*

But I knew what I was doing. I had my fifteen-year plan. This kids' play was just part of the process.

3. Leaders Are Generous

I used to play against Jerry Rice. It was a nightmare to play against this dude. But toward the end of my career, I got traded to the San Francisco 49ers. And now the greatest player in the history of the game and I were on the same team. And I said, "Good. I want to see what he's made of. I want to see what he does."

Up until this point, I had always been the first person on the field at practice and the last person to leave the field. I'd made that contract with myself when I was a kid, and I'd kept that contract. No one ever beat me.

Then I met Jerry Rice.

On the first day of training camp with the 49ers, it's like 110 degrees. Unbelievably hot. An hour and a half before practice starts, I'm in the locker room getting dressed. No one else is in there. Joe Montana is not in there. Ronnie Lott is not in there. Randy Cross isn't in there yet. Just me. And I'm thinking, "I'm beating them all again, and I'm going to keep this roll going. No one is going to beat me."

So I walk out into that heat and I look around at the practice field. "Good, I'm the first one here." Then I look over. And guess who's right there? Jerry Rice. The greatest player in the history of the game.

By now, it probably makes total sense to you, but to most people it won't. They're thinking he should just be chilling somewhere. He has nothing to prove, right? He's already the best in the world at what he does. But he's out there on the field. I'm like, "Damn. No one's ever beat me onto the field before." So I'm a little pissed.

An hour and a half later, the rest of the team comes out for warm-ups. And the passing warm-up is sixteen guys in a line, all receivers. Jerry Rice is in this line along with everyone else battling to make the team. Joe Montana and Steve Young are there to throw some balls to these receivers, just easy, to warm everybody up.

First guy in the line comes up. Joe snaps the ball. The receiver takes off at half speed, breaks off on a little slant. Joe throws the ball. The receiver catches it and stops. He tosses the ball back to Joe and gets back in line. Next guy comes up. Same thing. All-pro guy, cool, breaks off on a little slant. Joe throws the ball. The receiver catches the ball. Stops. Walks the ball back to Joe. Hands Joe the ball. Back in line.

And then Jerry Rice comes up. This is what he does: Full speed. Bam. Breaks off on a slant. Catches the ball. Gone. One hundred yards. We're like, "Damn. Where the hell is he going?" A hundred yards into the end zone. Turns around, full speed, all the way back. Hands the ball to Joe. Back in line.

The next guy comes up. He's going to run a little out pattern. All-pro guy, cool, breaks off a little out. Catches the ball. Stops. Walks the ball back to Joe. Hands Joe the ball. Back in line.

Jerry Rice comes up again. Full speed. Breaks it off. Catches the ball. Gone. Gone, one hundred yards over and over and over again for three hours. He must have run ten miles of those sprints. I've never seen anything like it. I go up to him after practice, after the three hours are done, and say, "Jerry, hey, man, damn. What in the hell are you doing? The running—why do you do that?"

And Jerry Rice says, "Bo, that's very simple. I do that because every time these hands touch a ball, this body ends up in an end zone somewhere."

Now, that's a great story. That's the story Jerry Rice told himself, and that story made him the greatest football player ever. That day changed my life forever. You know those sixteen guys running drills? They were my teammates, too, and I can't remember most of their names. But Jerry Rice—we all know Jerry Rice. We know his name because of the story he told and the way he lived out that story on the football field.

Jerry Rice changed how I think about life. His generosity of spirit changed everything I do. He was willing to give everything he had, all the time. What would your life look like if you turned up in that way? What could your life be if you lived out that story in all your relationships, starting with your relationship with yourself? How profound would the changes be if you brought the spirit of Jerry Rice to your schoolwork, playing on a team, your relationship with your parents, your friendships?

Be like Jerry Rice. Give everything you have, every time.

That's what I want you to take away from this chapter. Be like Jerry Rice. Give everything you have, every time. Tell yourself that story, and live by it.

I guarantee that when you look back over a life lived that way, you'll realize that you were the best. I can't imagine living any other way.

—Bo Eason

An Introduction to Business Mentoring

Your College Education as a Business Major

Some students knew from the time they were in diapers that they were born with "business minds." If you spent afternoons toddling back and forth from the toy bin, removing your Steiff bears and bunnies, and selling them to your siblings for one dollar (because that's as far as you could count at the time), you might be a business major. If you started a sticker business on Instagram as a weekend pastime to while away the hours of social distancing and you wound up selling enough stickers to pay for a year of college, you might be a business major. If you thumb through HBS case studies for fun, taught yourself how to read a stock chart, and hang on every word from seekingalpha.com and Nasdaq.com, you also might be a business major.

I have students who have tried, failed, rebuilt, and succeeded in creating enviable small businesses and products that have garnered the attention of not-so-small start-ups. They have learned the valuable lesson that there is no singular path to success and no set number of times to expect failure—both will happen during the process of discovering your talents and building anything that matters.

There are a number of ways to integrate a business education into your undergraduate career: you can apply to impressive business schools like UPenn Wharton, UMichigan Ross, NYU Stern, Cornell

Dyson School of Applied Economics and Management, or Carnegie Mellon Tepper School (emphasizing quantitative and technological skills); or you can apply to schools that enable you to register into their business programs during sophomore year, as do Berkeley's Haas School for Business Administration and Emory's Goizueta (undergraduates apply to the BBA program after completing prerequisites and earning junior standing in their credit hours).

Freshmen might be interested to learn about Haas's two freshman-admit programs: the Management, Entrepreneurship, and Technology Program for those with both an engineering and business inclination, and the Global Management Program, which combines the Haas business model with international project-based study that leads to a concentration in global management.

At MIT, the Sloan School of Management offers undergraduates a Bachelor of Science in Management Science. Students typically select one of four concentrations: business analytics and operations research, finance, information technology, or marketing science.

For a rich liberal arts approach to business education, students might prefer the University of Virginia's program in which interested business students begin study at the College of Arts and Sciences and must then apply to the McIntire School of Commerce (so there is no guarantee of admittance). The University of Virginia's McIntire School of Commerce believes that the savviest business students are those with "a broad liberal arts education on which to build." After two years, undergraduates apply for admission into the McIntire School of Commerce's undergraduate business program, where they experience unique programs like Integrated Core Experience (ICE), courses in which students learn business theories in intimate study groups and then collaborate to apply those theories to solve real-world problems.

A third option is to apply to excellent liberal arts schools that provide majors in economics, mathematics, languages, psychology, English, and international relations (all of which shape a sturdy foundation for future business students), work for a year or two after graduation, and then apply for your MBA. Your GRE or GMAT score will be accepted for five years from the year you have taken it.

Whichever way you choose to pursue your business education, be sure that along with training in finance, accounting, business analytics, management, and marketing, you also devote time to persuasive communication and writing skills, because those are the key to bonding with an audience or a client.

Let's see how a twentysomething businessperson uses story to teach you about the role of marketing and collaboration in building your own business as a teen. Enjoy this mentoring chapter from Alec Urbach (Princeton University), marketing consultant.

YOUR MENTOR:

ALEC URBACH

(Princeton University), Marketing Consultant, Author, and Speaker

Building Your Small Business or Product as a Teen

First and foremost: if you want your organization or business to get off the ground, collaborate.

But you might say, "Collaboration is scary! What if someone runs off with my idea?" And you'd be right to some degree.

NDAs are routinely imposed by Silicon Valley companies—there's a concern that you might take their idea and run with it ... somewhere else. Ideas are stolen. It happens! But that creates a culture of fear that trickles down to college campuses throughout the nation. Students are afraid of speaking in depth about their projects. Well, that's a risk we need to take. Understand that if you've really got the talent, you can innovate faster than someone else can copy. No fast follow will ever outdo the original.

As a graduate of Princeton University, let me tell you about something I saw on campus every weekend.

If you're getting a cup of coffee at Princeton University's campus center on a Friday afternoon, what you will see is clusters of individuals—two or three to a table—all looking at a computer screen. Are they doing p-sets? Are they working on papers? Are they watching Netflix? No. Their conversations go something like this: "Hey, I'm working on a new product, and I've taken it as far as I can get it, and I need someone who can write code in C." "Oh yeah, my roommate, James, knows C. I'll ask if he can help you out." Or you might hear: "I'm building the website for my product, but my copywriting skills are sad. I really need a humanities person to do this!" "Okay, I can ask my girlfriend's roommate! She's an English major and does copywriting for *Business Today*."

So, what do these conversations tell us? They demonstrate that you can't have a start-up with all techies, all math minds, or all advertising or marketing whizzes. What you need is all fields. This blend of discussion, talents, and ideas can put your company over the top—yet not enough young people understand that. We all love to use the word *disruption*. You know what's disruptive? Having a multidisciplinary collaboration with no boundaries. In the start-up and marketing worlds, a disruptor or influencer is a person, team, product, or launch that gets everyone else talking, posting, pinning, tweeting, buying! Once you, as a leader, assemble and inspire minds and talents from all different intellectual and technical paths, then you can have powerful collaborations, and then you can talk about changing the

You know what's disruptive? Having a multidisciplinary collaboration with no boundaries.

world. Don't be afraid to take a risk and collaborate. Be afraid to go it alone in the "shark tank."

Mentoring and Benjamin Franklin ...

At age twenty-one, Benjamin Franklin formed a club of mutual improvement called the Junto. It was a marvelous exercise in collaboration for the purpose of learning as much as he could about as many subjects as he could. He invited other polymaths and amateur scholars like himself, in every field imaginable, to come together to pool their books, ideas, and specialized knowledge and debate worldly advice at regularly scheduled intervals. Franklin saw the Junto as his personal think tank and set of consultants. After each session, he had a wealth of new information to fill up his inventive pamphlets. Franklin understood the value of collaboration with one's intellectual peers. Think about your own after-school activities and the steps you might need to take to move your own projects, businesses, or organizations forward. Do you have a Junto or roundtable at your high school—a group of contemporaries who can advise, listen, and learn from each other? *A student think tank!* If you don't, I highly recommend starting one. Call up your friends, your family, your teachers. It's a way to take risks in an honor-bound community of thinkers where you don't have to worry that someone will run off with your idea, and no capital is lost by pitching your concept or project and getting feedback because it's yours. The group must be committed to each other and the process. Each person in the group is selected to bring value to the table in some way—meeting every month (whether by phone, Zoom, or in person). Collaboration as a means to success needs to be replicated in high schools, on college campuses, and in industry—whether you're in Silicon Valley, Silicon Alley, your nation's tech arenas, your school's student center, or your garage. The act of STEM, humanities, and social science minds sitting around a table and exchanging ideas is the single collaborative effort that can change our futures.

Since the discovery of the wheel and the invention of fire, there are no new ideas—just new applications and abstractions. From the Silicon Alley of New York to the tales from Silicon Valley, some of the best start-ups are not reinventing the wheel. You may think that you have an interesting way to improve an already functioning app, product, or algorithm, but you don't move on it because you think people will criticize you for not being innovative enough; not making something brand new; not changing the world with your little idea. Well, the truth is, you can decide to give it a try, or you can decide to do nothing. That's right—doing nothing is a powerful decision. Here's what I can assure you—trying might just lead to success, or it might lead to failure, redefining, and rebuilding. Here's what else I can assure you. If you don't try, there are dozens of young entrepreneurial enthusiasts who will be there to step right into the space you've left behind. Here are a few examples of tremendous successes that had nothing to do with innovation:

1. Instagram: The official Instagram Wikipedia page says that Instagram is "an online photo-sharing, video-sharing and social networking service." So, it's Flickr, Picasa, and TinyPic combined with a social network—an idea that's been around since the late 1990s and early 2000s. By September 30, 2013, it would have had a $5 billion valuation, according to *Forbes Magazine* (but eighteen months before, Instagram sold itself to Facebook for *$1 billion*).

2. Pinterest (influenced by and made in the image of Instagram) is also not innovative. Wikipedia says it's "a visual discovery tool that people use to collect ideas for

their different projects and interests." What we have here is a slightly broader interest Polyvore—Polyvore is a site that allows you to put together collages of thing you'd like to see or maybe like to buy. Polyvore launched on February 1, 2007. Pinterest launched in March 2010, and the only one the average person has heard of is Pinterest. The one who markets best wins.

So, what is this teaching us? Positioning: your brand must be positioned effectively. You occupy a certain space within a consumer's mind: Coke occupies the space for cola; Dr Pepper occupies the space for a cherry-flavored soda. Guess what? When Coca-Cola released Mr. Pibb (anyone ever heard of that?), a direct competitor to Dr Pepper, Mr. Pibb flopped. Coke tried to step outside its mindshare. It failed. If the Atlanta-based giant couldn't branch out with its sodas, what sense does it make for a start-up that's had success in one area to push its luck in another? If people know you and love you in one space—stay there. Listen to your fan base!

Let's take a company that all of us know, many of us love, and some of us love to scrutinize—that would be Apple. Why does Apple win? Because of their *fans*—the cult of Mac. Everyone knows someone who has an Apple computer. In fact, that might be most of your friends. Apple, with their brilliant marketing, has built a fan base instead of a customer base. They did this by constructing a powerful brand identity: their "Think Different" ad (to which every young dreamer can relate); their 1984 ad (the Super Bowl commercial that introduced Macintosh computers as the great disruptors); and their "I'm a Mac" commercials (casting Apple as the young, confident, and hip choice versus PC as the stuffy, corporate, shady choice)—these made Apple into the company that puts innovation and disruption first. This hip, innovative reputation combined with sleek design (their unibody aluminum construction) and cross-platform integration gave the brand rock star status.

And who doesn't love a rock star? This is the same thinking that launched supermarketer Mack Collier's book back in 2013 about how to turn your customers into fans. What a smart concept that is! A rock star knows that his longevity is validated only by the continued loyalty and adoration of his fans. Mack Collier understood that, and instead of advertising and pushing his book, he chose, instead, to **engage** with his public. He personally thanked everyone who wrote a post or tweet about his book and then requested that they review the book on Amazon. This engagement with the customers did two things for him: Firstly, it reinforced the apparent value of his book's techniques by turning customers into fans. "When I asked these strangers to please review the book, several of them **thanked me** for asking them to review it!"

Additionally, showing this kind of vulnerability and care for his customers' wishes made it very obvious that there was a human being behind the book and that he was open to communication with his fans. He was collaborating!

I would ask you high school students to help your generation build the "new" by collaborating with each other as early as *now*. Princeton University, along with all the other Ivies and Top Tier schools, seeks out builders and collaborators. I know because I interview high school applicants for Princeton annually. Choose a friend or two who has different talents from you, brainstorm an idea that you believe could help some segment of your community, and then start building it. Remember, your future is riding on your ability to network and utilize multiple mental models. So, collaboration, even in your most unique and winning ideas, is a risk you need to take.

—Alec Urbach
Consultant and Speaker
Author of *A Genealogy of Human-to-Human Marketing*, Princeton University and Co-author of Pangea, Penguin Random House, Grupo Editorial
https://www.linkedin.com/in/alecurbach/

A Creative Business Case Study

So, we've established that asking makes you smart! Let's look at an example of a student who built a business during high school by asking to collaborate with nonprofits and for-profit businesses.

GEORGE'S VIDEOMERCIAL START-UP

Let's take a look at George's story. George did community service through the filming of free PSAs for charitable organizations in his community. This made him feel as though he had value and was helping important causes in his hometown, like Foundation Fighting Blindness and the National MS Foundation, but George was not using his art as a for-profit business and really needed to see if he had it in him. The charitable organizations George served wound up being mentors in that they encouraged him to do more with his documentary film talent.

A storyteller by nature, George started a video company, producing what he called "videomercials"—they would highlight the work of entrepreneurs, nonprofits, and professionals with interesting stories to tell. These guys wanted to get their story out in a way that was more accessible and exciting to the public than static walls of text on standard "About Us" pages. The richness of George's experience in this business, and any success he achieved through it, was because of his unusual collaboration with his clients—a diverse group of high-achieving individuals, like the PhD holder who studies the mental and visualization strategies employed by top golfers and soccer players and adapts them to enable CEOs to operate at peak performance levels (the same tactics that those athletes use to sink that clutch putt for a birdie or thread the ball down the field to set up the game-winning goal can be adapted to help a CEO outpace his competitors in the business world). Then there was the personal trainer born without a hamstring who overcame his disability and now inspires others to achieve their fitness goals—this is a man who is missing a muscle necessary to bend his knee, and he's gotten past that fact to inspire and train others. George viewed these enterprising professionals not only as collaborators but as heroes who have added value to society in new, nonlinear ways.

What these experiences taught George is that he must take educated risks now while he is young, but not take them alone. Collaborate, find mentors, create a brain trust of students with confluent skills so you can teach and advise each other.

There are so many ways to succeed, whether you're a social entrepreneur or a for-profit entrepreneur—and none of them must include earthshaking innovation. They just require you to step up and take a risk, because if *you* don't, there are dozens of young entrepreneurial spirits waiting in the wings to take your place in that space. Risk, fail, rebuild: these are more than just three verbs. These represent an attitude for a successful life.

Introduction to Computer Science, Machine Learning, and Artificial Intelligence

Computers provide us with life-changing answers, as long as we continue learning how to ask ever-more pertinent and human questions that keep up with the pace of change. What the technology and big data revolution means for your generation is that learning has already become less about memorization of factoids and more about analysis and devising critical questions. Einstein would be thrilled by the prospect of cloud-based mega search engines responding accurately to almost any question in any field. According to a rumor handed down through decades, a reporter asked for Einstein's phone number at the conclusion of an interview. Without missing a beat, Einstein reached for a phone book and began looking it up. The reporter laughed and asked why such a brilliant mind would not be able to remember his own phone number. Einstein replied that there was no purpose in filling up his available mind space with something he could easily find elsewhere.

Advances in computer science (CS), artificial intelligence (AI), and machine learning (ML) now and in the future will create tectonic shifts in how we practice medicine, teach STEM, run businesses, research legal precedents, and even catalog the great works of literature that we have created as a civilization. Because humans are generalists who can perform a variety of tasks with little new data or learning, the original goal of AI was to build artificial general intelligence from the more specialist applications we have created. Those of you who presently study or seek to study AI will be faced with a similar goal: How do you overcome the obstacles to providing AI with *common sense, abstract ideas* (applying past and diverse experiences to new ones), and *creativity* (the boundary-less kind that children possess in abundance)?

The hope of technologists is that you will become adroit enough in ML to one day conquer these obstacles for society. ML tries to push the boundaries of AI systems to solve any complex problem without needing to be taught—by adapting and refining AI's performance based on experiences. Imagine the remarkable benefits to society at the intersection of human intelligence and AI!

"You cannot resist an idea whose time has come."

—Victor Hugo

With extraordinary software and computing power at our disposal, the future of technology for your generation will likely be as important to society as was the Industrial Revolution—with its accompanying dynamic, dramatic, positive, and ethically questionable solutions. Is there any wonder why high school STEM students have their heads in "the cloud" and their aspirations focused on shifting the course of medicine, business, and education through programming, ML, and AI?

Let's discover more about your opportunities in the fields of CS/ML/AI from Stanford University engineer and Founder/CEO of Breakout Mentors, Brian Skinner, who provides a project-based and long-term approach to learning and loving computer science, machine learning, and artificial intelligence.

YOUR MENTOR:

BRIAN SKINNER

Founder, Breakout Mentors, The Personalized Approach for Kids Learning to Code

"I have to rush home—the new Jordans drop in twenty minutes!" exclaimed the sixteen-year-old sneakerhead Nolan. "No matter how fast I tap on my phone, they are always sold out, so I'm going to try on my laptop."

Twenty minutes later via text:

"Did you get them?"

"No, sold out instantly again!"

The heartache of missing out on exclusive sneakers cut deep. Nolan had dreams of wearing them with his suit to junior prom and being the only one at his school with them.

Nolan was resourceful, though, and armed with the right skill set that our mentors had helped him learn over the past two years: coding. After building several exciting Python projects with us,

Nolan felt empowered to learn web development on his own. By junior year, Nolan knew he could program his computer to perfectly time loading the page and quickly clicking "Add to Cart." For the next sneaker drop, he would be prepared.

Next month's sneaker drop:

"Did you get them?"

"YES, MY BOT DID!" Fourteen or fifteen enthusiastic emojis followed.

This wasn't why Nolan set out learning to code. It was just an unexpected chance to solve his problem, a chance made possible through the years of effort he had already put in and the mentorship he'd received. "You can't connect the dots looking forward," Steve Jobs said in his famous 2005 Stanford commencement address. "You can only connect them looking backward. So, you have to trust that the dots will somehow connect in your future."

This learning experience turned out to be just the beginning for Nolan. With his newfound interest in sneaker bots, he returned to study even more from our mentors in advanced topics like networking and security as well as machine learning. Nolan then revisited his bot with new expertise and created a small business selling bots to fellow sneakerheads. He connected with various companies who defend against bots—like gig-work companies DoorDash and Instacart, who want an even playing field for all their contractors, defending against someone using a bot to quickly claim the most lucrative gigs before others see them. It all led to Nolan writing an article for a corporate engineering website and opened the door for a potential internship down the road.

Insights from Silicon Valley

Palo Alto is the epicenter of Silicon Valley, a nickname that started with semiconductors but now refers to a flourishing software industry.

Nearby, Stanford University oozes with talented entrepreneurs who spill out into the community. Companies like Google have been started in garages, and it is where I started my own coding company, Breakout Mentors. Though I'm a Stanford engineering graduate who started a company in Palo Alto, that's where the similarities end. My company isn't a scalable high-growth start-up with the goal of taking over the world. Instead, we aim to change the world one young person at a time through education. For the past decade, Breakout Mentors has focused on one-on-one mentoring for nine- to seventeen-year-olds learning to code. The mentorship is personalized for a wide range of ages, experience, interests, and abilities to challenge our students at the perfect level. The closest we get to the high-growth start-up industry is working with the sons and daughters of famous tech executives and venture capitalists—and we're fine with that!

For elementary and middle school students, our goal is to build an interest in coding while also laying a strong foundation. While the coding is challenging for these younger students, the time pressure isn't the same as it is for high school students with full schedules and expectations of quick learning progress. We start with plenty of beginners in high school whose only experience is a short online coding tutorial. And we support extremely advanced students, too, whether they have worked with us for years or arrive having mastered only the fundamentals. No matter which category any of our students belong to, the aim of Breakout Mentors is to help them reach their next level and often, to build innovative technology that impresses admissions as much as it helps society.

This chapter will explore coding education from my perspective. As you'll learn, there isn't one perfect way to go about it. However, there are many insights that can be utilized to form an approach, coming not just from my Stanford and Silicon Valley background but from working with talented high school students such as you. First, let's lay the foundation for how we approach coding education by rewinding the clock.

My Stanford Experience

I arrived at Stanford in 2004 with an interest in math, science, and engineering and an excitement to dive into difficult material. At the time, I didn't know anything about coding or computer science. Absolutely zero—which, perhaps surprisingly, was possible nearly two decades ago in a way that isn't today. I did not have a career determined, so I hoped to explore while keeping my options open. Mechanical engineering seemed to satisfy my preferences, so I went with that.

Right away, I was thrown in deep: my first math class had an assignment to code an infinite series and run a Fourier transform on an audio file. To say I felt lost would be an understatement. At the time, I didn't even know what a loop was: something typically covered in the first hour of an introductory coding class. Fortunately, in this particular class, I could get away with just understanding the math; the teaching assistants were able to help with the rest. So, I got by but realized I would need to be much more comfortable coding for future classes.

Stanford does an incredible job making computer science interesting for a wide range of students. I loved the initial classes, so I decided to keep going, adding a minor in computer science. By the end of my senior year, I had very little interest in a career in mechanical engineering (or graduate school, which would have been imperative given the broad major without enough specialization) and had finally built up enough confidence in my coding skills to want to keep going. However, I didn't feel on the same level as the computer science majors applying to programming jobs.

After several years as a technical product manager at a software company, I realized I wished I had started coding earlier. It is never too late to switch, whether a major or a career track, but it takes tremendous effort. The longer you are on one path, the harder it is to pivot. As I observed the multitude of coding courses that all the kids were signing up for in the San Francisco Bay Area, I was excited to see they were being given the opportunity I would have loved to have had when I was young. Yet, as I took a closer look at these courses, I was disappointed by the lack of rigor and options and decided to do something about it.

Starting Breakout Mentors

A certain percentage of kids come out of a coding tutorial or summer camp with an interest in continuing. That's terrific! It is the goal. Sometimes a spark is all you need: if the spark happens to fall on a pile of dry pine needles, it will develop into a roaring flame. However, most of the time these sparks land on the busy road of our lives and die out.

Unfortunately, the available youth coding options weren't helping those kids with the spark to nurture and transform their interest into rigorous projects and impactful deliverables—the kind that colleges and companies seek. So, I created Breakout Mentors, building a team of talented collegiate mentors from Stanford, UC Berkeley, and other top engineering programs.

There isn't a long progression of classes for coding and computer science. In mathematics, for example, you have prealgebra, algebra, geometry, precalculus, calculus. It was an option to create this progression for coding in middle school and high school to set the standards and create endless curricula. Yet, we at Breakout Mentors didn't do that. Learning to code is unlike other school subjects. It is an engineering discipline, best learned through hands-on experience.

We opted to provide one-on-one mentoring to take advantage of the unique traits of the subject.

A decade after I started Breakout Mentors, learning to code is still not organized on a linear path. You have to chart your own path, which is a great opportunity to work toward your particular interests and create exciting projects. I won't give the typical argument for why you should learn it: career, school, make stacks of money, et cetera. We don't always do things we are told we *should* do (like flossing daily). Instead, we will first dig into what makes the subject interesting and explore it, unlike any learning experience you've ever had. We will go through some of the principles of what makes coding unique, how it will build you into an adept problem solver in everyday life, and why we believe it is ideal to learn with one-on-one help from an experienced mentor.

If you already know how to code and want some exciting next steps, skip ahead a few pages to the section "Going Above and Beyond as Advanced High School Students." There we will explore fascinating areas you can dive into, like real-world machine learning projects and USACO programming competitions.

Embracing Abstraction

Coding is logical. The computer follows specific rules: whatever you type in, it does the same every time. When something doesn't work as you expect it to, it is because you told the computer to do it, so you have to locate where you did that in your code. Learning to code will help you develop broad logical reasoning skills, yet it is hard to put a finger on exactly how that will be beneficial to you. So, let's explore one concept of abstraction and how it applies well outside the world of computer science.

Firstly, we must define *abstraction*, since there are many different uses of the word. Here I use it as the act of dealing with ideas rather than details. Perhaps the best example in your day-to-day life is when you tell someone to do something, you constantly make use of abstraction by not thoroughly communicating all the details. This is exemplified by the humorous kids' challenge to tell someone how to make a peanut butter and jelly sandwich. It is an activity that is sometimes done in school to learn how to give clear and concise instructions. The teacher is in front of the class with all the supplies to make a sandwich, and chaos ensues:

"Put peanut butter on one slice of bread"—the teacher sets the peanut butter container on top of the bread.

"Open the peanut butter"—the teacher pulls out a knife and saws through the side of the container.

"Using the knife, spread the peanut butter"—the teacher spreads the peanut butter on his or her face.

Once the class can successfully explain to the teacher how to make a peanut butter and jelly sandwich, the list of instructions is shockingly long. Sometimes this activity is done in computer science classes, although in high school it might not be quite as funny and instead met with eye rolls. Yet it exemplifies exactly what is happening in coding, where the computer does exactly what you tell it to do without considering what your intention was behind the instruction.

Throughout programming you are making use of the concept of abstraction. You don't necessarily have to type all the details of how the computer should do something. I tell students to "abstract away the details" since you don't create more powerful programs by writing more code. Well, it may require more code, but the power or output of your program shouldn't increase linearly with the number of lines of code. It is accomplished through layers of abstraction. The same goes for a CEO of a five-thousand-person company. They can't possibly understand every tiny detail about what is going on, and if they try, it isn't a good use of their time. They rely on their vice presidents and directors to surface the relevant information, setting metrics to know if a division is producing the output it should.

Coding is the best way to practice the use of abstraction since you rely on it to get anything done. Code is always built on the backs of others. If you are using Python or Java, you are already comfortable with a certain level of abstraction: you don't worry about the 0s and 1s moving around the CPU and memory. Instead, you write code at what would be described as a higher level of abstraction, after which the computer compiles or interprets your code into millions of 0s and 1s moving around. How much do you think you'd be able to accomplish if you had to constantly be thinking about when and how to move 0s and 1s to exact locations?

Coding is useful beyond video games, but games provide an excellent example to illustrate the next point. In Pac-Man, there are multiple levels with several different mazes. How you code your own version will require up-front planning in designing your approach. This next section will get a little more technical, talking about the code itself, so don't get intimidated if some of it is inscrutable.

Design Decisions: An Art and a Science

The requirements of the project will dictate your approach to the solution. The programmer needs to strike a balance between a simple solution for the basic requirement and overengineering, doing far more work than the goal requires. This is also why changing the requirements on a software project midway through can be disastrous; sometimes it is best to just start over entirely.

The quickest way to create one working level of the Pac-Man game would be to litter throughout the code assumptions about how the level behaves. For example, you get to this spot and always have to turn because there is a wall. Then if you later decide to add a second level with new wall placements, it is going to be very painful to find all those locations throughout the code that need to be updated. A significant change like this is also likely to be error prone, considering it is easy to overlook a single necessary change.

When you already know you need to support multiple levels, you can code it that way from the start. A more general solution is to assign each tile type a number: corner, open space, vertical edge, horizontal edge, and so on. Then when you're programming the gameplay, the logic is based on whichever tile Pac-Man is on. Here is an actual Pac-Man number map:

```
{6,4,4,4,4,4,4,4,4,4,4,4,4,5,6,4,4,4,4,4,4,4,4,4,4,4,4,5},
{3,1,1,1,1,1,1,1,1,1,1,1,1,3,3,1,1,1,1,1,1,1,1,1,1,1,1,3},
{3,1,6,4,4,5,1,6,4,4,4,5,1,3,3,1,6,4,4,4,5,1,6,4,4,5,1,3},
{3,2,3,0,0,3,1,3,0,0,0,3,1,3,3,1,3,0,0,0,3,1,3,0,0,3,2,3},
{3,1,8,4,4,7,1,8,4,4,4,7,1,8,7,1,8,4,4,4,7,1,8,4,4,7,1,3},
{3,1,1,1,1,1,1,1,1,1,1,1,1,1,1,1,1,1,1,1,1,1,1,1,1,1,1,3},
{3,1,6,4,4,5,1,6,5,1,6,4,4,4,4,4,4,5,1,6,5,1,6,4,4,5,1,3},
{3,1,8,4,4,7,1,3,3,1,8,4,4,5,6,4,4,7,1,3,3,1,8,4,4,7,1,3},
{3,1,1,1,1,1,1,3,3,1,1,1,1,3,3,1,1,1,1,3,3,1,1,1,1,1,1,3},
{8,4,4,4,4,5,1,3,8,4,4,5,0,3,3,0,6,4,4,7,3,1,6,4,4,4,4,7},
{0,0,0,0,0,3,1,3,6,4,4,7,0,8,7,0,8,4,4,5,3,1,3,0,0,0,0,0},
{0,0,0,0,0,3,1,3,3,0,0,0,0,0,0,0,0,0,0,3,3,1,3,0,0,0,0,0},
{0,0,0,0,0,3,1,3,3,0,6,4,4,4,4,4,4,5,0,3,3,1,3,0,0,0,0,0},
{4,4,4,4,4,7,1,8,7,0,3,0,0,0,0,0,0,3,0,8,7,1,8,4,4,4,4,4},
{0,0,0,0,0,0,1,0,0,0,3,0,0,0,0,0,0,3,0,0,0,1,0,0,0,0,0,0},
{4,4,4,4,4,5,1,6,5,0,3,0,0,0,0,0,0,3,0,6,5,1,6,4,4,4,4,4},
```

{0,0,0,0,0,3,1,3,3,0,8,4,4,4,4,4,4,7,0,3,3,1,3,0,0,0,0,0},
{0,0,0,0,0,3,1,3,3,0,0,0,0,0,0,0,0,0,0,3,3,1,3,0,0,0,0,0},
{0,0,0,0,0,3,1,3,3,0,6,4,4,4,4,4,4,5,0,3,3,1,3,0,0,0,0,0},
{6,4,4,4,4,7,1,8,7,0,8,4,4,5,6,4,4,7,0,8,7,1,8,4,4,4,4,5},
{3,1,1,1,1,1,1,1,1,1,1,1,1,3,3,1,1,1,1,1,1,1,1,1,1,1,1,3},
{3,1,6,4,4,5,1,6,4,4,4,5,1,3,3,1,6,4,4,4,5,1,6,4,4,5,1,3},
{3,1,8,4,5,3,1,8,4,4,4,7,1,8,7,1,8,4,4,4,7,1,3,6,4,7,1,3},
{3,2,1,1,3,3,1,1,1,1,1,1,1,1,1,1,1,1,1,1,1,1,3,3,1,1,2,3},
{8,4,5,1,3,3,1,6,5,1,6,4,4,4,4,4,4,5,1,6,5,1,3,3,1,6,4,7},
{6,4,7,1,8,7,1,3,3,1,8,4,4,5,6,4,4,7,1,3,3,1,8,7,1,8,4,5},
{3,1,1,1,1,1,1,3,3,1,1,1,1,3,3,1,1,1,1,3,3,1,1,1,1,1,1,3},
{3,1,6,4,4,4,4,7,8,4,4,5,1,3,3,1,6,4,4,7,8,4,4,4,4,5,1,3},
{3,1,8,4,4,4,4,4,4,4,4,7,1,8,7,1,8,4,4,4,4,4,4,4,4,7,1,3},
{3,1,1,1,1,1,1,1,1,1,1,1,1,1,1,1,1,1,1,1,1,1,1,1,1,1,1,3},
{8,4,4,4,4,4,4,4,4,4,4,4,4,4,4,4,4,4,4,4,4,4,4,4,4,4,4,7}

Ready to add the second level? Just create a new number map. What a pain to create those level maps, though! You wish it were a little easier, and being a wonderful engineer, you see how it could be done. You can create a small program that is a level editor. Perhaps it is a grid where you can drag and drop the various tile options, then export the level into the necessary format. This is where you may be in danger of overengineering. Yes, you have the ability to create a level editor, but is it an efficient use of time? Perhaps, if you are creating one hundred levels, but not three. This decision is both an art and a science: balancing planning ahead with unnecessary overengineering.

These decisions are abundant in all types of engineering;, however, most high school coursework won't provide the opportunity to fully explore it. You must go beyond an overly structured curriculum to create your own projects.

Projects Are Integral for Engineering

We examined a couple of ways that learning to code develops thinking skills that apply outside of coding, including abstracting away the details and making design decisions up front while avoiding over-engineering. Unfortunately, the majority of middle and high school students in a computer science course, summer camp, or online tutorial won't actually reach the point where they realize these benefits.

The mind-bending book *Gödel, Escher, Bach: An Eternal Golden Braid*[28] shows the intelligence of a system is at a higher level than the individual components. Think of an ant colony. An individual ant running in circles in your kitchen appears idiotic without the right context. It is only by zooming out and noticing all the individual ants working together that you can understand the intelligence. They are working together in a system.

When you're learning to code, it is very easy to get bogged down in the details. There are many individual concepts to learn: loops, variables, "if" statements, functions, arrays, classes, and many more. In a typical curriculum these concepts are introduced followed by short fill-in-the-blank exercises with five to ten lines of code. Then, it is on to the next concept in the syllabus.

Since the intelligence is in the system itself, it is important for students to quickly use the few core concepts they know to make projects with fifty to one hundred lines of code. It is only through projects that you can master the logical thinking skills. Furthermore, projects are what engineering actually is. Wikipedia defines engineering as "the use of scientific principles to design and build machines, structures, and other items." It isn't the scientific principles, those individual components. It is designing them to work together in a system.

28 The Stanford major Symbolic Systems was inspired by this book, a major that is an interdisciplinary study of philosophy, linguistics, computer science, and psychology.

The Woodworking Analogy

A noncoder won't have intuition about how to program a computer using principles and components to work together in a system. The physical example of woodworking will better illustrate the engineering process, even if you have never done it yourself.

There are practically unlimited tools you can learn in woodshop class or on YouTube. Hammer and nails, hand saw, vise, tape measure, level, sandpaper, hand drill, screwdriver and screws—the list goes on. The important question is, Can you take a pile of wood and make a table out of it? How many tools do you need to know before you can make a basic table?

There are practically unlimited tools you can learn ... the important question is, Can you take a pile of wood and make a table out of it?

Remember that engineering is designing and building: at some point learning additional individual tools won't get you closer to a finished table. Yet an expert may encourage you to pursue a new skill. A master carpenter might tell you, "Use a lathe for the table legs," since that is what he would do. However, learning how to use a lathe would take longer to fully understand than all the other tools combined. Pretty soon you might give up before you even start on the table.

Don't make the mistake of requiring your first table to be perfect. Ignorance is bliss: make an ugly basic table. Once you have a finished table, you will notice room for improvement or can show it to someone for feedback. For example, they might tell you to use a corner brace to attach the legs under the table rather than drilling straight into the top and leaving a visible screwhead. Now it is time to make your next table, slightly better than the last.

Isn't it important to learn new skills, though? Of course it is, but a tool is only as good as what you do with it. This is subtly different from deeply understanding the individual tool. If you know fifty ways to use a hammer, you will also need to identify when it will be useful in a project. Can you go from a goal to a plan to execution? This level of mastery is forged only in the fires of many imperfect projects.

Engineering Should Have Personalized Learning

The engineering learning process should have a certain degree of chaos. An extremely structured curriculum, even one that involves projects, isn't going to produce the depth of knowledge and mastery to do it again on your own: to take a pile of wood and make something from the ground up.

Imagine a class that introduces ten tools one at a time and does a short hands-on exercise with each. Then at the end the class culminates with a large project with step-by-step instructions on how to make a chair. A step in the right direction might be doing an open-ended final project to make something on your own. Unfortunately, you skipped the steps of engineering small ugly projects along the way, so expecting to create a large project for a grade will be frustrating.

Chaos means embracing that there isn't just one way for everyone. Yes, there are the ten tools that are important to know, but the order in which you learn them doesn't matter. And once you have learned several, no matter what they are, engineer a project limiting yourself to just those tools. This type of learning is best achieved with individualized help, adjusting the plan as you progress. It doesn't scale well to a whole class, so it is disregarded as an option in most classrooms. For personalized learning you need to seek mentors outside of school.

Coding is not woodworking, but there are many parallels. The goal of the woodworking analogy was to show that engineering requires individual technical concepts (tools in your tool belt), but that the designing and building process requires experience. To gain this experience, you should make many projects along the way with the concepts you know, rather than always plowing ahead for a shallow understanding of a new concept. Coding and computer science are very similar to woodworking in this regard. There are hundreds of concepts you can learn, but the important thing is how you layer them together to get the desired result.

Breakout Mentors does one-on-one mentoring because we want to provide the ideal environment for the chaotic engineering learning process. Someone who can encourage the student's creative ugly projects. Someone who has learning goals in mind but understands there isn't a set order or timeline for everyone. Someone who can teach the student at the perfect time when a new tool may be useful. Someone who has been through the struggles before and can smooth out the bumps along the way.

You can certainly accomplish it on your own given strong motivation, so don't think that mentoring is the only way. We just know mentoring can save time and heartache and produce a higher success rate. After the coding fundamentals and problem-solving skills are well understood, coding really becomes exciting.

Going Above and Beyond as Advanced High School Students

Once you have some coding ability, the options for personalization truly open up. There isn't a set order of classes, projects, or programming languages to learn. For some, the assortment of options is paralyzing, but it is a great opportunity to chart your own path to stand out. This is where your coding efforts can merge with your school coursework and other interests, proving your knowledge for college applications as well as having something cool to write about.

For Breakout Mentors students, we categorize the options into three areas: classes and Advanced Placement tests, real-world projects using machine learning, and advanced computer science through USACO competitions.

Classes and Advanced Placement Tests

Classes and AP tests are a format you are familiar with already. What should a sharp high school student do?

We advise Breakout Mentors students to avoid the AP Computer Science Principles class. This AP course was designed to get more high schools to offer AP CS and thus more students exposed to CS. This is a great goal; however, for a gifted student who grew up around technology, the class is very easy. Knowing how to code isn't necessary; it is more about learning how computers and the internet work. We suggest you don't waste a class period on it. If you want to take more AP tests, this is a good one to self-study for, especially as an eighth or ninth grader, before you may have several tests in one year. You may only need to spend a few weekends on Khan Academy or with a test-prep book.

The real AP computer science class is called AP Computer Science A. This is the one where you learn Java and object-oriented programming. If your school offers it, we recommend taking it even if you are a strong programmer going in. It is rigorous and includes a broad assortment of object-oriented concepts. The number of concepts it covers is so broad that the course isn't necessarily an effective way to learn to code, especially the logic and problem-solving skills. Depending on the teacher, there might not be many projects requiring engineering from the ground up. Students who are thrown in without previous experience will often struggle and might not even come out as strong coders. You should at least spend dozens of hours over the summer to make sure your logical reasoning and problem-solving are strong enough before starting the class. Then it will be easy to add new tools to your tool belt at the fast pace they come in AP CS A.

What is beyond the AP classes? Some schools offer data structures or other advanced topics. However, most don't have this option. The first question is whether you want the knowledge or proof of the knowledge. If you require proof, our students sometimes enroll in an online college course or even in person at their local junior college. If you are disciplined and motivated by learning, many top colleges like Stanford, MIT, and Harvard have free online courses, which would be an excellent next step.

Advanced Computer Science through USACO Competitions

The most prestigious measuring stick for high school computer science is the USA Computing Olympiad. Four times a year there are online weekend programming-based problem-solving competitions with divisions Bronze, Silver, Gold, and Platinum. Only a few thousand US high school students each year reach Silver, and only a few hundred reach Gold! If you compare that to the over seventy thousand students per year who take the AP CS A test, you can see how exclusive this club is. One of the USACO Gold students we mentor was just admitted to her dream school of MIT!

USACO is a wonderful opportunity for the right students. If you enjoy puzzles, can code well, and are interested in diving into more advanced concepts, then USACO is definitely for you! The best way to explore some of the problems and concepts is the free website

USACO Guide,[29] which was created by former top competitors. You can go into much more depth there, but here is a short overview.

Competition programming problems start relatively straightforward and quickly become very difficult. For each problem you are given an input, and your program needs to output the correct answer. An example might be, "You are given a list of P pairs of names that denote friendships of people. If person A is friends with person B, and person B is friends with person C, then person A is also friends with person C. Answer a list of Q questions of this form: Given two people X and Y, are they friends?"

As these puzzles become harder, you'll eventually face the challenge of creating a program that can compute an answer both correctly *and* efficiently. Almost any problem can be solved with a brute-force solution, which can take various forms but typically involves looking at every possible solution one at a time. Unfortunately, brute-force solutions don't always run fast enough. You need to learn how to estimate the speed of your program given the constraints of the problem (e.g., are you computing the factorial of ten or ten thousand?). If you discover your approach is too slow, you might need to consider using more efficient algorithms like binary search. What is binary search? Let's say you are programming a computer to find a word in the dictionary. It would be slow to just start at the beginning of the dictionary and look at each individual word. Instead, you can cut the problem in half with each step: open to the middle of the dictionary, and ask if the word you are searching for is before or after that point. Then open to the middle of that half, and repeat the process until you arrive at the word. A computer running that algorithm will find the answer much faster. You may be shocked by how much faster. If the dictionary had one thousand words, you

29 "USACO Guide," Competitive Programming Initiative, accessed June 7, 2022, https://usaco.guide.

can expect to find the word in fewer than ten steps compared to likely finding it in the first five hundred words going sequentially. If there are one hundred thousand words, you can still expect to find the word in fewer than seventeen steps using binary search!

The data structures and algorithms required to solve these problems start to become more conceptual at the Silver and Gold USACO levels. If you advance past Bronze but aren't familiar with these concepts, it will be nearly impossible to continue advancing. If you enjoy it, one of the best ways to improve your skills is to participate in other contests and join a community of peers who have a similar interest. CodeForces is a website with free weekly contests, and big organizations like Google and Lockheed Martin even run events where you compete with a small team. Breakout Mentors offers one-on-one mentoring from an experienced USACO competitor. We believe having a mentor with this experience will save you massive amounts of time. The list of concepts to know doesn't change; however, we can cover specific tips and tricks for problem-solving insights, provide resources, and guide you through problems that stretch your comfort zone the perfect amount.

What if you know how to code well but aren't drawn to contests and advanced algorithms? Passing the Bronze level is still an impressive achievement, so you may want to consider doing that. Just clearing one division is worth the effort! If you're not interested and dedicated to continuing past that point, there are a ton of different options out there to set yourself apart.

Real World Projects Using Machine Learning

The hockey superstar Wayne Gretzky famously said, "I skate to where the puck is going, not where it has been." Armed with that information, are you just as good at hockey as "the Great One"? No. The hard part is knowing where the puck is going and executing. You might be wondering if this is the section where we show you how to set yourself apart by being a great hockey player. Actually, we are going to examine where "the puck is going" for coding: it's headed toward machine learning.

Machine learning is, like regular programming, a way to get computers to complete a specific task. But instead of telling the computer exactly how to do it, you provide a lot of data and feed it through a "learning" algorithm. The computer learns the pattern, and the next time you provide input data, it is able to produce an accurate output.

For example, maybe you work in the marketing department of a major movie studio and have a bunch of data about past productions. You want to predict how much money a new movie will make at the box office. If you have just one variable—the budget—it would be very simple to graph the relationship (*x* as budget, *y* as revenue), draw a best-fit line between the points, and see where your new movie's budget falls on that line (if you have *x*, you can find *y*). You were able to identify the pattern in the data yourself.

What if you have dozens or hundreds of variables, though? Director's pay, actors' pay, marketing spend, release date, genre, parental guidance rating, and more. Machine learning is vital when you can't find the pattern in the data yourself. That is the first key insight—then there are many different algorithms possible to use. Some work similarly to what you did by hand with one variable, graphing and finding a best-fit line. However, this would be a graph with a dozen dimensions, so instead of visualizing, you'd have some complex math. The good news is that you don't have to understand linear algebra at a postgraduate level to be able to benefit from it. Embrace the abstraction, as we explored before. In order to make machine learning projects, you need to know which algorithms are useful in different situations, not the complete inner workings and theory behind why the algorithms themselves work.

Machine learning enables impressive real-world projects because data can be just about anything stored on a computer. Text, sound, images, video. Suddenly you have the ability for impressive projects that tie into your other interests! One Breakout Mentors student was interested in mental health. She came up with a project to examine how a Twitter user's mental health varies over time to explore if there are normal mood swings or even warning signs. She built and trained a machine learning model to automatically detect the sentiment of a tweet on a "positive, neutral, negative" scale.

Other capstone projects include an automatic bank check processor that converts handwritten text into digital form using images of the text for automated bank check processing, automatic pneumonia detection that detects pneumonia using chest x-rays to help doctors provide better diagnoses and help patients receive proper care, and an app that writes poetry in the style of your favorite poet using automatic text generation from the prompt you provide (an inventive Valentine's Day project).

Once you're armed with the ability to make machine learning projects, suddenly the term *artificial intelligence* has new meaning. No longer is it opaque and despotic. You will know that if good data exists to train a model, then you can approximate what a human would be able to do. You will also know the strengths and weaknesses relative to a human.

Do you remember *Where's Waldo?* and similar picture-hunt books from when you were a kid? Perhaps it is generational, so I'll explain. Your task was to scan the page looking for a man named

Waldo in a red-and-white-striped shirt and beanie. This task is a perfect example to illustrate where machine learning can be expected to outperform a human and where it may be weaker.

The early pages are relatively straightforward: somewhere on the page is Waldo, dressed quite differently than everyone else. But sometimes there are hundreds of people, so it may take you about thirty seconds to locate him. What if you were tasked with finding Waldo on one hundred thousand of these pages? It would take you over a month! A machine learning algorithm would be much faster, on the order of minutes. Its accuracy may not be perfect, though: in roughly one in two hundred pages, it may identify the wrong person. Of course, these are rough numbers that depend upon the algorithm, but they exhibit the strength of machine learning, particularly when a few wrong answers are acceptable.

Understanding machine learning provides a new lens to look at the world. When you can think in terms of data and the insights you can glean from it, the possibilities are endless . Just building off this picture-hunt example, there are plenty of meaningful real-world projects. One idea would be to search satellite images for illegal logging operations in the Amazon or to look for the campfire smoke of Siberian tiger poachers.

Understanding machine learning provides a new lens to look at the world ... the possibilities are endless.

Ultimately for college applications it is important to showcase projects that are personally meaningful. Ideally you project can tie into your personal story, merging your unique interests and abilities. There may not be a more useful tool to achieve this than machine learning.

Chart Your Own Path

Whether you are a beginner or an expert, coding and computer science do not have a clear path to follow. It is natural to be intimidated by this—to see someone way ahead of you and have no idea how they got there. This can either shut you down or inspire you to chart your own path. When you meander through uncharted territory, you may not end up exactly where you thought you would, but the journey will be fascinating, and you'll end at your own unique location. It reminds me of the quote "Shoot for the moon. Even if you miss, you'll land among the stars."

Coding is perfect for learning the engineering mindset: embracing abstraction, design decision trade-offs, starting with an imperfect solution and iterating. Developing this mindset will pay off beyond computer science and beyond other engineering fields, whether you become an entrepreneur, a physician, an environmentalist, or an attorney.

Write your story. Coding is a tool in your tool belt that you can apply to any interest. Areas like machine learning can provide a new lens through which to view the world, looking at everything as data and searching for the patterns. Your unique experiences, interests, and the way you view the world are what sets you apart from the crowd.

A word of advice as you set out on your journey. If you are on a coding path because someone told you it would be beneficial, you likely won't end up very far. You won't have a strong internal "why" to keep going when things get tough. There is a path that you will intrinsically find interesting. Set off on this path and pursue your interests, since it will afford you the power to push through obstacles. You might not know where you will end up, but you will become an adept problem solver in everyday life. The world is full of exciting problems in need of a solution. We are counting on you!

—Brian Skinner
Founder, Breakout Mentors,
info@breakoutmentors.com

An Introduction to Debate

A debate is a highly organized argument. In high school debate, two students, representing alternate sides of an argument on a pressing societal issue, speak during an allotted time. Interruptions are assiduously controlled, and students are not given the choice as to which side of the argument they must defend. What is important is how you build your case and prove your point.

Are you thinking of joining your school's debate club? Start observing the art of good communication. Read some not-so-great books so you know what the great books are when you meet them. Experience weak arguments so that you know how to make strong ones. Listen to opinions you disagree with (I mean, really listen) so you understand the importance of disputation. Research statements rigorously before making them in public so that you know what a frothy, unresearched point of view sounds like.

To my mind, debate is one of the most important skills to learn before heading off to a campus of vibrant, diverse, and both popular and unpopular opinions. As far as real-world utility, debate practice trains students to communicate through research, mastery, clarity, and eye contact. Every profession benefits from practitioners who express ideas with ease, are light on their feet, and organize time and materials methodically.

Ultimately, the study and practice of debate celebrates the right of free speech—civilization thirsted for it at the time of Homer in Greece and Seneca the Elder in Rome—and your generation is powered by that right as well. So, whether you are always winning arguments at home over who gets the car keys or in student council about the rights of faculty to assign term papers over the December break, connecting with a debate coach might be the beginning of a beautiful friendship!

YOUR MENTOR:

JULIAN DOTSON

President, District of Columbia Urban Debate League

My Debate Philosophy

I am from South Orange, a small suburb in New Jersey about thirty minutes away from New York City. I attended public schools and graduated from an historically Black college in Alabama, the prestigious Tuskegee University. Growing up, the line I remember most from routine parent-teacher conferences was, "Julian has so much potential." However, I could not identify what my calling would be. I understand now that a particular program was missing from the slate of classes offered in middle and high school—a program that would, ultimately, ignite the spark inside me. Like many of you, I excelled in science and math, did well in history and English, participated on sports teams, and even joined the drama club because I thought acting was fun. Little did I know that, nearby, in some of the private schools, students were being offered a practice of persuasive argumentation that would allow me to use all my subject strengths, including drama—something I would eventually teach and coach for a living: debate and forensics.

> **Debate is the only extracurricular activity that encapsulates a skill set that every person ... can use in any career.**

Just ask Oprah Winfrey, Jim Carrey, and thirteen US presidents (although some will be hard to contact!). They would wax prolific about having been on the debate team. Debate is the only extracurricular activity that encapsulates a skill set that every person from any background can use in any career on the planet. No matter how many computers and robots are involved, people will still need to express their ideas in the future. People will need the skills to aptly defend what they know is right when they are faced with adverse ideologies. Most importantly, people will need to know how to speak up for themselves in an argument—whether academic or social. Academic debate prepares students for real-world interactions. For over a hundred years in the most elite public and private schools across the United States, debate even found its way into the official curriculum. However, today, there are many schools in which debate is often not even offered as an extracurricular club.

As both an English teacher and debate coach, I advocated for years to start debate teams while teaching in public and private school environments because I knew the value of the activity. I used debate as a teaching strategy when analyzing literature, character development, and author's purpose. I created a law and public policy academy with debate as a central focus. I grew debate teams from five to over seventy-five students and eventually led the only debate league in Washington, DC, at the time, which is now popularly known as the Metro DC Speech and Debate League.

Middle school and high school debate topics cover every hot-button issue in the world, from environmental dilemmas to advancements in artificial intelligence and universal basic income to strategic military policies. Therefore, a student beginning in fifth grade will have studied nearly one hundred challenging issues in depth by his or her senior year in high school. Moreover, debaters cross-apply what they learn to every single one of their classes all the way through high school and college. Students who enter careers in STEM will have a knowledge base that is amplified by working as a team. This ability to access stored knowledge is vital to success, especially with the level of competition for highly paid careers. Students who enter the arts and business will pull from the presentations and stylistic adjustments they practiced in debate competitions and call upon the etiquette and social skills that debate coaching underscores. Students entering law and public policy will undoubtedly use argument, logic, and reason and revisit the hundreds of rounds of feedback they received from judges. In all, the world our teens are facing as well as the future of work will be separated by students who were on the debate team and those who weren't.

What Does Debate Teach?

At its core, debate teaches students how to evaluate information. The debater's mind always thinks of the two or more viewpoints of a topic and how they intersect. Students learn research skills from the very beginning. Even students as young as ten years old read briefs with many sources of evidence they would never be exposed to in citizenship and social studies classes. Students are focused on reading academic articles, charts, graphs, and expert opinions, then taught how to synthesize that information. Debaters' training in critical thinking makes them less susceptible to disinformation, one of the biggest cyberweapons of the future.

In debate, students learn how to appeal to their judges, and in my tournaments, judges are from everywhere: from countries in Africa, Europe, and Asia; Canada; and all over the United States. When students debate in front of one or more judges, they are exposed to people who speak different languages and have different accents, cultural identities, ideologies, and personal biases. The debater-judge interaction is a key component of debate that few other activities can teach. When students get to college and have professors from all over the world, they remember their debate judges. Lastly, debate teaches students the value of winning and losing, a skill that many students need in the world of grade inflation, "everyone's a winner" fallacies, and outright alternate reality. When a judge says the other team wins, no matter what a student tries to do, there is no appealing to the director. A judge's word is final unless a rule has been broken. There is something valuable in accepting defeat.

Tournaments

Students are given a wide variety of dates each month, from one- to three-day tournaments. The local tournaments and some special-invitation tournaments are often one day in length. When students debate in person, a typical tournament is on a Saturday. Students wake up early and dress in professional clothes; then they march into cafeterias to await their first round. Rounds are announced, and everyone heads to individual classrooms in pairs of teams to find a judge waiting. Sometimes students have small audiences of spectators, but in fierce competitions with high stakes, students may find other debaters, coaches, captains, college scouts, and excited parents. Rooms can fill up quickly in the final rounds, so students are taught how to manage any anxiety about speaking in public just by the very nature of the event. There are divisions in debate from novice to varsity, and on each grade level a debater can enter the novice division and grow based on ranks and performance.

Most tournaments start on Saturday mornings and last three to five rounds. In the many virtual tournaments, it is not uncommon for students to meet international students and students from all over the United States. When tournaments are local, students typically travel about an hour away at most to compete. Depending upon the tournament, there are awards for each speaker, pair, and team.

The next level of debate is called the National Circuit. These tournaments are held on university campuses and may also include speech teams, which can increase the number of rooms. During the virtual-competition era, students are flooding tournaments they never were able to drive or fly to, so these are considerably more competitive. Some tournaments start on Friday, so students might need to be excused from school early, as is often the practice for student athletes heading to a game.

On Friday, these tournaments have a few rounds; then Saturday the preliminary rounds wrap up, and students look forward to "breaking," or making it to the elimination rounds. At a national tournament, when a student "breaks to elims," the excitement runs high, because any chance to break means another bragging right when applying to top universities. Debaters who make it to the semifinals and win big national tournaments are few, so even making it to elimination rounds can carry a lot of weight in the eyes of a college admissions officer. Debaters benefit from the experience of going to a college campus, creating unique memories, and walking the same halls they hope to walk as future college students.

Popular Formats

One reason public forum debate has become so popular is the high number of tournaments in a given month. Students can typically choose at least two tournaments per month in which to compete. In the new world of virtual instruction, debate has evolved to facilitate large and small tournaments.

Most students who enter speech and debate in middle school have a couple of options for formats to enter in debate competitions—the most popular being Public Forum and World Schools. High school debate formats are World Schools, Congressional, Extemporaneous, Policy, Lincoln-Douglas, Big Questions, and the most favored, Public Forum.

The teamwork involved in debating with a partner in Public Forum may be the central reason it remains the most popular format. The topic changes every two months in the beginning of the school year; then, starting in January, the topic changes monthly. This provides students with fresh new ideas and current events knowledge. Somehow the topics seem to always land at the same time as the news. For example, one year, students debated Offensive Cyber Operations, and then the Pentagon was hacked in the Solar Winds attack. Another coincidence was when students debated recognizing the president of Venezuela, and at that same time, the opposition leader tried to overthrow the Venezuelan government.

Public Forum Debate

The Public Forum debate format is a fast-paced style with only one prepared speech per team.

First, there is a four-minute constructive speech, where students present their case, filled with ethos, pathos, and logos. The evidence burden is heavy, so students are constantly upgrading their sources and testing their warrants. After the first speech, students question each other in cross fire for three minutes; this might be their favorite part of the debate because they can catch each other in traps and question the authenticity of evidence or challenge each other's claims.

Next, the speech for students who love to argue, the rebuttal—an unprepared speech that students must construct during the round. Granted, the rebuttal speech should be prepared in the form of answers to potential arguments, called blocks. The speaker draws from their knowledge, evidence, and the brief they worked so diligently building during practices in the month prior to the tournament. After this speech there is another question period.

Then, the power of analysis must take over. Students are evaluating the debate in real time, figuring out which impacts and arguments are persuading the judge the most. The first speaker from both teams takes part in a summary speech and must work with the second speaker to coordinate their ideas while planning their strategy. Then, there is a grand cross fire, when all speakers have a chance to question each other. Students must be taught to respect others' voices while speaking up when appropriate, one of the most overlooked skills in debate.

Finally, the second speaker crystalizes the argument for the judge. Students at this point have to prove why they win the debate and point out flaws made by their opponents. Students must command the debate and declare victory, making it as hard as possible for the judge to choose a winner if the debate happens to be a close one.

World Schools

The World Schools format is similar to parliamentary debate, which is the most popular format in colleges and around the world. The proposition must defend the House of Representatives in the status quo. The opposition simply rejects what the House believes. This three-person debate format is written from the perspective of what "This House Believes" These topics are called motions, and they can range from the ethics of predictive policing, creating graffiti in public places, to school vouchers. The topics certainly vary more in World Schools than any other format. Because of this, students in this form of debate follow a different research process; students have to quickly categorize and sort through more evidence. During rounds, students do not rely as heavily on the evidence as they do in Public Forum, but they have to retain information and synthesize ideas much more.

In general, first speakers in World Schools are expert presenters who must deliver the speech passionately and persuasively, while leaving time for points of information or questions from their opponents. During this speech the first speaker is allowed to choose when to answer questions or points of information. This skill is also important in future jobs, because everyone knows in meetings there are times when someone must interject, and the speaker must choose when to recognize the person raising his or her hand.

Second speakers in World Schools solely rebut the opening speech. They must respond to each point made by the first speaker, including any points of information that need clarification. When students are in rebuttals, they must manage their time wisely, because they have to touch on all points while simultaneously answering points of information.

Third speakers do the final analysis and need to pay close attention to all of the nuances of the debate. There is no time set in the final speech for points of information, so the third speaker must fill time with crystalizing arguments and pointing out why his or her team should win the debate.

Stories from the Debate Realm

The speech kids, debate kids, coaches, and judges are part of a vast ecosystem of language, mannerisms, and habits that only forensics people understand, which I call the Debate Realm. Nevertheless, when these students tell their stories, someone who was not on the team would be impressed with their eloquence. I will share a few stories of just how successful my students became in college admissions and beyond.

In my first practice, forty or so students entered the room and saw five books stacked on each desk. Some students left the room after taking one glance at all the books, others asked questions, and some remained silent and just listened intently to my presentation. One sophomore, whom I will call Tina, decided to join the team. Tina stands out because throughout the year she had managed honors and AP classes and debated a style called Lincoln–Douglas debate. She did very well and went on to win several local, regional, and state championships. Tina graduated and went to college on a full scholarship for debate and academic achievement. During college, she became the number one freshman debater in the country. Her time in debate shaped her goals after graduation. Tina did a fall internship in the White House's Office of General Counsel, which she called "the opportunity of a lifetime." She was the only University of Virginia Law School student to intern in the final months of Barack Obama's last term. Tina is now a lawyer, as are many others who were on my high school debate teams.

The next short story takes us to Qatar. In one of the schools I coached, my students had the opportunity to debate against Qatari students at the Cisco Systems headquarters in Washington, DC. Six students from my league were chosen to go to Qatar to debate with Todd Fine, the league's vice president at the time. Todd is a champion debater who had won several big tournaments and went on to Harvard, where incidentally 80 percent of applicants are valedictorians and 10 percent of accepted students were on the debate team.

Another one of my students, Roland, debated during his sophomore year and by senior year had won several championships. One championship in particular provided the opportunity of a lifetime; he and I flew to the Reagan Presidential Library in Simi Valley, California, to debate against the best debaters in the country, where he advanced to the semifinals! Roland is now working in public policy.

If a student enjoys debate, learns the art, and gains valuable skills, that is success.

Student success in debate is not limited to winning a major championship or always breaking to elimination rounds. If a student enjoys debate, learns the art, and gains valuable skills, that is success. A professor at American University told me she can spot her debaters on the first day of class when they raise their hands. A federal appeals court judge who argued cases before the Supreme Court emphasized to me that debate is the most valuable activity a student can engage in during in high school.

No matter where students start or what grade they are in when they sign up, given the right team, coach, and experiences, debate will shape a love and passion for learning. You watch your child's eyes light up when they come home (or log off) after a tournament and tell you what happened. When was the last time your teenager went on and on about a conversation in school?

My debate league is unique in that we accept any student from any school or homeschool and partner students across the country. Some of my California students are partnered with my Virginia students; my New Jersey students are partnered with my Maryland students. We also host schools from any city in the world. We have had Canadian schools regularly compete as well as speech and debate teams from India and Vancouver. The bond of friendship and networking through debate also create opportunities. One of my students was invited to Italy by one of her opponents!

So, whether you intend to be an architectural engineer like my daughter, a business and science student like my son, or a sociologist, psychologist, professor, lawyer, judge, accountant, or technologist like my present students, debate will provide a space for you to express your unique intellect, match wits with talented teens from around the world, develop lifelong friends, and make memorable impressions on admissions.

—Julian Dotson
President District of Columbia Urban Debate League and Metro DC Speech and Debate League,
Head Coach of the University Pro National Team
www.dcudl.org
jdotson@dcudl.org

An Introduction to The Value of Music Study

As a college advisor, author, speaker, and eternal student, I believe deeply in the liberal arts—especially the "arts" part. In fact, during my doctoral studies, I pursued an additional degree in music. I believe that music enriches life, changes the molecules in any audience, and transforms the thinking and capacities of every young scholar or professional, regardless of field.From everything I have witnessed, the younger children are when exposed to instrumental or vocal study, the better.

Before you hear from the eminent music professionals and educators on the following pages, let me address one argument I hear among middle school and high school instrumentalists. Students learn early that developing beautiful technical facility on their musical instrument, let alone intuitive and intelligent interpretative skills when performing a composition, requires an exorbitant amount of practice time. They are right. It takes many hours (not necessarily ten thousand) to become an exceptional performer.

If learning the Accolay Violin Concerto or performing pop songs on piano provides enjoyment enough, then such ability will certainly enrich your life and bring happiness to those around you. However, if you seek to push your boundaries of skill and mastery and take on the performance of a Tchaikovsky Violin Concerto or Liszt's *La Campanella*, or you're a baritone attempting Rossini's "Largo al Factorum" (good luck with that), you will notice that occasional free time for all-day romps at the mall or weekend sleepovers might have to suffer. Without those three hours of practice daily (and pre-college conservatory students will recognize that as a minimum), both you and your audience will notice. Sacrifice is involved, but payoff in brilliant recitals, respect among your peers, and the development of grit and empathy, as well as impressive college admissions offers, are also likely.

How can you view such portentous but seemingly annoying sacrifices as positives? Think of what musicians call "rubato," which means "robbed," but not in the literal sense. One robs a beat or a half beat from one note to give more presence and power to the next—shorten one beat to lengthen another. I think there is a life lesson in rubato. Perhaps we should decide which great things that give us joy or will lead to future success need attention now and then give that attention with resolute focus and a full heart—stealing a beat from some of our social activity to lend more time and creative play to another opportunity with bigger eventual impact. So, young musicians, remember that when used artfully, a little rubato at the right time in your life can change everything.

Enjoy these insights on the musical arts from classical vocalist and composer Pamela Stein Lynde (Peabody Conservatory–Johns Hopkins University) and GRAMMY-nominated violist and composer Jessica Meyer (the Juilliard School).

YOUR MENTOR:

PAMELA STEIN LYNDE

(Peabody Conservatory), Classical Voice and Composition

On the Versatile Applications of the Study of Voice and Composition

We are living in a time of great change for the landscape of learning and academia. The foundation of traditional forms of education is coming into question, and with it, the arts and humanities are fighting to delineate their value to society. In an effort toward survival, many colleges and universities are drawing students in with the promise of job placement—offering them skills that will make them more valuable employees. Yet, at the same time, the traditional workforce continues to change, shifting toward independent contracting instead of traditional forms of employment and favoring those who think outside the box, taking a chance on uncharted territory.

All these changes may seem tenuous, but they actually provide a great opportunity for you as a young musician or artist. In a world where the market dictates value, how can training in music—and specifically voice, a notoriously underpaid and underfunded field of study—maintain relevance? How can the study of this discipline help you in your journey toward successful college admissions?

I walked into my first voice lesson at the age of twelve. I had always loved singing and studied violin starting in elementary school. I was constantly humming Mozart melodies around the house. But I never thought much about it beyond an after-school activity. My parents wanted me to try voice lessons to build my confidence and self-esteem. Middle school is a tough time for most kids. Everyone is finding their path, or losing it, in some way. Maybe you have had such experiences.

My first teacher's name was Karen. She was, in many ways, the opposite of me. I was shy and intense; she was bright and outgoing, like a light that pulled everything around it into illumination. I didn't have any idea what I was getting into, but two months into lessons, I was hooked. It went beyond just enjoying singing. I distinctly felt called to music as my life's work.

I don't know if other musicians experience this at some point. I don't talk much about it. But I felt that I had been pulled full force into something so much bigger and so much greater than me. Music felt like a thread that connected me to both the past and the future. It allowed me to exist as a lightning rod for a powerful and profound force of nature. I felt humility in the face of what music is.

Once I decided I would dedicate my life to this study, my priorities shifted. Suddenly I had a whole new perspective on what was important. I went from milling about aimlessly at the mall on Friday night with my friends to spending my evenings at rehearsals for community theater productions or choir practice or anything else that gave me a chance to sing. Middle school drama slowly faded into background noise.

I started by delving into musical theater and quickly moved on to classical music and opera. I was fascinated by a form that combined so many artistic pursuits into one powerful experience. As a creative kid who excelled in literature and art, I longed to find ways to become both a performer and a creator. I became quite a busy tween, writing musicals and novels after I finished homework at night, determined to learn every line of *Carmen* and *La Bohème*, and reading up on opera history and music theory in my spare time. These pursuits created a clear and unique *why* on my college applications—something admissions committees love to see. Remember that delineating a clear statement of purpose is essential for helping differentiate you from the average applicant.

I think it's important to note that I was probably an extreme case. I thrived in activities that required self-discipline and working under pressure, so my personality lent itself well to the pursuit of music. Not all kids are like that. The question then becomes, What more general value does the study of classical singing and composing have for young students? The answer involves a look at the benefits of these studies in a holistic sense.

The Value of Physical Repetition and the Development of Kinesthetic Intelligence

As students prepare for college, there are certain skills that may appear advantageous, giving them a leg up on success. One such skill is the ability to successfully cram for an exam. There is certainly value in being able to memorize and integrate large quantities of information in a short amount of time. It frees one up for other tasks. In fact, the ability to successfully cram has long been secretly revered among teens as a virtue. However, what happens when a successful crammer is met with information that cannot be learned overnight but can only be integrated through precise repetition that develops muscle memory over a long period of time? This form of learning requires a very different kind of intelligence, which may seem foreign to students who have come to rely on their success in procrastinating. Studying vocal technique and developing musicianship skills related to singing requires devoted attention to the working of the muscles, the flow of the breath, and the sensations of resonance in the body. In the same way that one cannot build strength by going to the gym once a week, students of singing learn quickly that practice between lessons is essential for progress.

Developing the physical control and awareness of the body that is required for vocal technique is an important exercise in humility. In the face of learning skills related to singing, or really any musical instrument, we are all humbled by the sheer devotion to and depth of understanding behind something that outwardly seems like a relatively simple task. Achieving breakthroughs in technique is often accompanied by tears, and rightfully so. Students who can successfully navigate the process of learning vocal technique and the challenge of applying that technique to vocal repertoire in an artistically meaningful way are already set up for success in any postsecondary education setting. They are learning the value of achieving something that is more akin to scaling a mountain than to acing an exam. Admissions seems to know this secret, as we can tell by the preponderance of acceptances to top-tier and Ivy League schools from high school / precollege conservatory programs. As Dr. Bedor often notes in her college boot camps, "It is not that these schools are *all* looking for professional-level singers or musicians; it's that they are looking for highly dedicated and practiced students who have been through the wringer of rigor and performance and have come out the other side as interpreters, unflummoxed presenters, and artists."

While the study of vocal technique and pedagogy is based in anatomy and physiology, the implementation of technique relies highly on imagery and visualization. Creative visualization is a necessary tool for teaching the body and mind to work together in support of the voice. For example, I ask students to listen through a passage they are having trouble singing and imagine themselves singing the passage, including everything from the inhalation, the flow of air, the articulation, and the desired muscular involvement. As my advanced students prepare for auditions, I ask them to visualize the entire situation they are walking into and how they would like it to go (e.g., what will the judges think when they nail that difficult florid passage; how will they feel when they hear their voice fill the auditorium on that high C?). Developing this connection between mind and body allows students to have control in situations that can feel anxiety provoking or even harrowing. This same process can be used to guide students through their preparation for any performance: college interviews, internship interviews, class presentations, pitching a start-up, or any exercise in public speaking.

Tying Breath to the Body: Voice Lessons for Mind-Body Well-Being

One of the most important fundamentals in learning to sing is proper breath support. I talk about breathing with my students in every lesson, whether they are beginners or professionals. Breathing properly for singing is something that takes years to master. Why is it that this function, which is an automatic process of the brain, poses such a challenge in the context of singing? The simple answer is that it takes practice and discipline to gain control of the body's intake and output of air and to connect those actions to specific musical phrases.

Breathing for singing is a heightened and more intentional function of regular breathing. Control of the breath is related to mindfulness and meditation and can be used to quell anxiety and still the mind. A high school student who studies classical voice, therefore, inevitably gains control and emotional balance that other students might not achieve during those stressful years. That balance is part of what enables you to bond with an audience, interpret music freely, and present your ideas in a class or leadership position on campus. Professors notice when they have students with performance backgrounds in their classes.

I speak to my students often about yoga, drawing the parallel to singing in that they are both disciplines that connect the breath to motion. I remember questioning a yoga teacher about this work, asking if it was supposed to make one more calm or focused. She said, "No. It's not about making you feel calm. It's about stilling the waters so you can see what is underneath." This kind of introspection is valuable for young students to bring clarity to their goals and how their goals align with their well-being.

Creative Forces and Their Application to All Aspects of Academic Work

The study of voice is unique in its connection to other disciplines, including literature, art, drama, history, and even science. Learning the workings of the voice requires an in-depth study of anatomy and physiology, giving students an understanding of the function of breathing, the action of the vocal folds, and the structures comprising the pharyngeal mechanism. Studying vocal literature requires students to embark upon an exploration of text and poetry and the historical context in which that poetry exists. Bringing vocal music to life is an execution of dramatic prowess, which requires a deep understanding of musical meaning and nuance. Let's not forget, also, that students of classical voice will have sung in multiple foreign languages by the time they reach college, opening up an understanding of other cultures and inspiring a curiosity for further study in speaking and reading the literature of these languages outside the musical context.

If you are a student who thrives in the study of classical music, you may find, as I did, that you are inspired to be not only a performer but a creator. As I began writing music, I wanted to know, for example, what kind of stories make for powerful works of art, and what devices make for particularly effective storytelling. What kind of subject matter attracts audiences or provokes important kinds of thought?

These are important questions for creators of things like opera, art song, or a Billboard #1 hit. However, these are also essential tools for understanding other human beings, with wide-reaching applications to fields like business, psychology, advertising, politics, sales, and much more. Understanding what makes powerful art is just a function of understanding human nature.

Inspiring a specific feeling from a large audience of people at once also involves another art form: persuasive technique. Persuasion is something you will be using in every college paper you write! To take things a step further, the kind of self-motivation required to create a large-scale work of art, such as an opera or cycle of art songs, is not unlike that which is required to start one's own company from scratch, develop a new technology, discovery a novel remedy, or become a successful consultant or freelancer. It is equal parts fierce intellectual curiosity, deep-seated passion, patient experimentation, and many hours of work. Anyone with the motivation and skills to create a long-form series of compositions will be a highly attractive candidate for college admissions.

Singing as a Therapeutic form of Expression and Communication:

Singing can serve as a valuable tool for students to express that which they cannot discuss in day-to-day life. It is essentially therapeutic. In an environment where students are dealing with boundless pressure to remain academically competitive, artistic ventures can provide a form of respite and release. The process of learning to sing and create music is all about learning to let go and be honest and vulnerable with one's feelings. These are all characteristics that are valued on a college application.

In some cases, particularly goal-oriented and conscientious students may get caught up in the technical work and have trouble "letting go" when singing. When working with such students, I draw on some of my training in opera that taught me to decontextualize arias completely and reimagine the context as something absurd and over the top. This method may include having students singing while doing somersaults across the floor or imagining they are fighting with a grizzly bear. It may sound silly, but this allows students to connect to very raw emotion in their singing that aids in the physical integration of the composition's emotional content. This method of recontextualization helps students build a deeper connection between physical action and emotion, which is essential for singing.

The ability to take unconventional directions and commit to them fully is a valuable life skill for young minds hoping to become competitive in a world of quickly changing technologies, economies, and environments. If there is anything we have learned in recent years, it is that the conventional paths to success are no longer assured, and high achievement is reserved for those with the ability and studied talent to embrace the novel.

On Timelines and Goal Charting

I have guided many students through the process of achieving admissions to conservatories and competitive college music programs. Years ago, it was understood that admission to competitive conservatories could be achieved only after years of intensive study on one's instrument. These days, society has been sold on the false visions of overnight success achieved by raw, untrained talent, vended to us by TV talent shows and the music industry publicity machine. Nothing could be further from the truth. I make it clear to my students who express interest in a conservatory path that they must begin to focus on technique, repertoire selection, foreign-language study, and musicianship skills as early as possible.

Students who achieve the most success in conservatory auditions start working with me from the time they are in ninth grade, and some even earlier. Because prescreening recordings for the top schools are due in the fall of senior year, students must be ready to present a polished set of audition repertoire before many of their peers have even started their application essays. This repertoire is typically studied for months to years before it is recorded so that it can be presented with the most physically integrated and emotionally nuanced precision.

Students embarking on the conservatory or music major path learn the value of working toward a long-term goal. This can include creating a plan for their study spanning the course of years. I know that Dr. Bedor uses the same kind of goal charting and talent building over a series of years as a tool for developing special skill sets (artistic, intellectual, or entrepreneurial) that build a talented student into a more interesting and valuable candidate. If my students express interest in applying for a conservatory or a highly competitive music major, I insist they work on their long-term goals by personal development through a series of independent projects. In the past, these have included performing a full recital of music spanning multiple musical time periods and languages, producing chamber music concerts that address relevant contemporary issues, performing works by modern composers, and even creating music-related content for social media.

A few years back, I invited some of my talented and dedicated students to take part in a project with electronic music composer and sound sculptor Lesley Flanigan, where my students learned to work with tools such as loop pedals and Lesley's homemade electronic instruments. This collaboration culminated with my students creating and performing a new work with this celebrated contemporary artist. In a highly competitive field where reputations matter, it is important to begin building a presence as an intellectually curious artist from the very beginning. Reaching out to and working alongside professionals in the field is one of the best ways to begin building a reputation while learning in the process.

The benefit of music study for young students is well documented and need not be reiterated. What must be understood is the way intensive study of disciplines like voice and music composition create better thinkers and more valuable members of society. We exist in a climate of conditional emphasis on skills that have value to a market, and it becomes more difficult to quantify the value of any humanities-related discipline. However, when we examine the kind of work and skill building that goes into learning to sing and compose, it is clear that the application of this work is far reaching.

Intensive study of disciplines like voice and music composition create better thinkers and more valuable members of society.

Beyond the application of these skills, I ask that we return to the question of intrinsic value and examine what we will wish we had left behind at the end of our lives. Most people will wish they had shared something beautiful, powerful, or meaningful with the people they love. They will hope that they forged strong relationships, left lasting impressions, and changed things around them for the better. Those with the ability to create powerful experiences through the discipline of music will have gained a deep understanding of this basic aspect of human nature—our desperation to connect in profound ways. Those who have musical talent and devote themselves, even for a while, to the path of creation and interpretation will not only be prepared for both personal and professional success in any field they pursue but will acquire the keys to the universe.

—Pamela Stein Lynde
Composer, classical singer, and music educator,
Studio Pamela Stein Lynde
Author of *Voice Lessons for Personal Growth and Professional Success*
pamelastein.net@gmail.com
www.pamelastein.net

YOUR MENTOR:

JESSICA MEYER

(The Juilliard School), Instrumental Music and Composition

How Playing an Instrument and Regularly Tapping Into Your Innate Creativity Enhances Your Overall Development and Strengthens Your Capacity to Work in Any Field

Since I can first remember, I have been attracted to sound. When I was a child, I loved hearing a song that I could sing along to, playing a beat on whatever object I could drum, and especially making up my own music on any piano I could find. Thankfully I was born in the 1970s, where every kindergarten classroom had some kind of piano in it (along with blocks, dolls, finger paints, dress-up clothes, and various other developmentally appropriate ways to ignite the five-year-old imagination). I say this because the five-year-olds of today are often writing sentences when their fingers can't really hold a pencil well yet and taking tests on computers instead of engaging in play. Integrating myself within a group of children was difficult for me at the time, so I spent my hours on the piano in the corner happily re-creating the songs I'd heard while watching *Sesame Street*. I have since learned exactly how valuable that kind of play is and how studying to be better on an instrument greatly affects your capacity to learn, function, and be present in this world.

I say "this world" because technology has vastly changed how we, as humans, function and mature. Some things are quite positive about technology—we can learn anything we are curious about through deep dives into the internet. However, this kind of access available on a phone we carry around all day can also reduce our capacity for imaginative thinking and limit our frustration tolerance for not having all the answers immediately. Despite the many ways technology has allowed us to grow, it has also hindered the very capacities that make us resilient, creative, and happy human beings—the very capacities that colleges look for and that will help you live a rich and full life.

It is no surprise to me that employers like Google are not combing business schools for potential employees but instead are tapping into the art schools to find artists—those who are used to

- developing a skill over time that requires long-range planning,
- collaborating with others in order to make a whole better than its parts, and
- living in that vague space before the eureka moment of identifying and fleshing out a solid idea—something that is indeed not "Googleable" but something that comes only from you and your process.

In the following pages, I would like to address how learning and performing on an instrument as well as how composing or improvising your own music can be a conduit for amassing valuable skills that can be applied to any field—but perhaps more importantly, how it can also help develop your whole self and bring you joy.

My Story

In the few years following my impromptu kindergarten piano sessions, whenever my mom would go to her friend Barbara's house for tea, I would sit at her piano to keep myself occupied. Over the course of an hour, I would come up with my own pieces of piano music and repeat them over and over until I memorized them. When fourth grade rolled around, I decided I wanted to play the violin. However, they ran out of violins, and since I was tall, they assigned me the viola. I still want to personally thank whoever made that decision.

After starting private lessons in fifth grade, I learned two things: I loved viola, and I hated practicing; I just wanted to play. In retrospect, the bigger issue was that I really did not know how to organize my work into effective practice sessions. After being assigned progressively harder music to learn as a teen, I got better over time at dealing with the frustration of not being good at something right away once I realized I needed to be part of a process that takes time, but it was a struggle. However, it took only a few times of finding out the hard way what happens when a musician is underprepared for me to change my work habits. The embarrassment of not knowing your part well in front of others is indeed quite the effective teacher.

I also had the opportunity to take a class that would change my life—one where we learned about the nuances of music theory not by studying all the rules but by writing our own music using Mac computers and MIDI samplers. In other words, I learned by making and experiencing. All my teenage angst came pouring out in the pieces I created. I even wrote a concerto for myself on the computer, and by senior year, I was spending most of my time composing in our little computer music lab when I was not practicing for college auditions.

Oddly though, when I got into Juilliard, I never once thought of studying composition because I didn't deem it practical. I shared my family's concern over how I would make a living after conservatory, and being a violist always equaled "orchestra job" in my mind, so that was the road I chose. However, years passed before I finally acknowledged what was missing from my life: writing my own music. With that realization I found success that was far from anything I had imagined.

After many years of viola performances that have taken me all over the world, teaching kids your age how to harness their creativity, and building upon my success as a composer after finally harnessing my own creativity, I am writing to share with you exactly why practicing, performing, and creating music directly contributes to your overall success and uniqueness as a college applicant and beyond.

The Mind-Body Connection

When I began practicing the viola regularly, I finally observed the magic that our bodies are capable of. At first, there was a disconnect between trying to learn the notes on the page and getting my hands and fingers to play them in tune while being rhythmically accurate. I was so nervous that I could not even breathe, and I cried for a long time afterward.

However, after those initial experiences, I became better at visualization: imagining myself feeling calm, playing the notes perfectly, and having a successful performance. Those who play sports know this practice of visualization well, and colleges are always interested in those who have routinely shown the capacity to perform well under pressure. Visualizing a series of events that will happen over time is already a capacity many people do not use, yet one that can be life changing—both personally and professionally.

For many years I struggled with playing in tune when performing classical pieces on my viola. However, when I improvised my own music or performed a piece I wrote, my body was much more at ease, and the notes would be clearly in tune. Why was this? When I improvised music, I immediately played the sounds I heard in my head without any other thought getting in the way. There was a clear pipeline between my mind and my body, hands, and fingers. Later, when I composed and performed a collection of pieces that I initially wrote for myself and a loop pedal, I became a far more virtuosic player because I was always playing the music that I was hearing in my head so clearly, since I'd created it and had a connection to it.

The science behind this is simple: when you are fully present and in the moment, this kind of effortless mind-body connection is activated because you are mostly engaging the left side of your brain, experiencing a "flow" state. There are many studies that show how the more we become proficient at a skill while engaging in creative choices, the better we can perform using the intuitive left hemisphere of our brains rather than the analytical right hemisphere (where we could easily become so self-conscious that we could choke under pressure). This "flow" state is that magical moment where the mind and body are indeed acting as one, and music is one of the most celebrated examples of that. It is the reason we still go to live concerts, dance, or sing together in groups. Learning how to engage in "flow" with an instrument in your hand lays the groundwork for you to create that magic in other mediums or professions—and we need young people who know how to express that magic in the world now more than ever.

Being Part of a Process

The educational system is changing—and not for the better. Time exploring and discussing ideas that have multiple views and outcomes has given way to weeks spent on test prep. Being able to entertain and respectfully discuss multifarious points of view is given lesser status in school than getting "the right answer." This practice has been going on so long that many students, even at top universities, are regularly coming into class only interested in finding out what they need to know to pass the test, instead of growing their capacity for critical thinking. Life has become even more about who has the "right" answer, the number, the *product*.

When referring to the Latin origins of the word, to "educate" is to draw out what one is capable of and provide sequential instruction for one to develop and grow. Having studied music for many years, I would also say the best education is one where you also learn how to teach yourself so you are better prepared for the changes that will happen over the course of your lifetime. Our current educational system leaves people feeling the need to take a class to learn something. But your generation is one that requires constant independent learning to keep up—whether that's in sciences, education, the arts, or technology. Learning happens inside and outside of a class, and learning to play an instrument is a great example of this educational model because so much of your progress depends on what you are discovering on your own in between classes or lessons.

When you're studying how to play an instrument, there is a great deal of self-teaching that happens between each weekly lesson. Every time you sit down to practice, you are deciding how slowly or quickly to play a run or passage, how many repetitions you need to be confident, and how you are sequencing your practice time in order to learn a piece. This differs greatly from the sports world, where the coach is ever present, telling you exactly what drills you should do and in what sequence. In the music world, you are the coach and the student every moment you have your instrument out of the case—unless you are in front of your teacher once or twice a week.

Practicing an instrument, learning a piece by your own self-direction, activating the process of long-range planning to get ready for a performance, and executing the piece under pressure develop the very capacities that essentially define college and life readiness.

Practicing an instrument ... [develops] the very capacities that essentially define college and life readiness.

Furthermore, when you are creating something from nothing, getting comfortable with the "I just don't know right now" is integral to the process. The creative process—whether you are learning a piece, composing your own piece, or performing and interpreting that piece—takes time, like writing this particular part of the chapter! A few weeks ago, I had a general idea of what I would tell you; then last week I made an outline. Between then and a few days ago, I let my "back burner" mull it over—which is the subconscious part of your brain that works on things while you sleep (which is why the advice to "sleep on it" still exists).

This is where procrastination is helpful, because during that time your brain is working to make whatever idea or problem you are grappling with better. However, you still need to meet the deadline. Just remember, the bigger the project, the more time you will need to set aside on your calendar for your creative process and the discomfort of "not knowing." You will return to your composition or musical instrument or science project or research paper and try to move it forward with calm and focused attention, understanding you can't complete everything in one sitting. Give yourself permission to pause. The greatest inspiration comes from walking away and returning.

Learning to survive and thrive in that temporary "not knowing" space instead of being overwhelmed is something that studying music provides. The great news is that these music study skills are beyond valuable when making the leap from high school, where your education is structured for you daily, to college, where suddenly you are responsible for running your own timeline and performance.

The Art of Collaboration

Currently, much of my life involves writing music on my laptop, getting it to the ensembles who perform it, going to visit them to hear it during a rehearsal, then being present for the premiere when the public hears it for the first time. My music has been performed at Lincoln Center, Carnegie Hall, and around Europe. While all this is very exciting, I am still making time to perform as a violist—and not always as a soloist, but as a cog in a well-oiled machine: an ensemble.

There is a saying that there is no "I" in "team." Sure, there are some limits one needs to put on themselves when functioning as part of a team, but I would argue that there exists a different kind of "me" in "team." After you practice your instrumental part individually, once you get to the rehearsal, a very specific set of interpersonal and intrapersonal skills is activated. Roles fluidly change within the ensemble, and it is your job to know your function at all times. For instance, at one point you might be playing a solo feature over the group, in another your sound is a small part of the whole ensemble, and at other times you may be the glue that holds everyone together. Then, there are the various ways rehearsals are run: there could be a director whose feedback you must apply, there could be a hierarchy of individual players that one has to follow at different times, or there could be a collective decision among musicians about what best serves the music.

I have taught many workshops for high school students, and it is always wonderful for me (and the teachers) to see what happens in small group work: whose voices come out that we do not normally hear and the deep and rich ideas that can emerge when there is no teacher directing every single decision. As school curriculum focuses more and more on test prep, these kinds of creative and collaborative activities fall by the wayside—and to a student's detriment. However, if you have an instrument in your hand and can find a bunch of folks who want to jam out on a song you already know, or who want to play a piece you have written, know that you are inherently developing collaborative skills that are essential for better functioning on a college campus, in the classroom, and beyond when working in just about any professional field.

Music has been a tool used globally by people to become the best version of themselves. I have seen this happen with so many kids, including my own son. We are born with the ability to create beauty and express what makes us human in so many different ways. Make time to create your own sounds to express what you or the world are experiencing, and enjoy the magic and catharsis that music brings to life and learning.

—Jessica Meyer
Composer, violist, vocalist, educator
violajessicameyer@gmail.com
www.jessicameyermusic.com

Interviews with Your College Student Mentors

No one can commiserate with high schoolers and the tremendous effort needed to keep your eye on the prize more than college and graduate students who have "been there, done that." The entire admissions process is still fresh in their minds, and their vantage point for advising high school students on the future is unquestionable.

So, although mentorship is best left in the hands of experts, some of the most heartfelt mentorship can come from your own peers who have already made the journey to the colleges you seek and are now in the process of building their next chapter. Older adults cannot always predict what will resonate with a high school student, but college students have just been there and done that. What they say has meaning and impact for high schoolers.

I've interviewed dozens of my former students who are now attending some of the most competitive colleges in the nation to see what advice they can share with the next generation about creating a successful high school journey and college career.

Let's check out their responses.

The Best of Princeton (Students from Freshman through Senior Year)

What do you wish you knew about college academics that you know now?

College isn't going to be the last thing you do with your life, but maintaining your grades will open a lot of doors for you. Remember, you may not think you're heading straight to graduate school after graduation, but things are shifting, and a secondary degree is coming back into favor. Keep a comfortable middle ground between your newfound freedom and the new responsibilities that you have in front of you—no one is going to remind you about deadlines or assignments.

What were the three main skills you developed in high school that have been invaluable during college?

1. Compartmentalization: Being able to approach multiple seemingly insurmountable tasks by dividing them into smaller chunks, each with their own due dates and completable deliverables.
2. Self-motivation: In college and beyond, you won't have the luxury of someone else setting your motivations. Your successes or failures are determined by your willingness to do the work because you're hungry for that success.
3. Stress management: Eisenhower's theory of time use—there are tasks that are urgent and important; urgent but not important; important but not urgent; not important and not urgent. Being able to categorize the projects and do the urgent but unimportant only in your downtime allows you to prioritize the urgent and important during your best working hours (and make space for the important but not urgent) because those are the big rocks to put in the jar. This is critical to maintaining schedule, successful grades, and lower stress.

Have you changed your major since entering college and if so, to what?

I remained a history major from entering college to completing my degree.

In what internship opportunities should high schoolers engage?

Even if you have a tangential interest in a field, your time in high school is the time to find internships in areas that you are curious about. Remember that your high school internships come off your résumé once you start more professional internships during college (and that can be as early as freshman year).

What do you do just for you?

Since 2020, I have led a team of amateur game designers in a meeting every Saturday morning. We discuss mechanical questions and make decisions about where the line falls between game balance and the fun of the community engaging with the game. It's a way of enjoying one of my long-term fascinations and building up experience handling projects and managing disparate personalities even when they disagree in our meetings.

What do you think the future of college education should be?

I don't have a fully defined vision for collegiate education moving forward, but I understand that it is particularly important for students to be given a focus on practical skills while still being able to explore their intellectual curiosities. The current state of liberal arts educations at top-tier universities grants too much freedom to students, which results in their ability to make it through college without picking up any directly applicable skills to their intended future careers if, for example, those careers involve business, computer programming, or public speaking. Simultaneously, prerequisites force students to struggle through courses that are outside of their skill sets or will never be useful to them in the future. It's a dilemma. I believe that collegiate institutions need to decide whether they value student freedom to explore intellectual curiosities more highly than the opportunity to take courses that prepare students for specialized careers.

From my standpoint, a student should be required to choose from courses in a liberal arts core that speaks to them and then be able to specialize in any number of career-course modules to prepare them for a future in the job market. I know it's very easy to poke holes in an honored system when you don't have to be the one fixing it. My view is that students need P/F or audit for full credit options (without getting a grade that can be averaged into your GPA) in the courses they are afraid of but know they should take to become well read or keen analysts. Through such a system, there would be greater openness to take the classics or ancient literature when one is a math major; computer science or economics when one is a humanities major; creative writing for engineers; or ORFE (operational research and financial engineering) for history majors.

What do you believe that other people think is crazy?

Life is made of little steps—decisions made at such a fine scale that we can't see the difference between making the sixty decisions that get us to breakfast every morning and making the one decision to have breakfast.

Yes. That's a microscopic example of a decision, but most decisions are just that small.

If you want to make something happen, the only thing you really have to ask yourself is, "Do I want this enough to make the next tiny decision?" And if you do, then the next question is recursive. Most people think in whole decisions, but that leaves room for too many surprises and bumps on the pathway to reaching your goal. So tiny decision-making is not as crazy as it sounds.

How important is a liberal arts education to you? To your future profession? Please explain in full.

Liberal arts education holds a strange value-proposition for me. These courses unquestionably sharpen the mind by allowing students to explore questions outside their own fields of intended employment. At the same time as a liberal arts education focuses on skills that can be applied outside of obvious professional employment, it often lacks the ability to prepare students for the realities of the occupations they will be entering. This experience gap can sometimes be supplemented with internships and part-time roles, but it is important to remember that not every field benefits equally from on-the-job experience, and that some "entry-level" positions may require years of apprenticeships, regardless of your level of liberal arts education.

What advice would you give your fourteen-year-old self?

I remember hearing once when I was in my sophomore year of college that there was a shift in the way people approached individual strengths and weaknesses. When I was in high school, there was a focus on all-around knowledge. Colleges accept students based on their universal skill in math, English, history, science, and any other subject that can be evaluated with a standardized test, but the college experience has very few situations in which a student benefits from generalizing rather than specializing in their area of study. Covering your weaknesses means you are not working on your strengths. There will rarely be a case where it is necessary for you as an individual to be the CEO, CMO, CFO, and COO of your own enterprise. Specialize and be the best you can be at the things you care most about. Let other people support you by filling in the gaps.

What class needs to be given in college?

One course that should be part of every undergraduate institution's core curriculum is a basic primer on personal finance. Students do not all need to understand the financial structure of every company for which they will work, but they do need to understand the principles of personal investment, savings, and taxes.

The Best of Harvard (Freshman and Sophomore Students)

What were the three main skills you developed in high school that have been invaluable during college?

- Developing ways to emotionally distance and detach myself from school and extracurricular work. This was critical to ensure that my well-being was not dependent on the approval of my teachers, parents, admissions officers, etc.
- Being comfortable spending time alone (which is *not* turning my brain off to watch that sweet YouTube).
- Imagining ways to understand and "be with" the people behind pieces of writing, music, and art.

How has your leadership in high school continued or laid the groundwork for your continued leadership in college?

My high school serves a predominately white, wealthy, suburban community. On paper, one of my most prominent high school leadership positions was student government. All of my contributions were based on advocating for the cultural and social interests of a homogenous and overrepresented student body; daily executive meetings involved debates over whether prom should be "Wild West" themed or space themed; working with authorities to shut down our town's main road so the homecoming queen and king could be paraded from the recreation center to the high school; or making glitter-and-glue posters advertising what the theme of each day for spirit week is. Spending time with my college classmates of marginalized cultural backgrounds, many of whom felt isolated and dissociated in tackling colossal questions ranging from identity to homelife, accentuated the dissonance I felt in this sphere of leadership—and it sharpened my (counter) devotion to building spaces for the muted experiences and communities I and my classmates share. This very coincidental groundwork has become a major motor for my present motivation in leading student coalitions and art projects where I and my classmates may heal and build collective power *for ourselves*.

Have you changed your major since entering college and if so, to what?

I changed my major from social studies to history and literature. Social studies starts you off with an intensive dive into Western social theory, and those interpretations form the genetic material for the body of scholarship you generate. History and literature appears to be more open to topics and perspectives in ethnic studies; studies in women, gender, and sexuality; and literary theory.

What are the books you've read recently that have made an impact? Why?

Joan Didion's *Slouching towards Bethlehem*: Her writing is beautiful.

Saidiya Hartman's *Wayward Lives, Beautiful Experiments: Intimate Histories of Riotous Black Girls, Troublesome Women and Queer Radicals*: Approaching such a terrible and incomplete archive, Hartman writes a history that both loves and liberates.

What internship opportunities should high schoolers engage in?

Anything related to the arts—I feel you will have fewer and fewer opportunities to pursue arts in the competitive, utilitarian, meritocratic environment of college, which is unfortunate because one must always draw on art to improvise new ways of inhabiting the world. So, get as much of it as you can! From econometrics to performance theory, to English literature, to statistics, all the brightest minds in my classes are from people who adore reading and creating art. I think it's causation going on here.

How is college different or the same as your expectations?

In this environment, it is actually harder than I thought to cultivate a sense and pride of self. The most natural thing here is to define yourself—everything from your habits to your accomplishments to how you speak—against the circles of individuals around you. For example, a self-reflection that was very eye opening to me was that I had let my sleep schedule slip partially because I would always hear my peers talking about how poor their sleep schedule was. This did not seem to bother them or change their success in class, so I initially felt it was okay to mirror their "up all night" antics. I now felt more comfortable prioritizing other things over sleep because of the people I was surrounded by. That was not a good idea, and I eventually developed my own, more healthy sleep schedule based on my personal needs.

Escaping high school doesn't mean you escape its cliques. On the contrary, the "mega-cliques" of college are so sophisticated and prominent that they are truly *cultural* forces—forces that can modify your language and life. This can sound pessimistic, so I want to maintain that I have significantly expanded my horizons in encountering others within these brilliant "subcultures." But at the same time, I think it is critical to be less dependent on the monologues of these circles to bring coherence and structure in your own life. Learn what works for you.

To what extent is time organization important in high school and college?

Time organization is critical. How you spend your time is the most immediate way of *investing in yourself*. This is complicated: you shouldn't try to put your time into an opportunity cost framework either (e.g., studying for this exam will be more "useful" to me than hanging out with friends who will be my lifelong compatriots and mentors), but you should ensure that whatever you spend your time doing, you feel it is strengthening you physically, intellectually, emotionally, or spiritually.

What do you do just for you?

I like to bike, jog, read, and think about writing … actually writing is too hard.

What have you done that has made the biggest impression on your professors? Your friends?

It has always come down to rejecting the script of flattery, obsequiousness, high performance, etc., and feeling fully comfortable and confident in presenting my idiomatic qualities. You have to express who you are and what you believe without being afraid of good-natured sparring or differing opinions. If your dialogue is researched and thoughtful, that makes the best impression on friends and professors alike.

What is your five-year plan?

Graduate college, spend a couple of years teaching in public school, go to graduate school to pursue some theory-focused humanities topic.

What do you think the future of high school education should look like?

I think it would be pretty neat if we lived in a society where high school is one avenue out of many for rigorous study and socialization.

How important is a liberal arts education to you? To your future profession? Please explain in full.

I don't think we should be so dependent on institutions to pursue liberal arts. To be clear, institutions can drain you of all energy/time to gather with others and engage in art, but they can also preserve and present the most beautiful spaces for you to do just that. Without liberal arts, I fear that perceiving the world can become just a habit, rather than a ritual for healing and expanding one's existence. Without a liberal arts education, I fear that one will become just a clever corpse. Art is the seedbed not only for one's sense of self but also for any sense of community. Ultimately, it would be preferable to not have to rely on a college education to receive the value of liberal arts thinking. One should be disciplined and deliberate in carving out spaces to create art with others—independent of whether one is in a university.

What advice would you give your fourteen-year-old self?

1. All your interests are legitimate and valid.

2. Read more.

What do you want parents to know?

Happiness is a generative affect that empowers individuals to care deeply for themselves and the world. I believe the primary goal we want for our youth is for them to be happy—to be a ray of positive light. Please remember that neither wealth nor merit is positively correlated with happiness. On the contrary, there are too many instruments, cloaked as portals to wealth and merit, that only stress and isolate young people and drain their inner sources of happiness and connection.

I think it's parents' responsibility to think about this while contemplating their child's future.

The Best of Duke

What do you wish you knew about college academics that you know now? What is the best preparation?

A big misconception that I had from high school is that the arts are just a "nice to have." I had always loved music and composition and had a talent for orchestrating my own original compositions, but I believed that I needed to heavily pursue internships and summer jobs instead. My high school guidance counselor emphasized that those internships and jobs would be looked upon as impressive by Admissions. So, it was a shock to find out that what ultimately pushed me into the acceptance pile at Duke was my essay on creating music and hearing the natural collaboration of orchestral instruments in my orchestration. I know this made a difference because my regional officer remembered my essay and spoke about it after I accepted admittance. So, I wish I had pursued my musical talents at a higher and more intensive level during high school—maybe at a pre-college conservatory. It turns out that some of my best preparation for college came from my music: being a musician means you learn how to listen deeply and juggle multiple projects simultaneously. Being a composer means taking the rules and skills of composition seriously but being willing to bend them in the name of originality and something daring. I think that these two skills are vitally important for those of us heading into business, politics, or research.

What do you wish you knew about college academics that you know now? What is the best preparation?

I wish I was more aware of how much you need to find and develop your own study support systems. During high school there are set times for activities that are established for you—you're in class or you're at an after-school club and then take the late bus home to begin homework and study. But in college, you are the master of your time, and there are tons of diversions waiting around every corner. It really helped me to literally schedule my study time into my calendar and set fixed weekly study session times. Preparation-wise, I would say the best metric would be to learn how to learn. Take the time to find what study environments and ways of learning are most effective for you (e.g., are you a library studier, a study group studier, or a solo practitioner who needs to study in the quiet of his room?). Then, when you enter college, find places and support systems that work for you!

What were the three main skills you developed in high school that have been invaluable during college?

Learning how to write persuasively is probably the most important skill for a future journalist. I learned that skill unsurprisingly from AP Language and Composition as well as AP Literature. However, more surprisingly, I learned just as much from AP European History, where discussing the course of events requires the formulation of background and analysis, and from my debate team, which taught me the value of couching a successful argument in evidence.

What were the three main skills you developed in high school that have been invaluable during college?

Sending emails, consistently following up, and learning how to meet new people and build connections. The best opportunities I have been a part of in college are because I simply sent an email after a conversation with a new friend, a professor, or lab director. I advocated for myself that way, and people responded, allowing me to get to know my professors, TAs, invited speakers, and new classmates.

What internship opportunities should high schoolers engage in?

I think that high school students need to embrace the multidisciplinary. When you get to college, you will see that although it's important to specialize and become super knowledgeable about your major, you will fall behind if you do not have other pockets of knowledge and understanding from fields outside your own. So, I would tell a high school student who wants to study business to take a research internship one summer and learn the scientific method in a hands-on way. I would suggest that a future scientist should work on a political candidate's campaign to learn how communication can change minds and the dissemination of facts. I would tell future attorneys to work at a nonprofit to understand the plight of the people it serves. All these internships will make you more worldly—something that is helpful on a college campus.

What internship opportunities should high schoolers engage in?

My lab internships are the ones that taught me translatable skills towards my pre-med track in college. Especially given they were research skills, I was able to use my internship in microbiology research, as well as my broader scientific writing skill set to gain the only undergraduate position available in my current research lab on campus. Gaining confidence in your work is critical, and that can only come from your past experiences.

How is college different or the same as your expectations?

It's tough, but that's okay. I knew the transition was going to be hard, and I had to keep an open mind. I also think you grow a lot more than you expect. Being alone and with true agency for the first time in your life, you mature so much and so quickly.

To what extent is time organization important in high school and college?

Critical. Being able to get into college and thriving in college is all about maintaining a good work-life balance and making sure you do what you need to. That's where time organization comes in to ensure you get everything done! Don't get the books you need from the library the day before a paper is due (you won't find them there); don't give yourself only a weekend to study for a final; do make time to blow off steam with good conversation, exercise, and leadership on campus that is exciting to you.

How did you find your college friend circle?

I have a good group of close friends—many of whom I met in my classes or in my dorm. Especially toward the beginning of your journey as a freshman, people are open to talking and gathering. Embrace that! Meet as many people as you can in your first couple of months, and build relationships with those with whom you have the best conversations and experiences.

What do you think the future of college education should be?

Provide a platform and opportunities for students to find and explore what fields they are passionate about, and limit requirements that do not support that.

Favorite podcast?

I love a couple of movie podcasts, most notably *Beyond the Screenplay*! I have also really gotten into the *Vox Explained* podcast.

What do you believe that other people think is crazy?

That it's okay to be busy! I find doing work a bit therapeutic, and I don't like to just sit around with nothing to do! Work doesn't have to be high stakes—it can be a hobby such as reading a book or building a project with friends.

How important is a liberal arts education to you? To your future profession?

Critical to who I am and my future! I love to learn, and a liberal arts education enables me to pick and choose whatever is interesting to me across fields—fields I would never have engaged with otherwise. I am also premed, so having an education that takes into account multiple perspectives is critical to being a good healthcare provider in the future.

What are the books you've read recently that have made an impact?

Atomic Habits, by James Clear, really helped me better shape my learning environment to maximize studying and focus. I would recommend it to anyone.

The Best of Brown University

What do you wish you knew about college academics that you know now? What is the best preparation?

The biggest difference between college and high school academics is that in college, the entirety of your grade in a class is derived from three, or maybe four, exams. There are rarely graded homework assignments, participation opportunities (outside of seminars), or projects to pad your grade. This means that it is on you to keep up with classes and study well in advance. The best strategy to do well is to watch lectures when they occur and study very often for every class so you do not get behind and risk failing an exam worth a significant portion of your grade.

What were the three main skills you developed in high school that have been invaluable during college?

In my opinion, the most important tool for success is not intelligence or innate ability but rather discipline. Success is not about working twelve hours a day for a week to complete a project or ace a test but rather working two hours every day for a year to create something meaningful or master a skill to set yourself ahead of your peers. The tool for practicing discipline is time management, an invaluable skill I began to learn in high school. Keeping a detailed planner and planning out my days, weeks, and months allowed me to achieve more than I ever thought possible in high school. If a test was six months away, I would take the time to make a detailed study schedule. In addition to making sure I was on track to do well, making schedules also alleviated any stress, as I knew simply sticking to the schedule would prepare me adequately. When I walked into the testing center, I was calm and able to focus because I knew that there was nothing more I could have done to prepare.

Planning so many hours of every day, and even planning out free time, may sound restrictive and even neurotic, but it gives one more free time and takes away any associated guilt. So, when you see friends on a Saturday night, you will not feel guilty about having fun, but rather will feel the fun is well deserved as you've completed everything you needed earlier in the day and have your next day already planned out. As marathon world-record holder Eliud Kipchoge said, "Only the disciplined ones in life are free. If you are undisciplined, you are a slave to your moods."[30]

Another skill I started developing in high school was learning how to communicate appropriately with superiors. In the professional world, most communication is over email. Therefore, it is of great importance to learn how to write emails with the correct formal tone, respond promptly to bosses and supervisors, and send follow-up and thank-you emails when appropriate. So, high school students: starting an email to anyone other than your friends with "Hey ..." is not acceptable.

Finally, never be afraid to ask for help. Oftentimes, our egos get in the way of our asking for help despite there being absolutely no shame in doing so. For example, in high school I was able to do very well in most of my classes but struggled with physics. Instead of wasting hours and hours in misery, I sought a tutor to help me. Although it was a bit of a hit to my ego to hire a tutor for high school physics when many of my friends barely had to study, it was supremely useful and helped me deeply understand the concepts. In college, I advise everyone to ask for academic and personal help when they need it. Although it may not seem like a special skill, knowing when to ask for help, before it is too late, can make a dramatic difference in one's life.

Have you changed your major since entering college and if so, to what?

My major did not change! I came into college planning to be a neuroscience major and will be graduating with a neuroscience degree, then heading off to medical school.

30 Eliud Kipchoge Quotes. BrainyQuote.com, BrainyMedia Inc, 2022. https://www.brainyquote.com/quotes/eliud_kipchoge_1044566, accessed June 7, 2022.

What are the books you've read recently that have made an impact?

Noise, by Daniel Kahneman, had a big impact on me. The book discusses how our moods and seemingly tangential external factors influence our big decisions. The book tries to explain why two doctors in the same hospital give different diagnoses to identical patients or why parole boards are more lenient on sunny days versus rainy days. The book also contains advice on how to evaluate the "noise" present in our own lives and optimize our decision-making.

What internship opportunities should high schoolers engage in?

It is never too early to think about your career. If a high school student has any interest in any professional area, whether it be art, medicine, business, or law, they should seek an internship in that field. An internship may, in part, consist of seemingly menial work. However, being part of an organization in any capacity and interacting with organization members can still provide valuable information to high schoolers and help them learn more about a career path of interest. Remember, while you're doing those mundane tasks, you are observing what makes the company or organization or medical center tick. That's valuable. Internships can also be difficult to attain as a high school student. To address this, working with an experienced college advisor is very helpful, as is cold emailing and leveraging connections.

How is college different or the same as your expectations?

Honestly, college was about what I expected it to be. I understood that there would be a lot more independence, as was the case. No one is there to tell you to go to class, to wake up before noon, or to eat lunch. This is both good and bad in the sense that you can spend your days pretty much however you like, but it also puts the burden of staying organized squarely on you. Additionally, I expected the classes to be more rigorous than high school. Again, this proved to be true. With this said, though, you are in class for fewer hours each week, so you have more time to study compared to a busy high school schedule, when many of us are in school from early morning to late afternoon.

To what extent is time organization important in high school and college?

Time organization is the single most important skill for success in life. Being able to stick to a preplanned schedule and not waste limited time is in many ways the singular key to success. Furthermore, setting at least three hours aside every day for deep work—writing, memorizing, analyzing, ideating—free from the distraction of our phones and screens can make a big difference and allow one to accomplish an incredible amount over time.

How did you find your college friend circle?

I was very fortunate to have found amazing friends in college that I still live with to this day. I met my main friend group during my first year. We lived in the same building and were in many of the same classes, so we were able to spend a lot of time with each other. One piece of advice I would give when it comes to making friends is to be patient. You do not necessarily have to click with the first group of people you meet. If you spend a couple of Friday and Saturday nights alone, that is totally okay. It takes time to find people who share your values and who you enjoy spending time with.

What do you do just for you?

I practice yoga and exercise. We spend so much of our days sitting down and staring at screens. I think it is of the utmost importance to stay active and disconnect from technology every so often. The health benefits of stretching and exercising are profound. So, taking the time to maintain your body will ensure that you will be able to enjoy your academic success for years to come. At the end of the day, you cannot enjoy all the fame, fortune, and success you might achieve if you are in poor health.

What have you done that has made the biggest impression on your professors? Your friends?

I give my full attention to people. Even if you are in a class of thirty people and sitting in the back of the room, the professor will know if you are on your phone constantly. When you spend time with friends, even if you check your phone subtly, they will be able to tell and will remember. Giving people your full attention and being wholly present when you are with them goes a long way and makes a significant impression. Additionally, being honest, responding quickly when someone reaches out, and doing something nice without expecting something in return can make a memorable impression on someone.

What do you think the future of high school education should look like?

The quality of education that high schools provide varies widely across the country and the world. I would love to see increased access to education for the poorest in our society.

In recent thinking about reforms for high school education, there is a train of thought that seeks to decrease the number of tests and make grading more subjective. While I understand the possible positives of this point, I would suggest that exams still have a place. If any of us chooses to pursue law, medicine, finance, or graduate school, we will have to take licensing tests in the beginning if not for the entirety of our careers. Developing test-taking and studying skills early in high school would thus serve very useful to many picking careers that require lifelong exams. Additionally, I would hope that the top professionals pride themselves on not having to run to a computer to look up the right answers to every patient or client question. Testing keeps you sharp, and with voluminous information at your fingertips, and the earlier we are engaged in such testing, the more mundane and process oriented it feels.

What do you think the future of college education should be?

Liberal arts colleges generally do a good job of emphasizing writing as a core skill to be developed. I think this trend should continue. Requiring writing intensive classes or humanities courses with writing components is important in that it teaches students how to synthesize many pieces of material into a cohesive piece of communication. This is an extremely useful skill in pretty much any job and should be emphasized in college given that professors are experts in the field and can provide beneficial feedback to students.

What do you want parents to know?

I know when I was a teenager, I was hard on myself. When I came up short or felt like I wasn't doing enough, I would take it to heart. As a parent, it is important to push one's kids to have high expectations but also make sure that they always have a safety net in you. Whether their child achieves all their goals or not, a parent should always reinforce the fact that their love is truly unconditional and not dependent on their child's success. This creates a sense of comfort in a teenager and allows them to push themselves harder because they know even if they fail, if they tried their hardest, their parents will still be proud of them. I was lucky to have parents like this. Knowing that they loved me unconditionally actually pushed me to want to make them proud and to make their sacrifices worth it. My motivation for working was not a negative motivator: fear of failing or fear of falling from their graces. My motivation was instead a positive motivator: wanting to push myself to my limits, because I knew that even if I came up short, I still had people who cared about me supporting me. Having an unconditional support system in my parents grounded my mental health and never made stress existential.

The Best of Brown PLME (Eight-Year Program in Liberal Medical Education)

How has your leadership in high school continued or laid the groundwork for your continued leadership in college?

Seeking leadership opportunities in high school gave me useful skills that equipped me to perform well in college. When you organize a group in high school, you learn how to delegate, communicate with people, push projects along, and deal with multiple personalities. These skills are all invaluable when you join organizations in college and are easily scaled up when you lead major projects as an undergraduate soon to apply for medical school. Medical schools care about your soft skills—your leadership, community organizing, creative pursuits, and ability to persuade (so debate is a great activity in which to succeed) and communicate with diverse populations of students (because eventually, you will have diverse populations of patients to tend to). I recommend that everyone try their hand at founding or independently running a group in high school. This will give one the confidence and soft skills for college.

What is your five-year plan?

Because I am in medical school, my five-year plan is established for the most part. I will finish my four years of school and then hopefully match into a specialty of my choice. As to what that specialty is, I am still in the process of figuring it out.

Favorite podcast?

My favorite podcast is *Hidden Brain*. The show expertly blends biological science, social science, psychology, and storytelling to reveal the unconscious actions that shape our lives. Whether it is answering why risk is hard for humans to assess or how groups we belong to shape our decisions, *Hidden Brain* consistently offers thought-provoking responses to phenomena we rarely pause to consider.

How important is a liberal arts education to you? To your future profession? Please explain in full.

When I was in high school, I could not define a liberal arts education and could much less understand its value. I knew I wanted to pursue medicine, and that meant studying STEM. Of course, to gain admittance to Brown–PLME, I did my share of humanities pursuits and building of meaningful community organizations and projects, but I did not believe they would impact me as a thinker, diagnostician, voice for reform in medical policy, or clinician. Now that I am on the other side, I have realized a liberal arts education is invaluable, allowing you to critically understand the world. A broad education that combines history, English, literature, politics, economics, and science truly helps you contextualize the workings of humanity. When you read an article in the news, a liberal arts education allows you to place the story historically and understand the various associated political tensions and historical patterns. A liberal arts education also emphasizes writing and speaking in classroom settings. Writing and speaking are arguably the most important skills someone can have. If you have a strong liberal arts background, every paper, talk, email, and report you deliver will be better received and place you ahead of your peers who do not have a strong writing foundation. And in interviews and meetings, if you can communicate well and summarize ideas from various sources, you will be more likely to get the job or promotion. While a liberal arts education will not equip you to write a computer program or build a plane, it will help you communicate your complex ideas to others.

What advice would you give your fourteen-year-old self?

The first thing I would tell myself is to enjoy all the time I have with my parents. Shockingly, by the time many of us turn eighteen, we will have already spent over 90 percent of the time we will ever spend with our parents. During college, many will see their parents for maybe a month in total every year. And during our professional lives, we will see our parents for maybe a week every year. So, savor every minute with your parents, because before you know it, there may not be many minutes left.

The second piece of advice I have is to realize that now is a good time to work hard. Many will tell you that your teenage years should be carefree and fun. And they should, but I urge high schoolers reading this to also work hard on their passions and in school in addition to spending time and having fun with friends. For better or for worse, if one works hard from the ages of fourteen to twenty-two, they can reap the benefits for literally the rest of their lives and actually work less hard later in life. While becoming professionally successful by no means necessitates a degree from a "prestigious" college, going to a well-regarded, academically rigorous school makes achieving success exponentially easier and more likely. By putting in the work now, one can set themselves up for the rest of their lives.

Students from a Potpourri of Universities (UPenn, Columbia, Yale, Stanford, Cornell, Duke, U Chicago, Carnegie Mellon, the UCs, Northwestern, Rice, Bowdoin, NYU, and Vanderbilt)

High school students become very nervous about not having taken certain APs or advanced mathematics courses because their high schools don't offer them. But admissions officers receive an updated packet of information on each high school and know which courses are offered, so that they do not automatically dismiss students without those courses. They recognize that not all high school students have the same opportunities. They also understand that some students live in communities with active arts, computer science, and athletic programs whereas others would have to travel hours for the same advantages. The thing to remember is that Admissions at top schools might look less at those extra, expensive courses some take but more at how you have made the best of the opportunities available or, even more importantly, how you have built the things in your community that you want to leave as your legacy to other students. Just taking the available courses in your school and doing the same activities as everyone else does not make you interesting to top-tier schools. You become very interesting when you create original value for yourself and your community. We have the world at our fingertips, and sometimes, we are only an outreach letter away from a research internship. Take things into your own hands! **(U Chicago)**

Does the Top Tier prefer students from less populated states?

Geographic diversity is a plus in admissions to the top tier and Ivies and has been for quite some time because a more diverse class leads to more diverse experiences and perspectives on campus. I have seen this to be true at Yale. **(Yale)**

Does your school prefer EA/ED applicants?

The early pool is usually made up of students who are at the top of their class in academics and leadership, so, as Dr. B says, it's a self-selecting group. When you think about it this way, it is not easier to be admitted early; in fact, it can often be more difficult. Some of my peers think they would not have been admitted to Columbia or UPenn if they had applied early. **(UPenn)**

Do you think it matters what you major in? Should you strategically choose a major?

At some schools the answer is absolutely, yes. At many of the Ivies, I hear from friends, you cannot apply for engineering or computer science unless you have years of building and coding apps or internships for a couple of summers. So, if you've discovered a love for product development or app development in the summer before senior year but have made a name for yourself as a writer and school magazine editor throughout high school, it's best not to suddenly put down comp sci or engineering as a major. Admissions won't see your capability in the fields. In some schools, like Princeton, for example, Admissions insists that they don't care what you say you'll major in because they know everyone tends to change once or twice before end of sophomore year. They do want to see a thread of academic interest in high school, though. However, if you are applying for art or music, you should have a portfolio or great conservatory-worthy recordings to share because the Ivies and top tier receive such applications and videotapes from the most celebrated student artists in the nation. It's definitely that way at Yale. **(Yale)**

How important is research experience?

Science students with research and STEM competition experience are looked at very closely at my school. It says something about you if you have pursued research, written abstracts and papers, or been published and celebrated in your area of research during high school and you now hope to win a place in one of Stanford's STEM majors. Again, though, if students have not had access to research mentors or local fairs, that is considered. **(Stanford)**

How does the process of application reading and decision-making work at many of the top-tier schools?

When Admissions has received a completed student file, an officer does a first read-through. Everything is under a microscope—from grades to scores to essays to teacher and guidance counselor recommendations and additional artistic or research submissions. Transcript and advanced curriculum along with leadership and large-scale extracurricular projects are weighed. At some schools, like Cornell, faculty members will review supplementary materials submitted in their area of specialization.

After the admissions officer writes a short summary of the applicant's highlights, the file is read by a senior admissions officer who has background on the student's high school and region.

Ultimately, the application is then sent to a committee with everyone of note in the Admissions office.

After weeks of review and summaries read aloud (with the regional officers pitching their preferred candidates), the committee votes: accept, defer, or reject. After speaking with many classmates about this process, we all agree that it never pays to hang your hopes on a waitlist. **(Cornell)**

How Do You Determine Your Best-Fit College?

Most students will say that your choice usually comes down to a gut reaction that you feel when you set foot on campus. Campus visits provide a chance for prefrosh to talk to current students, sit in on classes, watch the mood on campus, and speak to faculty. Of course, everyone is on their best behavior for prefrosh visits, but you can absolutely get a good sense of campus attitude, vibe, and faculty engagement from a visit.

For candidates who have not yet been accepted but are visiting campus for information and tours, always make sure to sign in and let the school know you were there. That's considered demonstrated interest. **(Columbia)**

How is college different or the same as your expectations?

I entered college a technologist: AP Bio, AP Chem, AP Physics, AP Statistics, multivariable calculus, you name it! I coded in Java, JavaScript, Swift, Python, Ruby on Rails. I expected to major in computer science, become the best, build new things, learn novel tricks of the trade, and go off to Silicon Valley to seek my fortune. What happened along the way is that I found philosophy, economics, psychology, and Victorian literature (useful in understanding the value of commodities and consumers) and wound up a double major in computer science and behavioral economics with a minor in societal and human impacts of future technologies through the philosophy department, because the best way to set yourself up for success in a global economy is to become intellectually dexterous. **(Carnegie Mellon)**

What general advice can you offer?

Most of us think about the extracurriculars and passion projects we engaged with and created during high school as high school projects. We toss most aside when we get to college, thinking new is better, or sometimes, none are better for a while because we are so burnt out. Here is something you should think of: many of you will be going for graduate degrees or first jobs immediately out of college. Do you know what those interviews care most about aside from your GPA and internship experience? The projects you have led or created on campus! So, you should not think of becoming a couch potato in college. Continue following the projects and causes you enjoy with an eye toward becoming the most interesting and take-charge applicant for any job or academic program you choose. **(Rice)**

How is college different or the same as your expectations?

A political science and government enthusiast who has been planning on law school since I've been in elementary school, I never expected to be pursuing a JD/MBA program. No one expects to be bitten by entrepreneurship (unless you were the kid constantly creating business schemes in high school), but our world is changing: lunchtime conversations are revolving around everyone's ideas to change certain fields, businesses, or medical practices. On college campuses, perhaps because of greater fear and uncertainty about the future, students are brainstorming differently. So, I am not as sure where I'll end up, but I know for the short term, it will include a dual graduate degree. **(NYU)**

What are the books you are reading now?

The Man Who Mistook his Wife for a Hat, by Oliver Sacks, because I am a neuroscience major **(Northwestern)**; *Sapiens* and *Homo Deus*, by Yuval Noah Harari, because I am an anthropology and history double major **(Bowdoin)**; *Noise* and *Thinking Fast and Slow*, by Daniel Kahneman, because I am an economics major **(Vanderbilt)**; *Kiss, Bow, or Shake Hands*, by Morrison and Conaway, because I am a business student. If you're going into business or law, it's valuable to learn the traditions and communications methods of professionals from around the world **(UC–Berkeley Haas)**; *Plato, Complete Works*, because I am a CS major and would like to base my future work in programming around a profound knowledge of human beings **(UPenn)**; *The Checklist Manifesto*, by Atul Gawande (**Rice-Baylor Direct Med student**).

PART FIVE:

KEEPING THE STRESS DOWN AND THE FAMILY HARMONY UP DURING HIGH SCHOOL!

Now a section for you to read with your parents!

Students, your family is the backbone of your success; so thank you, parents, for encouraging your children to read books that inspire and set them on the road to their college dreams, providing them help and perspective on the overwhelming but thrilling rite of passage that is college admissions.

Let me start by suggesting that parents begin a weekly tradition of family meetings:

Encourage your child to talk about problems encountered academically or socially, and ask a lot of questions. This is key to your child's health and to family well-being. Parents will speak to me confidentially about how they feel the window of communication closing a little more with each passing year. That's because our children grow up and they grow out; but it's also because kids are becoming worried earlier and earlier about college applications, and when kids get worried, they retreat. So often, in a weekday filled with classes, sports, school newspaper meetings, the late bus, and SAT/ACT tutoring, there is barely enough time to eke out a fifteen-minute dinner break, let alone a thoughtful conversation with parents. So, parents become programmed to ask the same questions: "How was your day? What did you get on the test? When is your next one?" And students become automatons at answering with few words and adeptly close their doors. As George Bernard Shaw said, "The single biggest problem with communication is the illusion that it has taken place."

The stress of uncertain academic outcomes, a barrage of damaging social media, and the feeling of helplessness when thinking about how to differentiate themselves for college make kids feel a little like a freight train is barreling toward them. They are overwhelmed and scared. But a weekly family meeting will help break down the fear and open up communication channels.

Let's look at how you can use the family meeting:

It's best not to wait for your child to do poorly on several tests (that creates stress). Find out during a family meeting which subject your child is struggling in, and jump right into action.

1. Are you or your spouse adept in that subject? If so, schedule a half hour per night for teaching and working with your child until he or she gets out of that learning valley.

2. Does your child need professional tutoring? Call a neighboring high school department chairperson and find out who the best teachers are in that subject.

3. Does the National Honor Society do free tutoring in subjects? Find the name of the coordinator at your high school.

4. Do teachers give extra help at school—once, twice, or three times a week? Make sure your child is at every single session; not only will extra learning take place, but a bond will be formed with the teacher, and perhaps that teacher will be more merciful on the next test. All this is to say: catch the learning problem before it becomes a transcript problem!

If you are not receiving satisfaction from the high school guidance office, don't get mad! Get going! Do a work-around! Perhaps there's a special course your son or daughter wants to take or needs to take to learn an additional STEM skill like AP Computer Science, but

- it doesn't fit the schedule,
- **or** your school doesn't offer it,
- **or** your child didn't score high enough in math the year before to be selected for it,
- **or** there is an inadequate teacher whose students never score well on their AP tests and your child wants a better learning experience.

Don't stress about it! Instead, (1) sign up for such a course at a nearby college; (2) take the course online through an eminent program like Johns Hopkins Online or Stanford University OHS, and make sure your child receives a certified transcript for the course; or (3) homeschool your child for the course with a certified instructor who can give your child quarterly grade reports that can be bundled at the end of the year and walked into the high school guidance office to be sent along with your child's high school package to colleges during senior year. Did you know you could do that?

Do the little things that help your child get noticed by their dream schools. For example:

1. **Networking**: Learning to connect with fellow students, professors, and possible future mentors and employers will be part of your teen's reality throughout college. Well-taught networking skills will help teens access opportunities and create relationships that could last a lifetime. Someone your teen meets at a business breakfast could wind up providing a high school internship or a college job, and the skills involved in such connecting and communicating will be valuable during alumni interviews for college.

   Bring your child to networking events, introduce them around, and then set them loose. Beforehand, you can explain that any event with other students or adults can be viewed as a networking event, and that at such times, it is as important to listen as it is to speak. Ask your teens to research some of the key players or speakers at the event so they know something about the people with whom they might be communicating. Take them around with you, initially, to show them the ease with which professionals and coworkers tend to connect.

2. Brainstorm small research projects in fields of interest to your teens. Ask them to create an annotated bibliography of books and articles with a summary of key points that will provide preliminary information on the topic and support or dispute their analysis and conclusions; then set aside a school vacation for them to focus on writing a ten-page research paper on the topic. Teach them how to cite footnotes via Chicago or Turabian notes. Turabian is best for high school

students as it involves a simpler version of Chicago style that one uses when the paper is not meant for publication.

3. Help them connect with your network to nab a couple of public speaking opportunities—anywhere! Have them prepare elevator pitches on their latest charitable project, speak on an issue of school importance at an education board meeting, talk about a new business idea at a business breakfast, or start a TEDx Studio and invite the most interesting teens and professionals to come and speak each year. TEDx Studio talks can be produced by students and uploaded to TED. Studio licenses give student organizers who do not have a TEDx at their own high schools the ability to produce TEDx Talks unaffiliated with an in-person event—just ask your speakers to videotape themselves presenting the talk and upload.
4. Teach your children that neither their life nor their professional path will be linear. This generation's signature will be its ease with consistent independent learning, multidisciplinarity, improvisation, and entrepreneurship—regardless of field.
5. To that end, I leave you with an insight from writer and entrepreneur Taylor Pearson. Pearson suggests that the days of specialization in one academic or artistic path that winds up being one's professional path for life are coming to an end. Students who believe that if they study hard and major in one field, they will find the perfect job upon graduation might find themselves disappointed. He likens such thinking to the life experience of a turkey: From the day a turkey is born, it is kept safe and fed, led to believe that every day will be like the one before. But

"at the moment that the turkey has the most historical data to show that its life is likely to keep improving, on the fourth Wednesday of November," it finds out it's not so great to be a turkey! We can represent the assumption as a syllogism: "Every day the turkey farmer feeds me. Tomorrow is another day. The turkey farmer will feed me tomorrow."[31]

In whatever way we look at it, the messaging for this generation's students is clear: of course, they should become experts in their chosen field of specialization, but they can no longer rely on learning what is needed for their careers by their twenties. Every field is requiring a grasp of diverse mental models and interdisciplinary understanding. The theoretical or technical tools students might have learned for their selected professions today will likely be obsolete in the future. So, it's wise to teach teens to embrace a lifelong process of learning and relearning—and the more diverse that learning process, the better. In a society where traditional assumptions and study of rote specializations might waylay a student ten years from now, learning the mindset of an entrepreneur through building their own creative or community projects and organizations teaches solutions thinking. Learning to learn, build, and pivot now, in high school, can only help young minds advance as problem solvers and innovators of a world in flux.

31 Taylor Pearson, *The End of Jobs* (Austin, Texas: Three Magnolia LLC, 2015).

6. What about families who live in rural areas or communities that do not offer many extracurricular or internship possibilities? I am hoping now you can see that where you live in your mind and heart—in your curiosities and passions—is far more responsible for what you create than where you live physically. If you schedule brainstorming sessions with your family about what you could fix in your community, meaningful ideas will emerge. But then it's up to you to make them happen. Very often, I find, it's easier for students to do the best projects when they are living in rural areas or small towns that offer little extracurricular engagement—because you get to create everything! Every town has fractures or gaps that need to be healed or filled. Determine what those are, and fill them with your unique talents.
7. If your child has decided to study on a pre-medical track in college (regardless of major) and pursue medical school postcollege, discuss the elements colleges are looking for from students whose applications speak about a future in medicine. This is important.
8. Here is what Admissions will expect from students with this interest: (1) research over an extended high school career; (2) students who compete in regional, national, and international competitions with their research; (3) those who receive certifications in allied fields; (4) those who write papers or articles in their field of interest; (5) students who shadow physicians; (6) students who take ancillary courses in the field; (7) those who demonstrate dedicated artistic talent in music, writing, fine arts, or dance; (8) those who

present a compelling story of *why* their future is in medicine; and (9) those who create a community project that shows human-to-human interaction, because regardless of all the technology entering the medical field, the essence of medicine remains how you relate to your patient—human to human.

Come up with a plan for your child to give back to the community (to any community).

Let your child understand that it is as valuable and weighty a thing to be a good global citizen as it is to be a good student.

Let me give you an example of how one of my students journeyed from stress to inspiration to his dream college.

Sean, a hardworking and overstressed high achiever, decided during a family meeting that it would be a wonderful thing to spend a summer on a medical mission to Guatemala. He taught classes at a clinic each day on preventive healthcare measures for children. The kids at the clinic and from neighboring areas loved Sean, packed his classes, and stayed after to hear his stories and jokes. One day, Sean received a disturbing phone call from home. There had been a serious fire in his area of California, and his home had been destroyed. Thankfully, no one in his family was on site at the time, so everyone was safe. Sean was understandably distraught and visibly sad—and the children at the clinic noticed. What happened next was astonishing. The kids went around to all the patients and their families, collected small handfuls of coins, and presented the tiny sum to Sean upon his departure for the United States. Sean was humbled. He could not believe that these children who came from so little and had so little would think about giving to him. After all, Sean had come to Guatemala to help them! When Sean returned to the United States and to a new normal, he founded an organization called the Don't

Get Sick Library. He compiled his healthcare lessons and had them translated into Spanish and illustrated. Sean's organization shipped the manuals to clinics all over Central and South America.

The next time I spoke to Sean, he told me that stress had just melted away because he could get up every morning knowing that children he had never met, from halfway around the world, were benefiting from something he created.

Who got the greater gift from this experience? I don't know, but Sean is now studying on the premed track at Duke University and majoring in global studies.

A point to consider with teens is that students do not learn when you tell them something or even when they engage in something. They create new neural pathways and learn when they have the time and mind space to reflect on something they just experienced. That's when they start to "become." So, parents, teach your children that instead of making to-do lists, they should make "to be" lists and then reflect on those attributes and become the person they want to be. They'll notice, you'll notice, and Admissions will notice. Look at the power of a family meeting!

All these proactive decisions will dial back the stress at home during high school and will allow you guys to fulfill the dreams on those dream boards.

A Note Looking Forward to Your College Freshman's Mental Health

Have your calls via Zoom, Skype, or some sort of video conferencing app. Why? Because when you see your child's facial expressions and behaviors as well as hear your child's voice, you will have an abundance of cues, a fuller picture of your child's mental health.

With the rise in mental health issues on college campuses, please have your child sign a HIPPA waiver and medical power of attorney before the college move-in date. These forms give you the right to review information or speak with mental health specialists.

Parents often feel powerless when trying to determine how their child is actually doing in courses at the end of each semester. It is less an invasion of privacy and more a proactive way to be sure your child is not spiraling downward. Often poor grades are either a sign of or lead to depression and hopelessness. Before classes begin, ask your child to sign a FERPA waiver form permitting you to check end-of-semester grades. Students are the ones who benefit from this kind of continued connection with parents because they may feel that they are letting parents down by not operating at peak performance without them. As parents, it is so helpful for you to assure your child that you are on their side and understand they are doing the best they can. Alternately, you might be a voice of reason that assesses a particular course of study is not well suited for your child. All this input helps rather than hurts. Ultimately, you want to let your child know that you have "broad shoulders" and can handle any worries they discuss with you.

Finally ... It's Not You, It's Them

Students, under no circumstances believe less about yourself because a few Ivy League or top-tier institutions say no. I assure you that if you have a stellar academic record (grades and scores); a deeply designed, long-held thread of intellectual or artistic passions; thoughtful and powerful essays; and glowing recommendations, Admissions sees you. The committee understands your intelligence, they understand how special you are, and they realize you belong at their school. However, they have their own agendas, space issues, and annual departmental needs (perhaps comparative literature or music majors are in demand this year); there are changing socio-political factors in our nation that resonate through our halls of learning (we want to embrace more veterans, more first-generation college students, more diverse experiences); there's the question of geography ("Are there any students from X state? We have not had many applications from their best high schools for two years"); and there are athletic or celebrity considerations. Admissions decisions may have nothing to do with your exceptional work in high school, and you cannot let the results bring you down. Maintain a growth mindset (through which setbacks and challenges are only the beginning of the story, not the end for you), and you will create transformational success in your studies wherever you go to school. Let's examine what a growth mindset is.

At Stanford University, Professor Carol Dweck ran a fascinating experiment with children, the result of which might put some things in perspective.

In her presentation to children of increasingly difficult puzzles, she expected that they would all eventually become frustrated, feel incapable, and give up. But some didn't. Some children became even more determined and exuberant, rising to the challenge. The gist of the experiment showed that students who viewed their inability to solve a second puzzle as a detriment decided they were simply not smart enough to handle the challenge. It was as if their internal monologue sounded like this: "Well, I'm not really good at puzzles, and I don't like feeling inadequate, so I might as well not try anymore." However, the children who persisted through the challenges they had been handed were the ones who enjoyed seeing what they could learn from the experiment and how they might problem solve around the difficulties. Their intelligence never entered their decision to soldier on. The puzzle solvers who stopped solving saw their abilities as fixed; the ones who continued rising to the occasion believed their success was flexible—they could develop that skill and become super-solvers in the long-run.[32]

So, if you do not get accepted to your top choice school, yes, there are things you can do to, perhaps, nudge a deferral into a spring acceptance. You can write a full-length "why" essay for schools that do not incorporate one into their supplement; you can request another beautiful recommendation; you can scale up your passion project to have even more measurable value to society and receive media attention and send the social proof to Admissions. However, you can also understand that there can be many dream schools, and being admitted or not admitted to the ones that top your list is not something to take personally. Admissions in a postpandemic world will take some years to sort itself out. In the

32 Carol S. Dweck, *Mindset: The New Psychology of Success* (New York: Ballantine Books, 2007).

meantime, remember that you own your own story and have the agency to make it extraordinary—wherever you are. And wherever you are, will be someplace great.

"You contain multitudes."

PART SIX:

IN CLOSING

You have any one of several futures before you. Make yours dynamic and imaginative; be curious and research; speak up and ask questions; be kind and intentional, finding ways to positively change the world just a little bit. Then, feel good about knowing that you had an exceptional high school adventure, and that, dear student, will make you an *Exceptional Applicant.*

Baccalaureate

A show of hands, please: [33]

How many of you have had a teacher at any stage of your education
From the first grade until this day in May,
Who made you happier to be alive,
Prouder to be alive,
than you had previously believed possible?
Good!

Now say the name of that teacher to someone sitting or standing near you.

All done? Thank you ...

33 Kurt Vonnegut, *If This Isn't Nice, What Is?* (New York: Seven Stories Press, 2013).

APPENDIX

A Look into Direct-Med Programs

For those of you headed toward direct-medicine programs in college, a seven- or eight-year medical course of study, I will attempt to pull back the curtain right now on how to craft exceptional medical school applications, what questions will be asked during interviews, and how to prepare your volunteer and creative life for an eye-popping résumé.

Here are some questions that frequently pop up during direct-med program interviews and applications—a few you might have expected, but most I'm sure you haven't:

Sample Questions

1. How do you know you want to be a doctor?
2. What was your most meaningful clinical shadowing experience?
3. Describe the most difficult adversity you have faced and how you dealt with it.

4. In what ways would you contribute to a diverse campus?
5. Outside of academics, what do you enjoy doing most?
6. What aspirations, experiences, or relationships have motivated you to study in an eight-year medical program?
7. Please explain why you wish to study in the specific medical academic areas you selected.
8. What life perspectives would you contribute to the BS/MD community?
9. Describe an intellectual challenge or an ethical dilemma that you have faced. How did you resolve it?
10. Explain a complex message to someone. How do you approach it?
11. On a group project, what would you do if someone isn't doing their share?
12. Describe a project you worked on that required significant attention to detail.
13. Discuss a time you sought out a new experience to learn more: What actions did you take?
14. Please discuss an experience in each of the following categories and why it was meaningful in your decision to pursue a medical career: (a) clinical, (b) research, (c) community, (d) publication, (e) fascination with one field of science.

To apply for a BS/MD program, be very sure you want to study medicine. The competition is more brutal than ever, as most applicants are in a self-selecting pool. This means that they know they have the grades, scores, research, and extracurriculars that would typically make them stand-out candidates. So, if you are not similarly prepared through high school, you might want to destress your application process and apply for excellent colleges as either premed or perhaps as psychology, biochemistry, or neuroscience majors. This approach will afford you a stimulating and interdisciplinary college career that provides more time to engage in things like research, shadowing, and community healthcare leadership before applying to medical school.

How to Prepare before Applications

- Shadow physicians for long stretches of time over two years, if possible. Ask questions about the dark side of medicine: dealing with how to address the needs of terminal patients; how physicians cope with feeling overworked and burned out; keeping up not only on medicine but on the technology required for use in medical practices as well; handling angry patients; long hours that might keep you away from family, etc.
- Journal, journal, journal so that you have cases to discuss, methods of diagnosis to compare, and human-to-human interactions to observe. All these components will find a place in your BS/MD essays (and there are many, many supplementary essays for such applications, so you will need material to write about).

Details to Know for the BS/MD

- Make sure your grades are mostly As in the most advanced courses your school offers (BS/MD programs look for rigor of curriculum and academic success in all your subjects).

- Standardized test scores are still of vital importance. Make sure you score in the high 700s (above 750) on each part of the SAT or above 34 on each part of the ACT. The competition is serious.
- Of course, excellent grades and scores are only the gateway to a positive admissions decision. Your extracurriculars must demonstrate leadership, not membership. Your community activities must demonstrate devoted volunteering and outreach that have had positive impact. Additionally, whenever possible, be able to demonstrate that you founded or created a project, program, product, or podcast that can positively affect the field of healthcare in some way.
- If possible, plan on spending some time in another country volunteering in clinics or research labs. Diversity and global understanding have become important aspects of the BS/MD and MD applications.
- Have you considered the fields of medicine that most appeal to you? If your fascination is with neurology, have you, for example, ever spent volunteer time with those suffering from Alzheimer's? If you are considering pediatrics, have you spent time observing children with learning disabilities or ADHD?
- Have you engaged in science research, competing in regional, state, national or international fairs? If you have not competed, have you researched and written an original research paper on your niche area of interest in medicine? Are you epistemically curious—always asking your STEM teachers for further reading on subject matters of interest and devotedly building your own independent home library on STEM literature and medical breakthroughs?

- Have you studied additional college coursework in your fields of interest online for free?
- The aforementioned steps will build you into an empathetic, knowledgeable, and competitive candidate for admissions to BS/MD programs.
- Go get 'em!

Some of the Nation's Best and Most Nurturing BS/MD Programs according to My Students

- Rensselaer Polytechnic Institute/Albany Medical College
- Rice University/Baylor College of Medicine
- Baylor University/Baylor College of Medicine
- Boston University Accelerated Medical Program
- Brown University PLME (Program in Liberal Medical Education)
- Case Western Reserve University School of Medicine
- City College of NY Sophie Davis BS/MD Program
- Drexel University BS/MD
- Hofstra/Northwell School of Medicine (The Donald & Barbara Zucker School of Medicine)
- University of Cincinnati College of Medicine
- The College of New Jersey/Rutgers New Jersey Medical School
- Stevens Institute of Technology/New Jersey Medical School

- University of Connecticut's Special Program in Medicine
- George Washington University School of Medicine and Health Sciences
- University of Pittsburgh School of Medicine's Guaranteed Admission Program (GAP)
- University of Colorado Denver/U of Colorado School of Medicine
- Northwestern Honors Program in Medical Education (HPME)
- Penn State University/Thomas Jefferson University Premedical Medical (PMM) Program
- UMKC School of Medicine BA/MD Program
- Temple University's Medical Scholars Program to LKSOM
- The University of Rochester Early Medical Scholars (REMS)

Test Optional / Test Blind: What You Need to Know for a Postpandemic Future

A welcomed but confusing result of the pandemic is that many top-tier universities, including the University of California system, have gone test blind, requiring no SAT or ACT for admissions, while others have gone test optional in a show of support for the unmitigated mess resulting from a difficult educating-at-home scenario during the crisis. However, it's this very same test-optional language among universities that is really making decisions tough for students.

Wording on college websites and in counseling offices is problematic. Test-optional schools do not say, "We will not look at any standardized test scores" or "don't send any standardized test scores." They are simply optional. This means that those students who have been studying the "ways" of the SAT/ACT for months (and in some cases, years) will still submit their scores, so those applications will be viewed with extra data points. For bright students in the most-tested generation in history, the "belt and suspenders" approach of taking an SAT/ACT plus AP exams to demonstrate that they can score above a 750 or a 4 or 5 on all APs, respectively, is still the approach.

Where does that put you if you don't have the scores?

The Common Application has noted that application entries with test scores during this test-optional period dropped below 45 percent. That is quite a testament against the test! What would it really mean for a test-blind process to be officially approved by all top-tier schools?

Students immediately become very excited about the thought of one or two or five fewer tests to study for, and that is certainly understandable. But what are they not seeing? My students know that I speak all the time about the missing pieces, the missing evidence, the missing perspective that goes into that Admissions decision. The test-optional or test-blind approach is no different. With a test-optional or test-blind approach, your GPA will be examined under a microscope from freshman year through senior year first semester: slip-ups will be noticed. Your AP tests will be weighed more heavily. What you build and accomplish **outside** of school, whether it's a business, a few apps, a line of sneakers, an international organization, or a unique internship, will become increasingly important. Are you all ready for that? Such "progress" in the admissions process might encourage students as early as middle school to begin honing their talents through free online courses, mentors, and subject experts who can help them become minimasters of their art, science, or academic field of choice. The truth is, your teen years are some of the most imaginative, idealistic, and intellectually stimulating times of your life. Why wouldn't you want to begin thinking like this?

What the future holds for testing and college admissions is anyone's guess (even as MIT brings back the standardized exams to ensure that students have the very highest analytical ability and intuitive mathematics skill). One thing that seems evident is that Admissions will have to be more holistic than ever before. We're counting on them to put your exceptional examples of adaptability—your unique passion projects—front and center. Outside of school intellectual pursuits, research, glowing teacher recommendations, and leadership—all those things will make up your new admissions decision in a big way. Start making them work for you!

For help on your pre-college journey or on college applications, please know that you can contact me at: CollegeHelp@CollegeAdmissionCentral.com

A CHECKLIST ON HOW TO GET REJECTED (DON'T TRY ANY OF THIS!)

1. Be a member of five clubs
2. Excel in nothing but academics
3. Have an internship in a company or medical practice that has the same last name as yours (it will raise red flags about whether you've done anything yourself)
4. Assume that your forty hours of volunteer service at a hospital during senior year will impress Admissions

5. Send 1400 SAT scores to the Ivies
6. Ask four different people to read your perfectly lovely, polished essay and then piece together all their "suggestions" into your revision (congratulations: you now have four different essays in one 650-word personal statement and will not be accepted to your top colleges)
7. Suddenly build a nonprofit the summer before senior year
8. Use your personal statement to brag about an accomplishment instead of to tell a story
9. Say you want to major in international relations and then know nothing about foreign affairs during your college interview
10. Assume that being part of two varsity teams is going to impress Admissions when your GPA is subpar.
11. Spend your summers on "pay to play" programs (like a two-week minicourse at Brown University or a one-week intro to Python through ID-Tech) instead of on a job through which you are supplying real value, or an undergraduate course that provides a transcript or specialized certification or enables you to craft a minithesis or original research paper.
12. Apply to college as a computer science major when you have not spent your high school career building things (for example, apps, algorithms, biomedical devices, household inventions, or robots that pick up your socks before mom gets on your case.

Notes

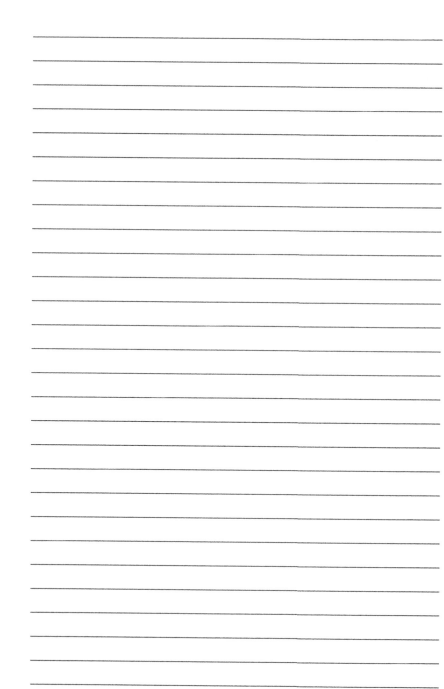

Made in the USA
Las Vegas, NV
18 March 2023